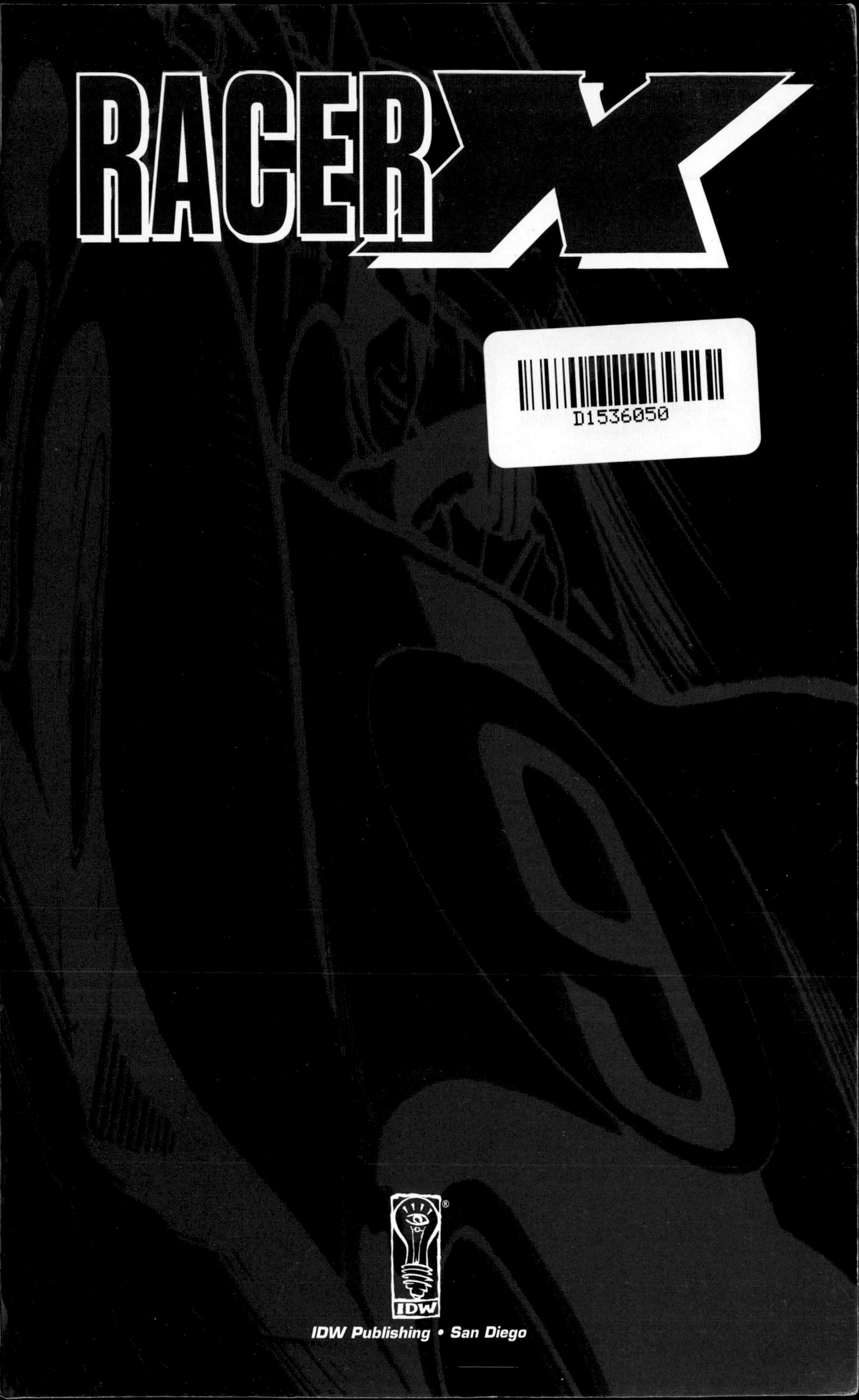

RACER X

IDW Publishing • San Diego

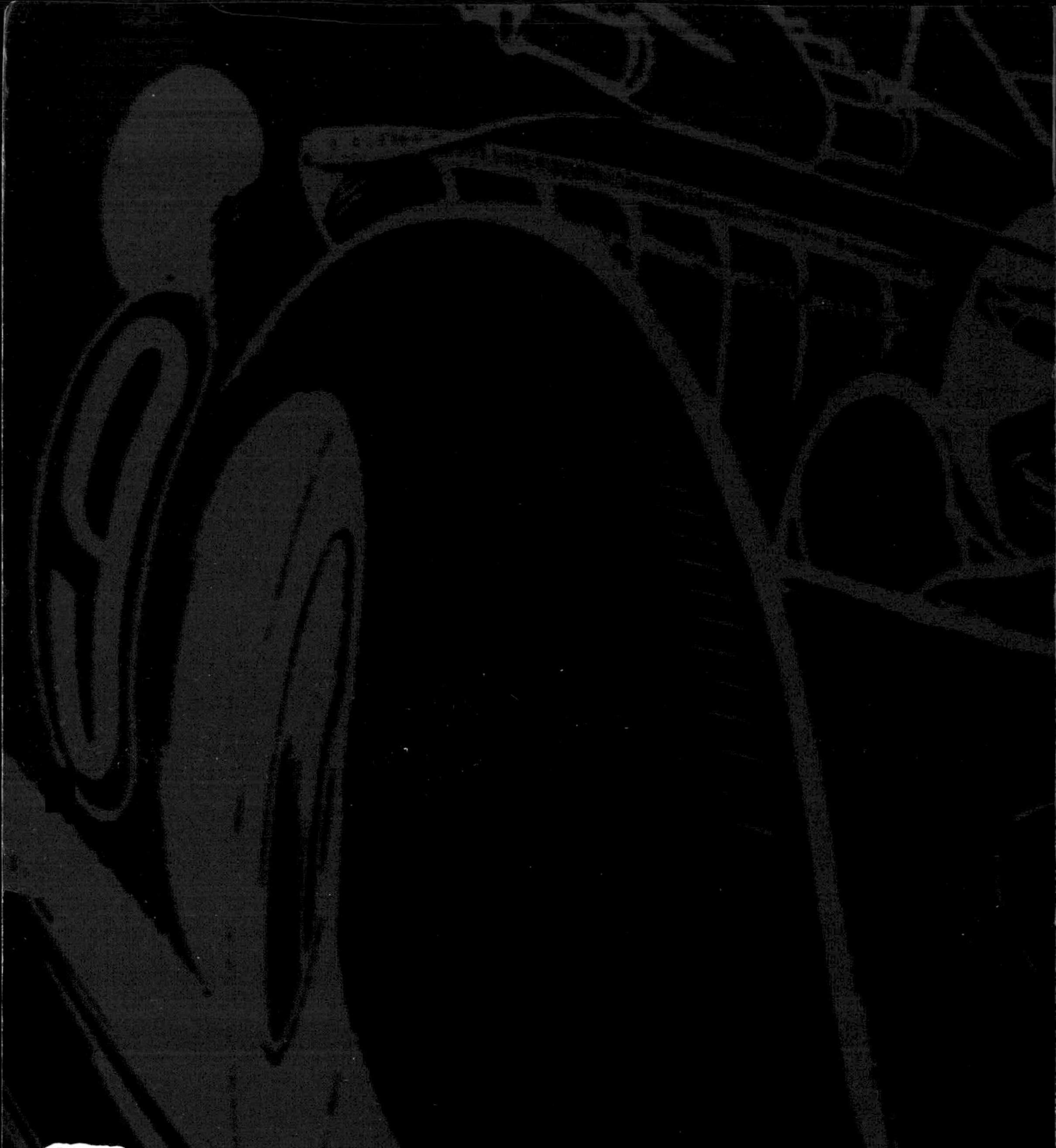

IDW Publishing is:
Ted Adams, President
Robbie Robbins, EVP/Sr. Graphic Artist
Chris Ryall, Publisher/Editor-in-Chief
Clifford Meth, EVP of Strategies/Editorial
Alan Payne, VP of Sales
Marci Kahn, Executive Assistant
Neil Uyetake, Art Director
Tom Waltz, Editor
Andrew Steven Harris, Editor
Chris Mowry, Graphic Artist
Amauri Osorio, Graphic Artist
Matthew Ruzicka, CPA, Controller
Alonzo Simon, Shipping Manager
Kris Oprisko, Editor/Foreign Lic. Rep.

www.idwpublishing.com
www.speedracer.com

ISBN: 978-1-60010-214-1
11 10 09 08 1 2 3 4 5

Racer X #1
page 6

Written by ***Fred Schiller***
Pencilled by ***George Booker***
Inked by ***Brian Thomas***
Lettered by ***Ken Holewczynski***
Colored by ***Rich Powers***

Racer X #2
page 34

Written by ***Steve Sullivan***
Pencilled by ***Vince Argondezzi***
Inked by ***Brian Thomas & Thomas Baxa***
Lettered by ***Kurt Hathaway***
Colored by ***Marcus David***

Racer X #3
page 64

Written by ***Steve Sullivan***
Pencilled by ***Vince Argondezzi***
Inked by ***Brian Thomas***
Lettered by ***Kurt Hathaway***
Colored by ***Marcus David***

Racer X #4
page 92

Written by ***Steve Sullivan***
Pencilled by ***Vince Argondezzi***
Inked by ***Brian Thomas***
Lettered by ***Kurt Hathaway***
Colored by ***Marcus David***

Racer X #5
page 120

Written by ***Steve Sullivan***
Pencilled by ***Vince Argondezzi***
Inked by ***John Dell III***
Lettered by ***Kurt Hathaway***
Colored by ***Marcus David***

Racer X TPB

Cover by ***Ken Steacy***
Edited by ***Dene Nee***
Design and Remaster by ***Tom B. Long***

RACER X

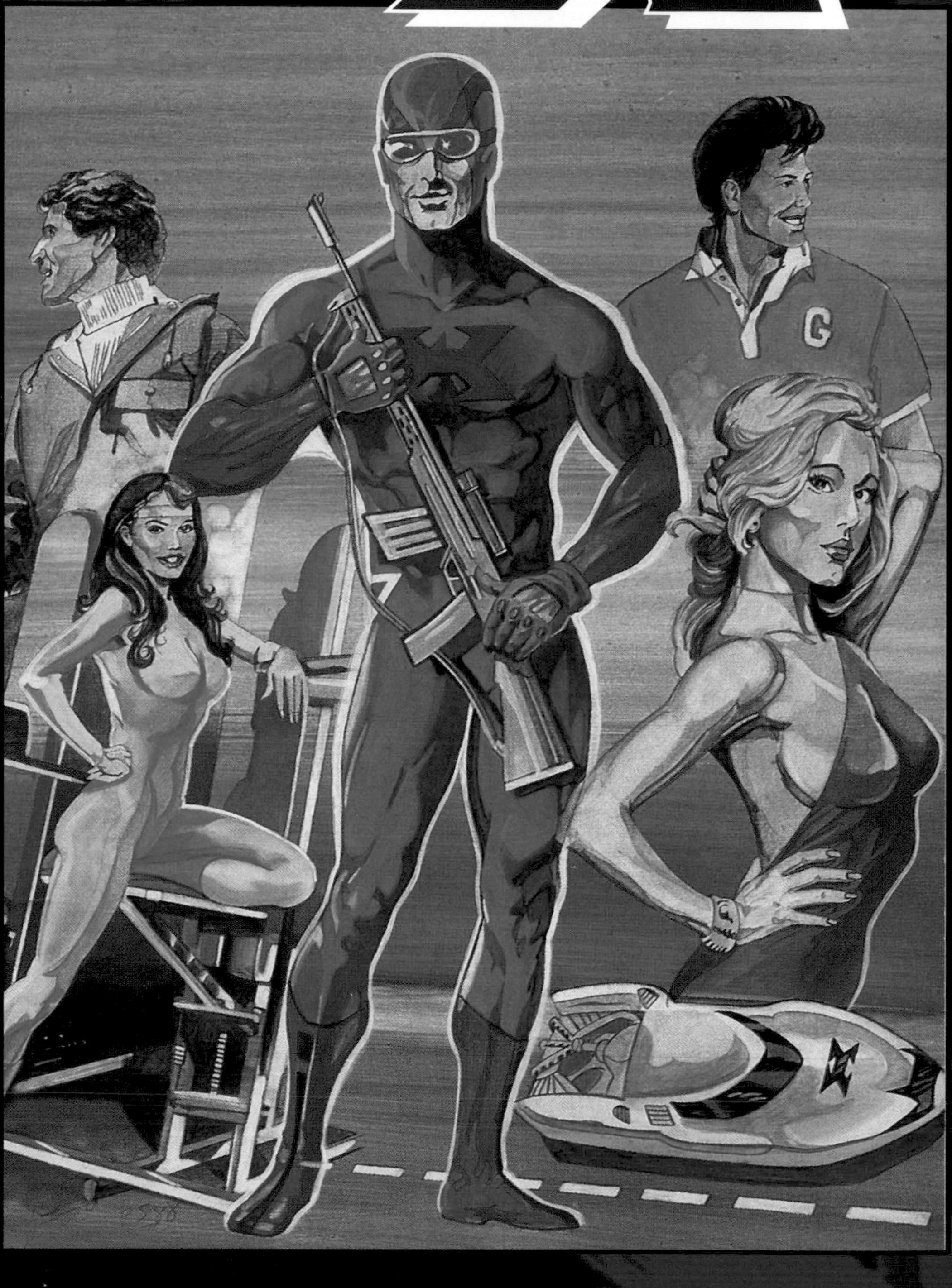

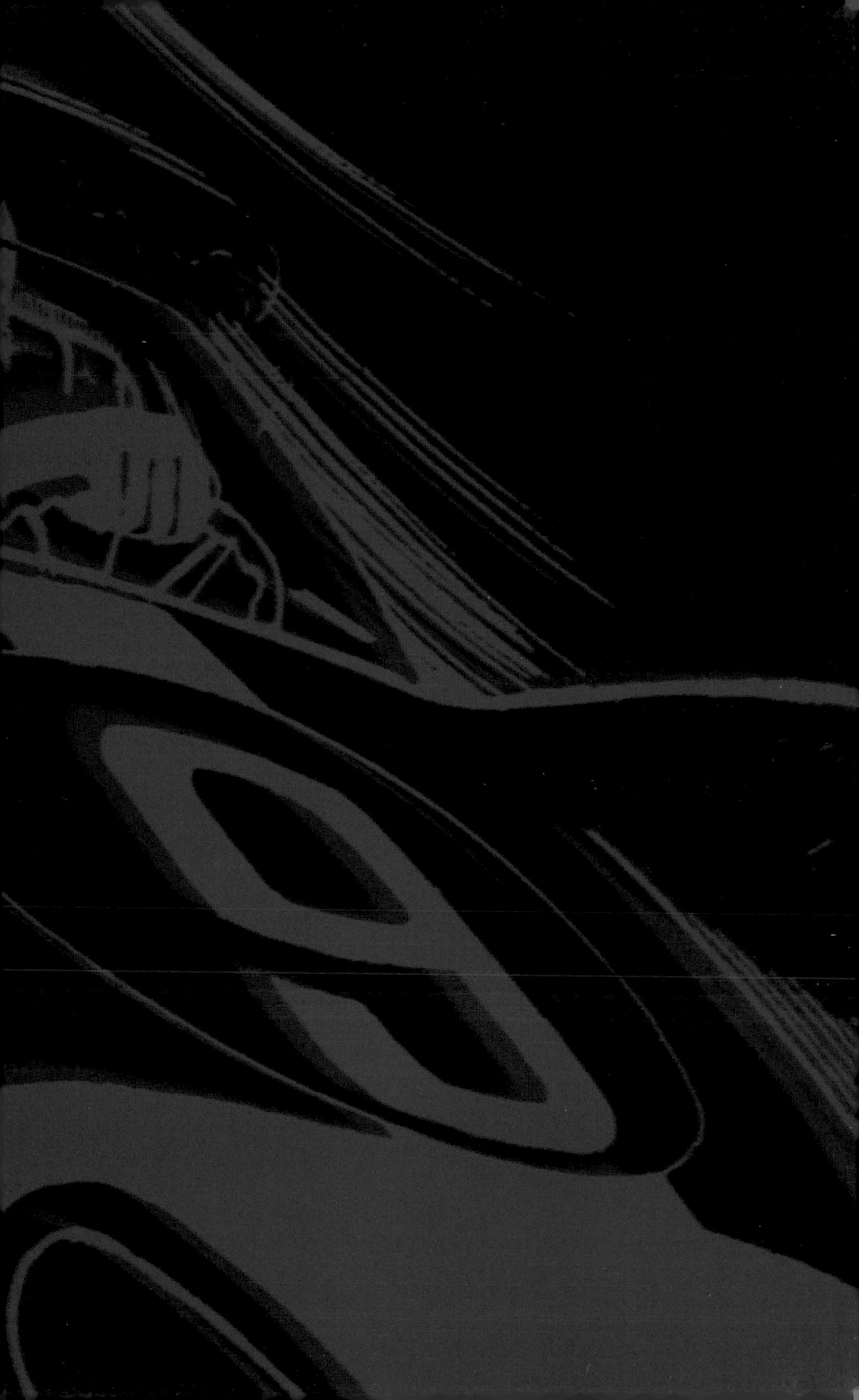

Racer X #1

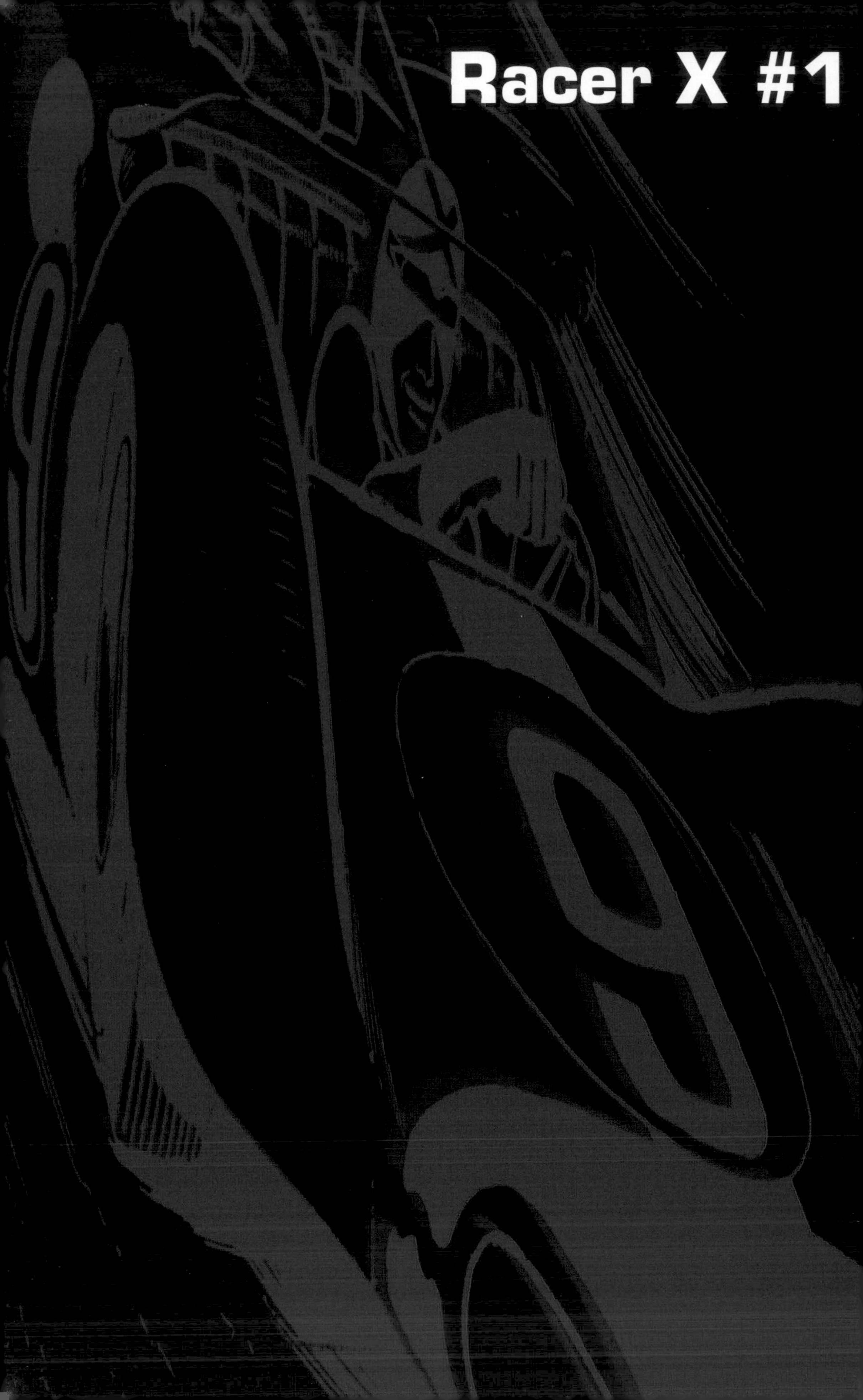

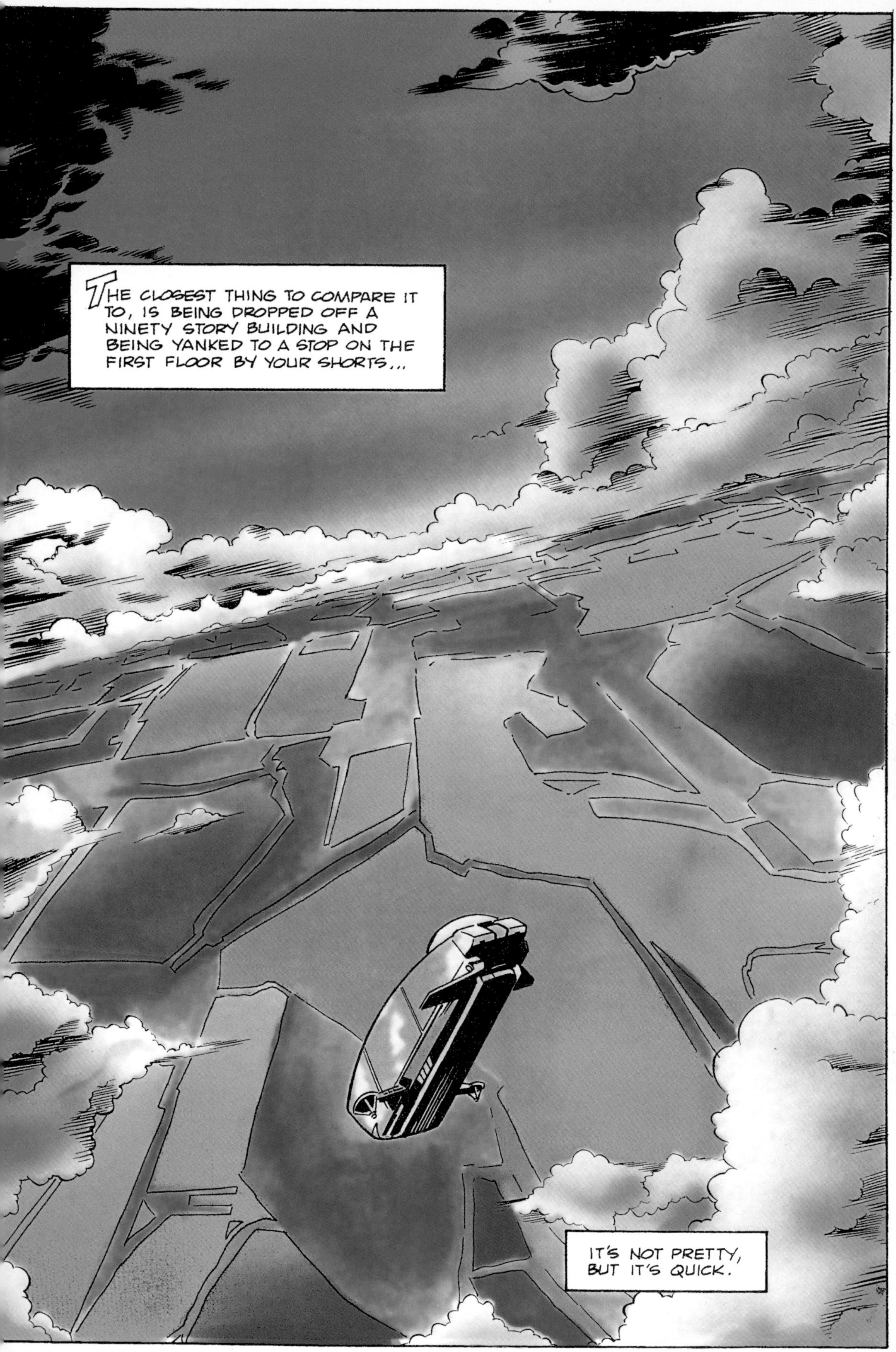
THE CLOSEST THING TO COMPARE IT TO, IS BEING DROPPED OFF A NINETY STORY BUILDING AND BEING YANKED TO A STOP ON THE FIRST FLOOR BY YOUR SHORTS...
IT'S NOT PRETTY, BUT IT'S QUICK.

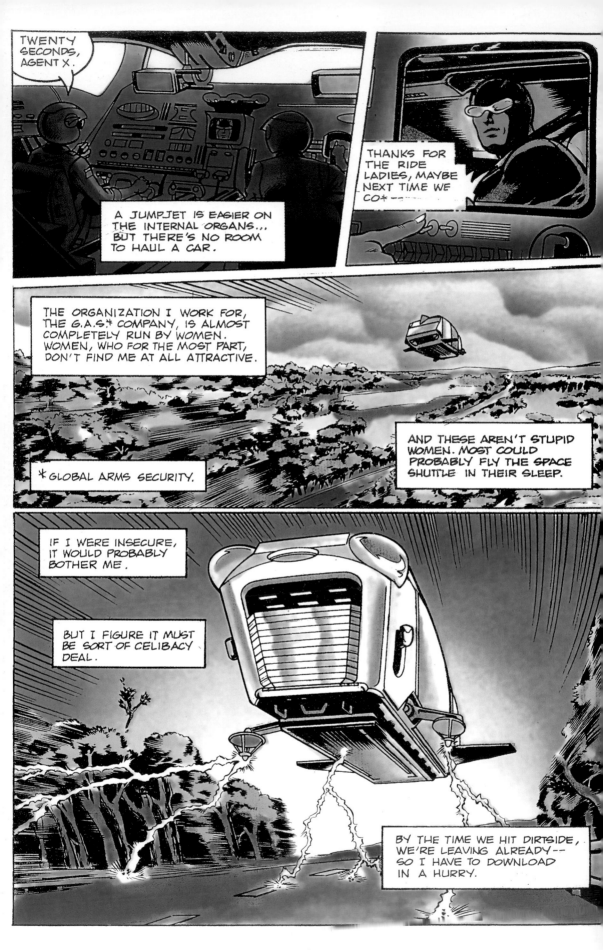

TWENTY SECONDS, AGENT X.

A JUMPJET IS EASIER ON THE INTERNAL ORGANS... BUT THERE'S NO ROOM TO HAUL A CAR.

THANKS FOR THE RIDE LADIES, MAYBE NEXT TIME WE CO*--

THE ORGANIZATION I WORK FOR, THE G.A.S.* COMPANY, IS ALMOST COMPLETELY RUN BY WOMEN. WOMEN, WHO FOR THE MOST PART, DON'T FIND ME AT ALL ATTRACTIVE.

*GLOBAL ARMS SECURITY.

AND THESE AREN'T STUPID WOMEN. MOST COULD PROBABLY FLY THE SPACE SHUTTLE IN THEIR SLEEP.

IF I WERE INSECURE, IT WOULD PROBABLY BOTHER ME.

BUT I FIGURE IT MUST BE SORT OF CELIBACY DEAL.

BY THE TIME WE HIT DIRTSIDE, WE'RE LEAVING ALREADY-- SO I HAVE TO DOWNLOAD IN A HURRY.

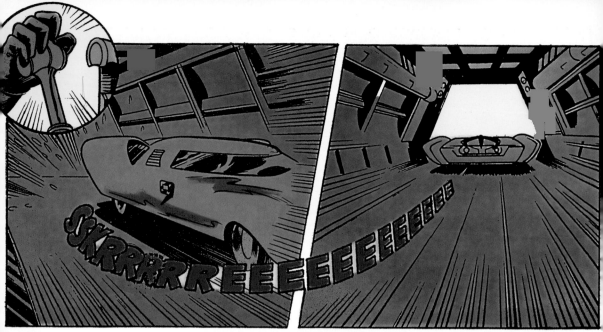

SKKRRRREEEEEEEEEEEEEEEE

I TOUCHDOWN DOING A GOOD THREE HUNDRED MILES PER HOUR.

MY OLD 980 GOT TRASHED A FEW MONTHS BACK. *

*SEE RACER X PREMIER #1

I HATE DRIVING A CAR I DIDN'T DESIGN, BUT THIS ONE'S NOT BAD.

THE WINDSHIELD PROJECTOR'S A NICE TOUCH.

IT SHOWS ME WHAT'S COMING UP, MILES AWAY.

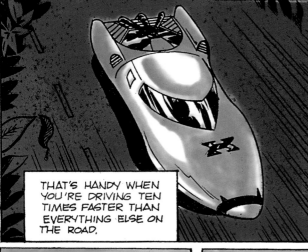

THAT'S HANDY WHEN YOU'RE DRIVING TEN TIMES FASTER THAN EVERYTHING ELSE ON THE ROAD.

WHEN I COAST DOWN TO NINETY, I FIRE UP THE MAIN ENGINE,

THE CAR HAS TWO.

ONE FOR WHEN I HAVE TO RUN IN A TYPICAL ROAD RACE OR DRIVE IN TRAFFIC.

AND THERE'S ANOTHER ONE...

FOR WHEN I'M IN A HURRY.

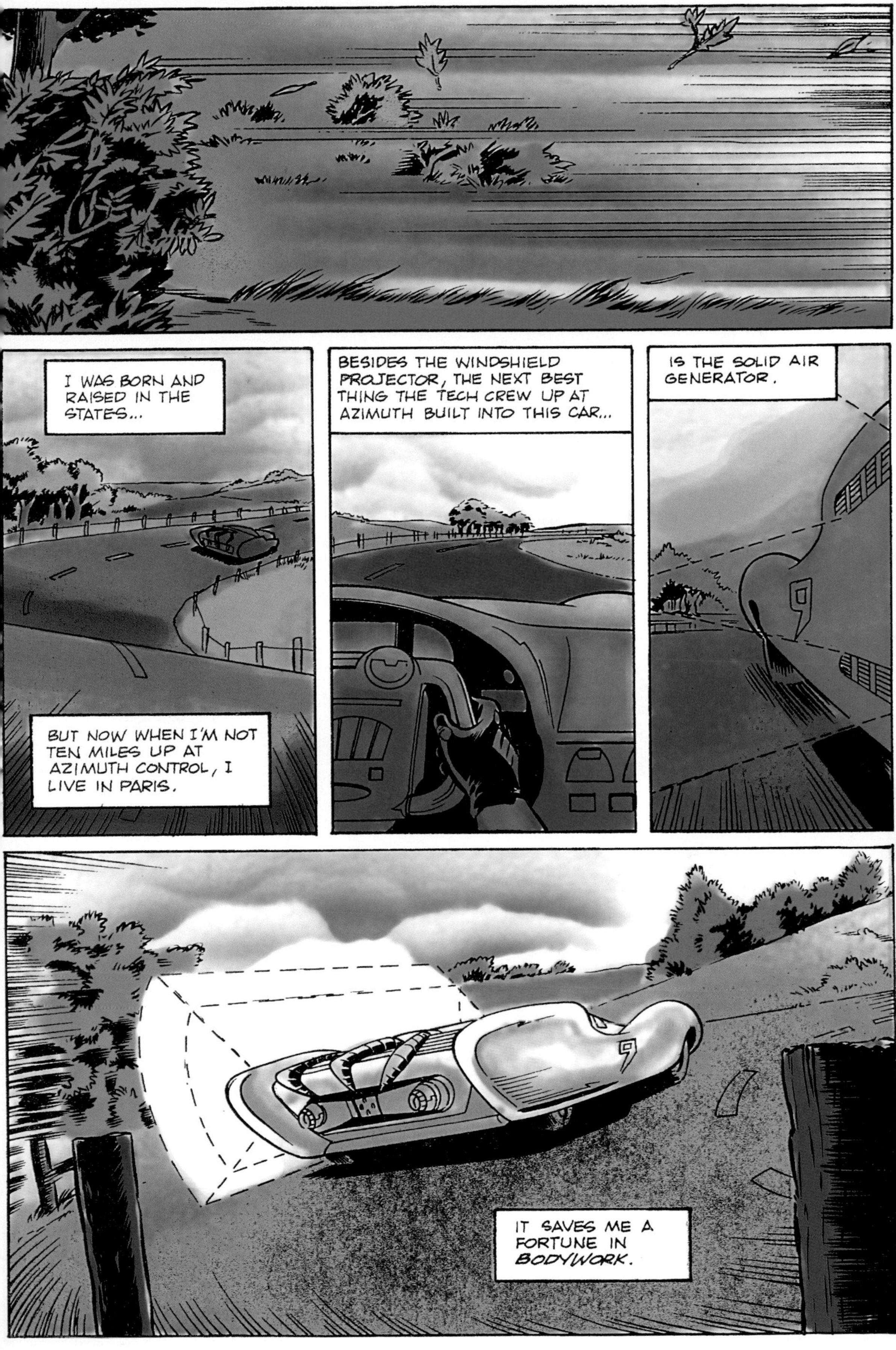
I WAS BORN AND RAISED IN THE STATES...
BUT NOW WHEN I'M NOT TEN MILES UP AT AZIMUTH CONTROL, I LIVE IN PARIS.
BESIDES THE WINDSHIELD PROJECTOR, THE NEXT BEST THING THE TECH CREW UP AT AZIMUTH BUILT INTO THIS CAR...
IS THE SOLID AIR GENERATOR.
IT SAVES ME A FORTUNE IN *BODYWORK*.

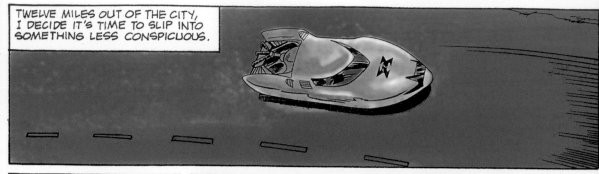

TWELVE MILES OUT OF THE CITY, I DECIDE IT'S TIME TO SLIP INTO SOMETHING LESS CONSPICUOUS.

AN AUTOMATED TRANSMITTER ANNOUNCES MY ARRIVAL AT THE G.A.S. STATION SUB-STATION.

.GAS HER UP AND CHECK THE TIRES -- AND DON'T PLAY WITH THE RADIO!

'YER A REGULAR RIOT REX.

"WHAT WOULD YOU PEOPLE DO WITHOUT ME...

...TO LIVEN YOUR DAY?"

WE'RE WILLING TO TRY.

THEY'RE ALL GREAT PEOPLE... EVERY ONE OF THEM WOULD DIE FOR ME. THAT THOUGHT STILL SCARES ME.

WASHINGTON, D.C.

AWW, I'M JUST KIDDING. LIZ STEVENS, THE COMMANDER UP AT AZIMUTH, SAYS I KID TO MUCH.

I GUESS IT'S A FAULT OF MINE.

ANOTHER ONE I HAVE IS THIS THING AGAINST BULLIES.

I HATE THEM.

YOU GUYS ARE REALLY LUCKY.

I'VE GOT SOMETHING IN THE TRUNK THAT COULD RE-ARRANGE YOUR DNA STRUCTURE.

BUT FOR NOW I'M ONLY GOING TO USE MY FISTS.

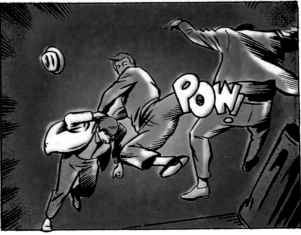

POW!

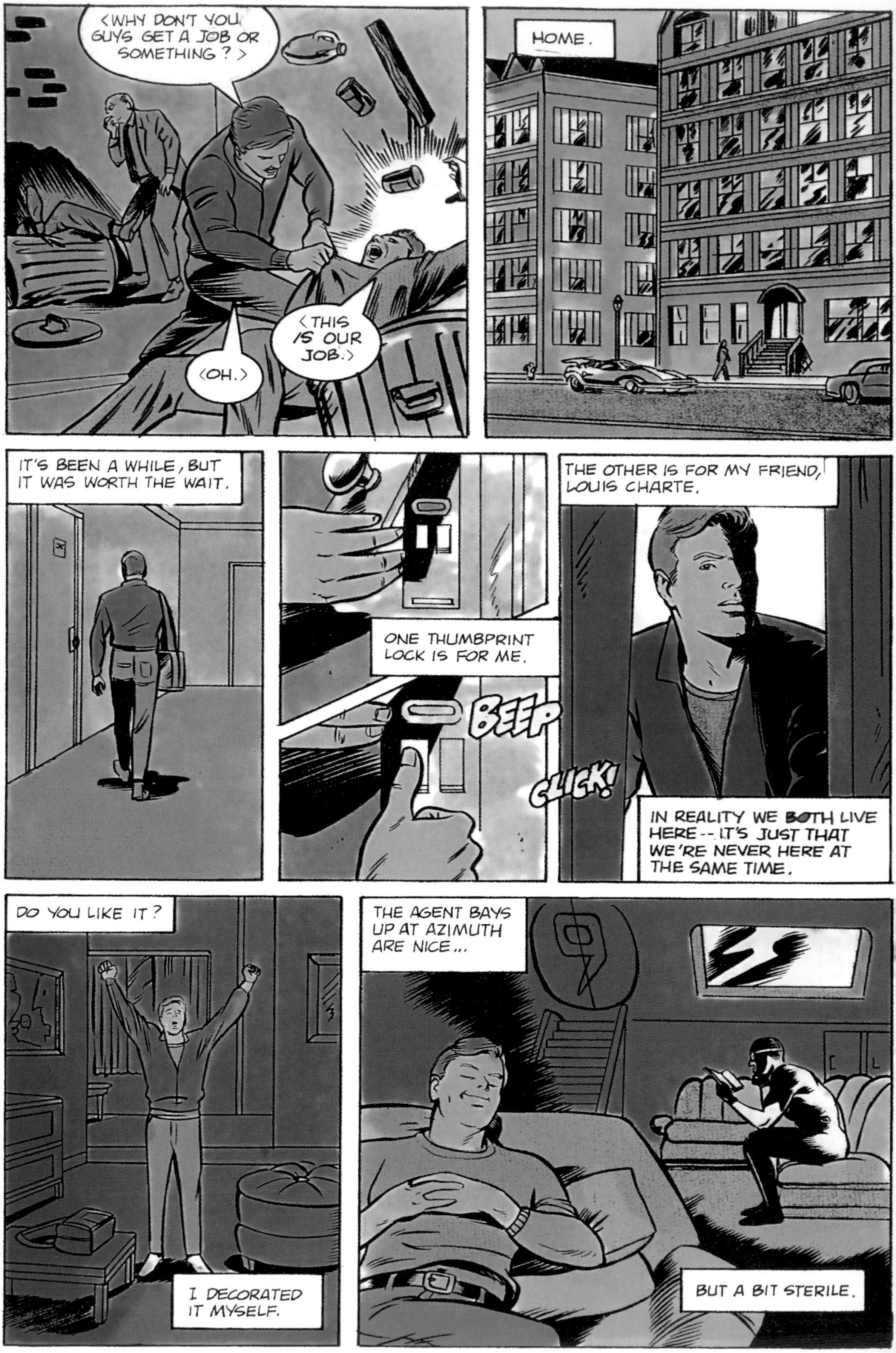
<WHY DON'T YOU GUYS GET A JOB OR SOMETHING ?>
<OH.>
<THIS IS OUR JOB.>
HOME.
IT'S BEEN A WHILE, BUT IT WAS WORTH THE WAIT.
ONE THUMBPRINT LOCK IS FOR ME.
BEEP
CLICK!
THE OTHER IS FOR MY FRIEND, LOUIS CHARTE.
IN REALITY WE BOTH LIVE HERE -- IT'S JUST THAT WE'RE NEVER HERE AT THE SAME TIME.
DO YOU LIKE IT?
I DECORATED IT MYSELF.
THE AGENT BAYS UP AT AZIMUTH ARE NICE...
BUT A BIT STERILE.

...REX *WHO*? SHE ASKS...WHY I OUGHTA...

I GUESS I DESERVED THAT, THOUGH. I HAVEN'T CALLED HER SINCE I RAN OUT ON HER AT DISPINEA'S LAST MONTH, AND LEFT HER *WITH* THE *BILL*.

HOW COULD I EXPLAIN THAT IT WAS A MATTER OF *INTERNATIONAL SECURITY*?

I'LL MAKE IT UP TO HER TONIGHT. I'LL TURN ON THE OLD *RACER* CHARM AND SHE'LL BE... EH? I FORGOT ABOUT THAT *SCAR*...

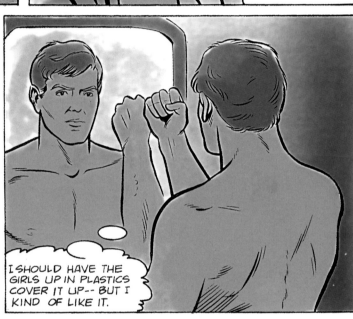

I SHOULD HAVE THE GIRLS UP IN PLASTICS COVER IT UP-- BUT I KIND OF LIKE IT.

IT'S SORT OF A *REMINDER*... A REMINDER OF THE DARNDEST PARTNER I EVER HAD.

HANG TIGHT, RANDY-- I'M GOING TO PULL THE CORD!

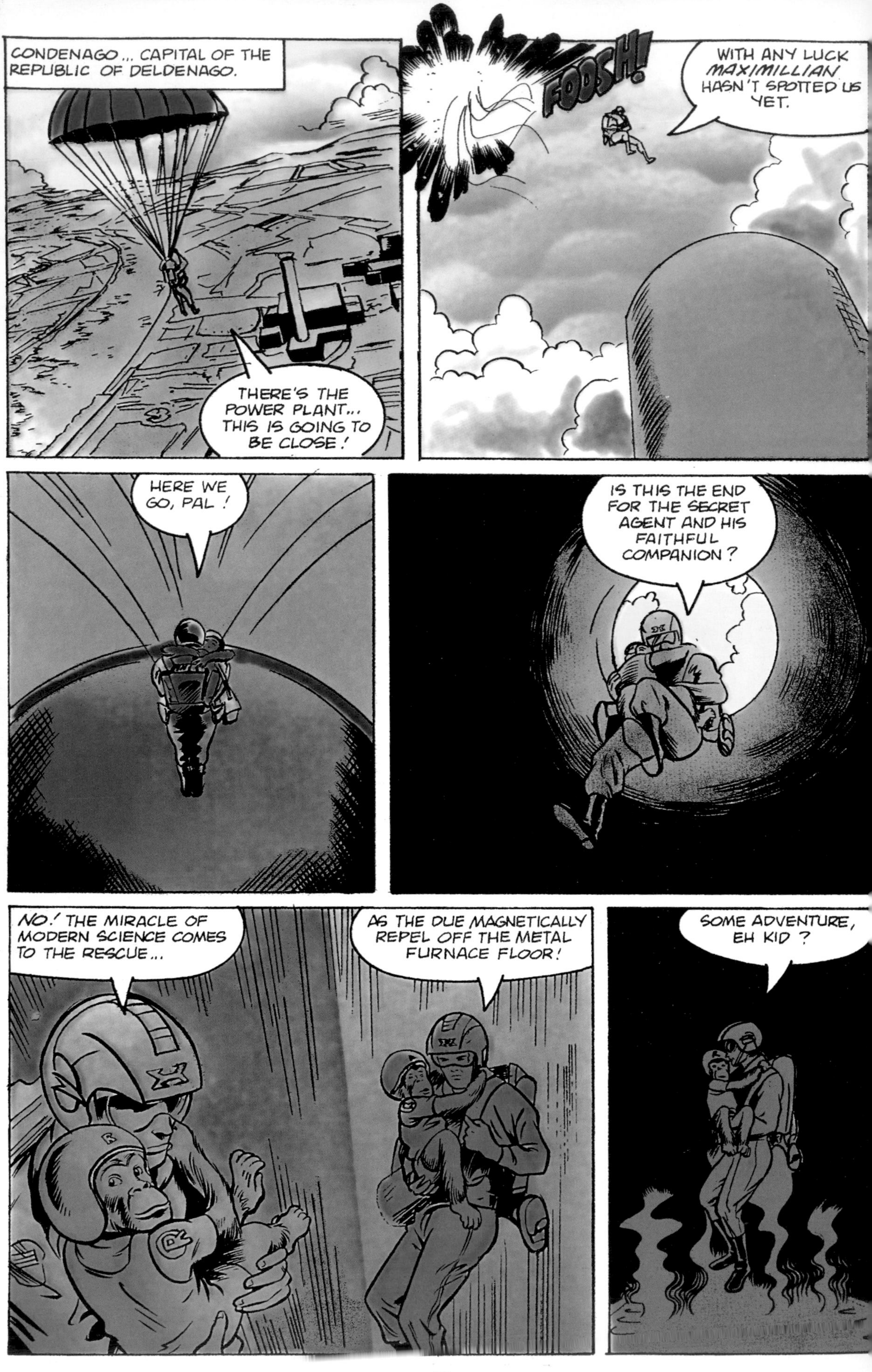
CONDENAGO... CAPITAL OF THE REPUBLIC OF DELDENAGO.
THERE'S THE POWER PLANT... THIS IS GOING TO BE CLOSE!
FOOSH!
WITH ANY LUCK MAXIMILLIAN HASN'T SPOTTED US YET.
HERE WE GO, PAL!
IS THIS THE END FOR THE SECRET AGENT AND HIS FAITHFUL COMPANION?
NO! THE MIRACLE OF MODERN SCIENCE COMES TO THE RESCUE...
AS THE DUE MAGNETICALLY REPEL OFF THE METAL FURNACE FLOOR!
SOME ADVENTURE, EH KID?

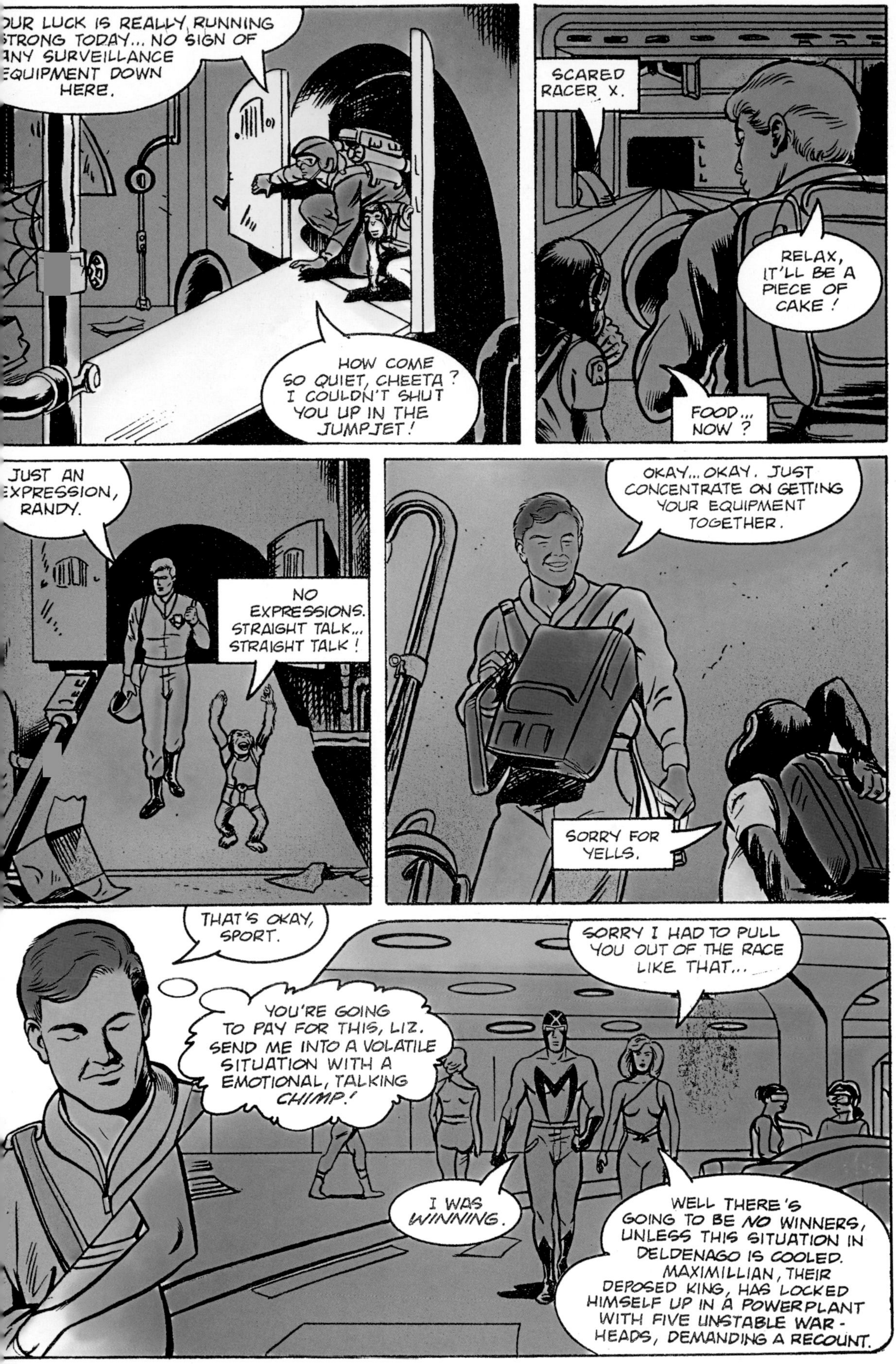
OUR LUCK IS REALLY RUNNING STRONG TODAY... NO SIGN OF ANY SURVEILLANCE EQUIPMENT DOWN HERE.
HOW COME SO QUIET, CHEETA? I COULDN'T SHUT YOU UP IN THE JUMPJET!
SCARED RACER X.
RELAX, IT'LL BE A PIECE OF CAKE!
FOOD... NOW?
JUST AN EXPRESSION, RANDY.
NO EXPRESSIONS. STRAIGHT TALK... STRAIGHT TALK!
OKAY... OKAY. JUST CONCENTRATE ON GETTING YOUR EQUIPMENT TOGETHER.
SORRY FOR YELLS.
THAT'S OKAY, SPORT.
YOU'RE GOING TO PAY FOR THIS, LIZ. SEND ME INTO A VOLATILE SITUATION WITH A EMOTIONAL, TALKING CHIMP!
SORRY I HAD TO PULL YOU OUT OF THE RACE LIKE THAT...
I WAS WINNING.
WELL THERE'S GOING TO BE NO WINNERS, UNLESS THIS SITUATION IN DELDENAGO IS COOLED. MAXIMILLIAN, THEIR DEPOSED KING, HAS LOCKED HIMSELF UP IN A POWERPLANT WITH FIVE UNSTABLE WAR-HEADS, DEMANDING A RECOUNT.

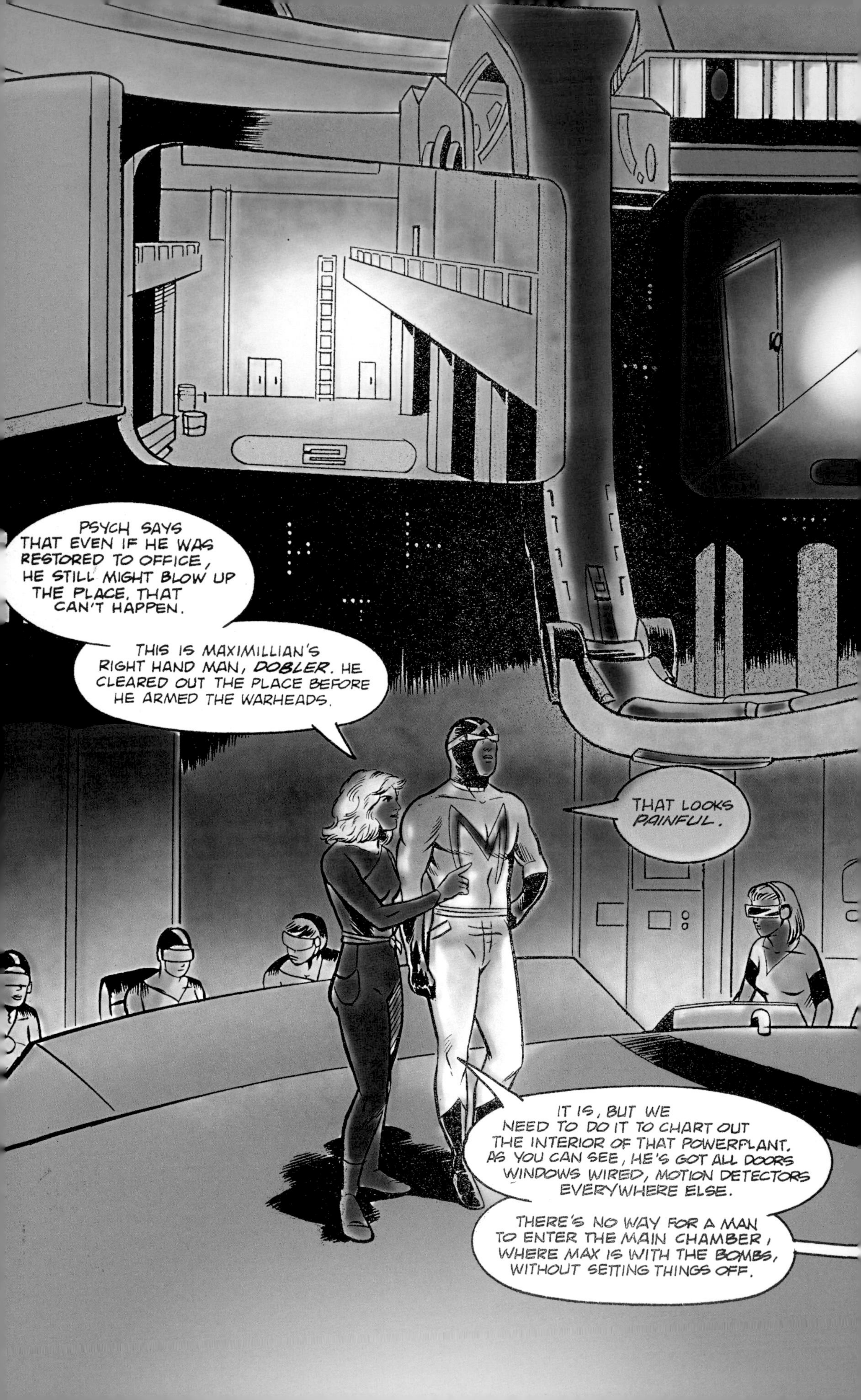
PSYCH SAYS THAT EVEN IF HE WAS RESTORED TO OFFICE, HE STILL MIGHT BLOW UP THE PLACE. THAT CAN'T HAPPEN.
THIS IS MAXIMILLIAN'S RIGHT HAND MAN, DOBLER. HE CLEARED OUT THE PLACE BEFORE HE ARMED THE WARHEADS.
THAT LOOKS PAINFUL.
IT IS, BUT WE NEED TO DO IT TO CHART OUT THE INTERIOR OF THAT POWERPLANT. AS YOU CAN SEE, HE'S GOT ALL DOORS WINDOWS WIRED, MOTION DETECTORS EVERYWHERE ELSE.
THERE'S NO WAY FOR A MAN TO ENTER THE MAIN CHAMBER, WHERE MAX IS WITH THE BOMBS, WITHOUT SETTING THINGS OFF.

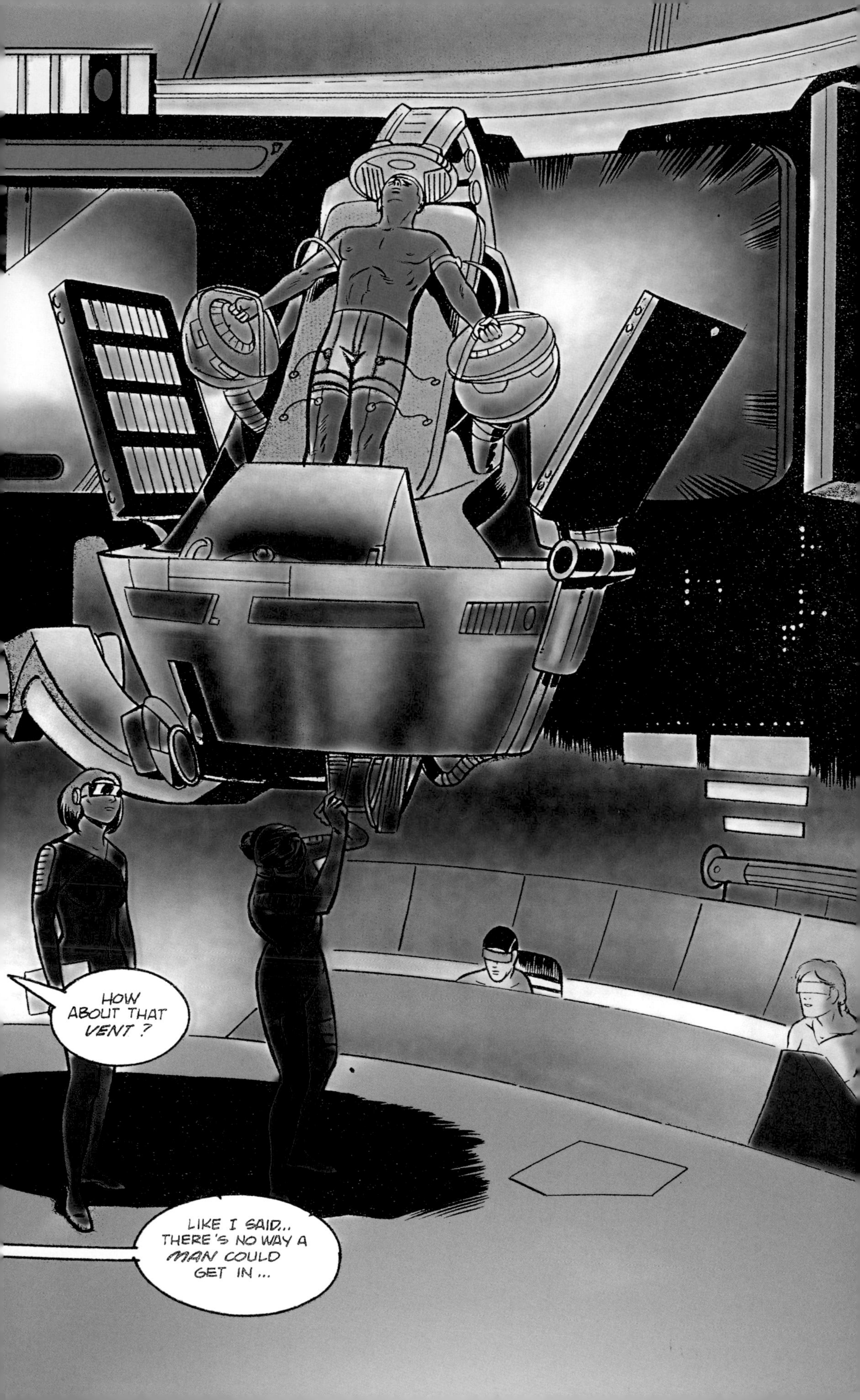
HOW ABOUT THAT VENT ?
LIKE I SAID... THERE'S NO WAY A MAN COULD GET IN...

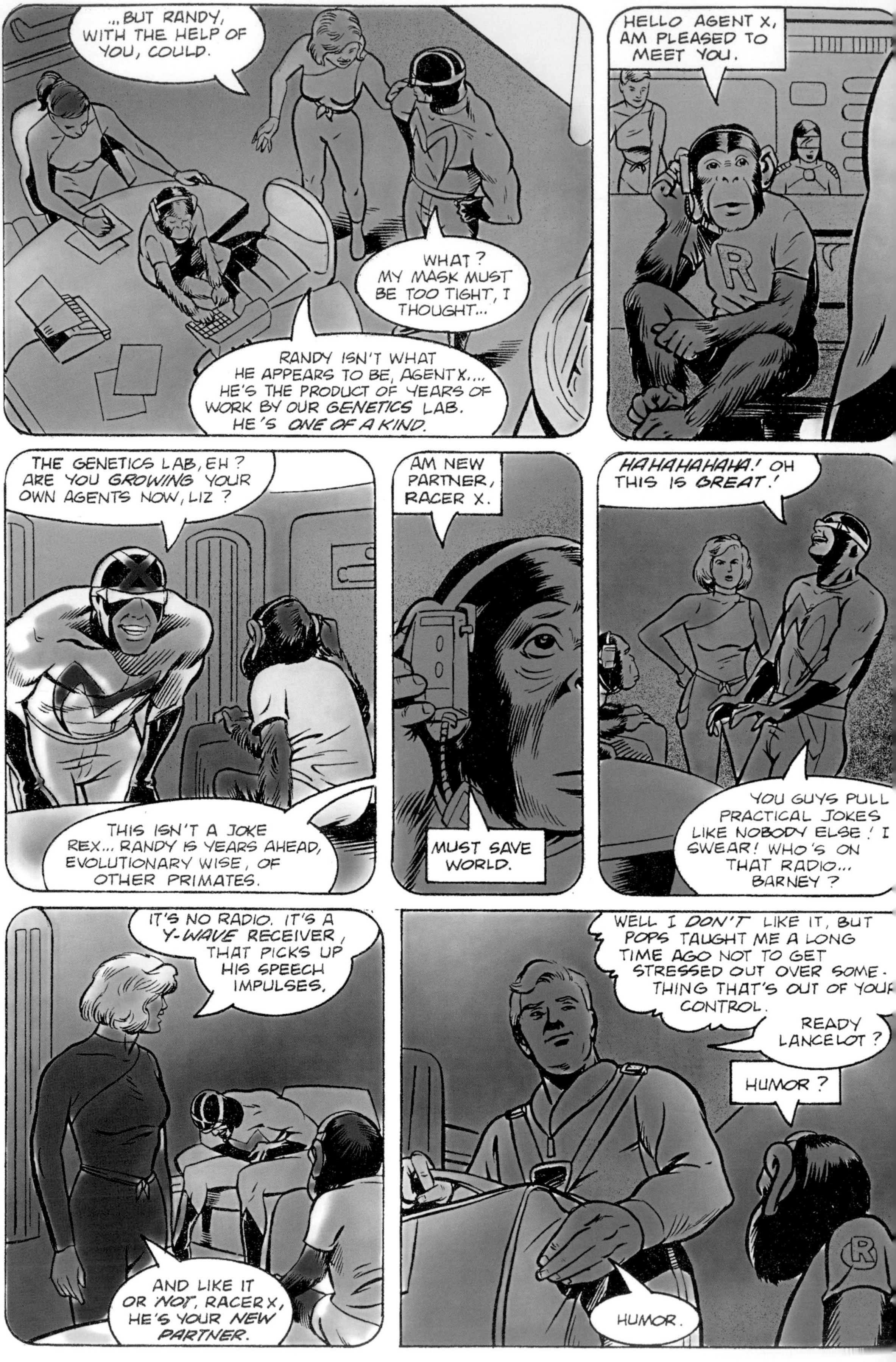
...BUT RANDY, WITH THE HELP OF YOU, COULD.
WHAT? MY MASK MUST BE TOO TIGHT, I THOUGHT...
RANDY ISN'T WHAT HE APPEARS TO BE, AGENT X.... HE'S THE PRODUCT OF YEARS OF WORK BY OUR GENETICS LAB. HE'S ONE OF A KIND.
HELLO AGENT X, AM PLEASED TO MEET YOU.
THE GENETICS LAB, EH? ARE YOU GROWING YOUR OWN AGENTS NOW, LIZ?
THIS ISN'T A JOKE REX... RANDY IS YEARS AHEAD, EVOLUTIONARY WISE, OF OTHER PRIMATES.
AM NEW PARTNER, RACER X.
MUST SAVE WORLD.
HAHAHAHAHA! OH THIS IS GREAT!
YOU GUYS PULL PRACTICAL JOKES LIKE NOBODY ELSE! I SWEAR! WHO'S ON THAT RADIO... BARNEY?
IT'S NO RADIO. IT'S A Y-WAVE RECEIVER, THAT PICKS UP HIS SPEECH IMPULSES.
AND LIKE IT OR NOT, RACER X, HE'S YOUR NEW PARTNER.
WELL I DON'T LIKE IT, BUT POPS TAUGHT ME A LONG TIME AGO NOT TO GET STRESSED OUT OVER SOME-THING THAT'S OUT OF YOUR CONTROL.
READY LANCELOT?
HUMOR?
HUMOR.

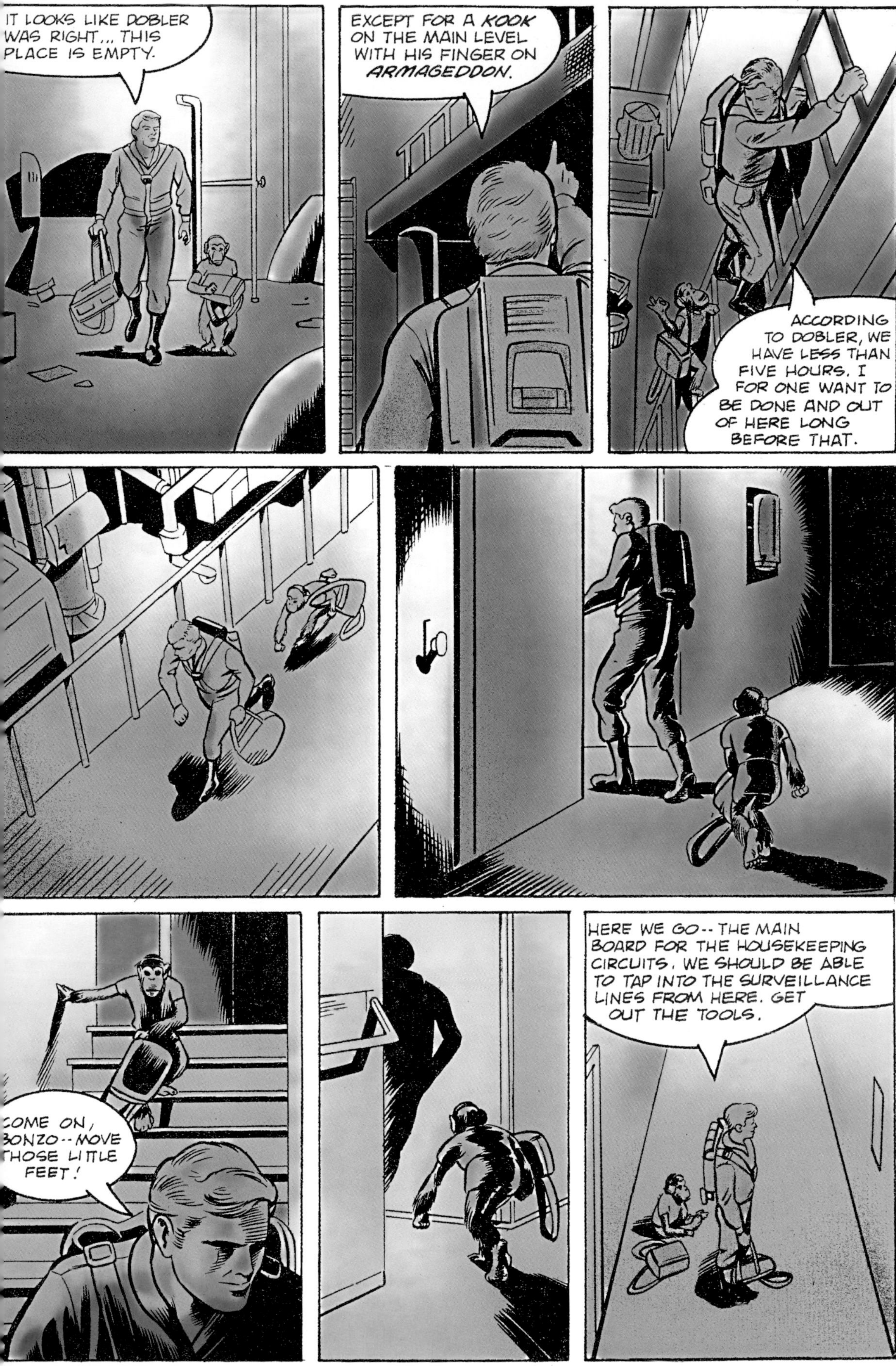
IT LOOKS LIKE DOBLER WAS RIGHT... THIS PLACE IS EMPTY.
EXCEPT FOR A KOOK ON THE MAIN LEVEL WITH HIS FINGER ON ARMAGEDDON.
ACCORDING TO DOBLER, WE HAVE LESS THAN FIVE HOURS. I FOR ONE WANT TO BE DONE AND OUT OF HERE LONG BEFORE THAT.
COME ON, BONZO--MOVE THOSE LITTLE FEET!
HERE WE GO--THE MAIN BOARD FOR THE HOUSEKEEPING CIRCUITS. WE SHOULD BE ABLE TO TAP INTO THE SURVEILLANCE LINES FROM HERE. GET OUT THE TOOLS.

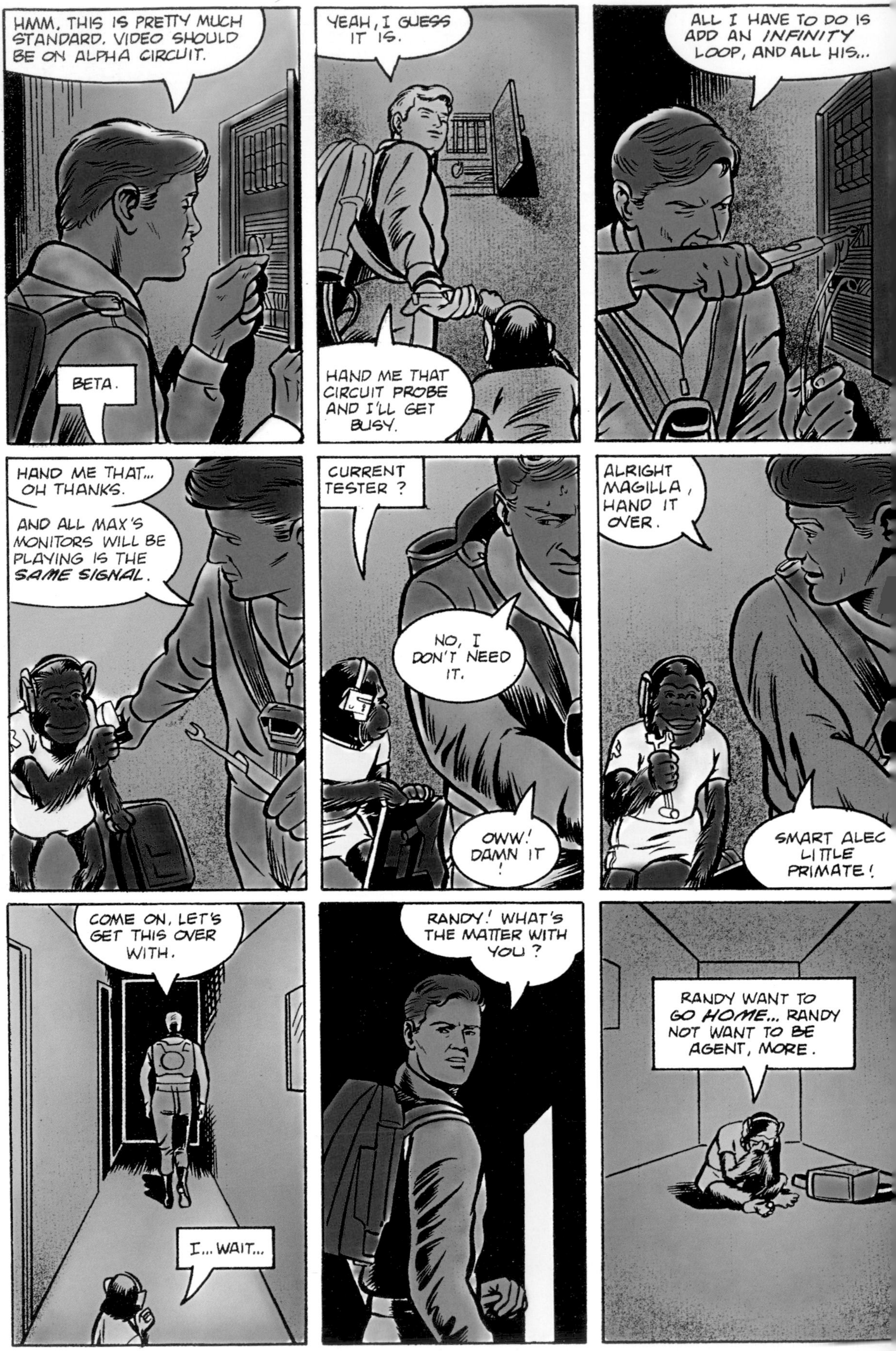
HMM, THIS IS PRETTY MUCH STANDARD. VIDEO SHOULD BE ON ALPHA CIRCUIT.
BETA.
YEAH, I GUESS IT IS.
HAND ME THAT CIRCUIT PROBE AND I'LL GET BUSY.
ALL I HAVE TO DO IS ADD AN *INFINITY* LOOP, AND ALL HIS...
HAND ME THAT... OH THANKS.
AND ALL MAX'S MONITORS WILL BE PLAYING IS THE *SAME SIGNAL*.
CURRENT TESTER ?
NO, I DON'T NEED IT.
OWW! DAMN IT!
ALRIGHT MAGILLA, HAND IT OVER.
SMART ALEC LITTLE PRIMATE!
COME ON, LET'S GET THIS OVER WITH.
I... WAIT...
RANDY! WHAT'S THE MATTER WITH YOU ?
RANDY WANT TO GO *HOME*... RANDY NOT WANT TO BE AGENT, MORE.

THIS ISN'T A GAME, FRIEND. THIS IS SERIOUS BUSINESS.

RANDY SORRY... WORLD KILLED BECAUSE OF RANDY.

KILLED?! WHAT ARE YOU TALKING ABOUT? WHAT'S WRONG WITH YOU?

WHY YOU HATE RANDY?

HATE? WHAT DO...

CALL RANDY OTHER NAMES... BONZO, MAGILLA, CHEETA, LANCELOT... BAD NAMES.

WELL, I... I GUESS I HAVE A CHIP ON MY SHOULDER. IT'S JUST THAT I'M USED TO WORKING SOLO.

HANS SOLO? STAR WARS?

NO... SOLO, ALONE.

YOU'RE THE FIRST PARTNER I'VE EVER HAD.

MY FIRST ONE.

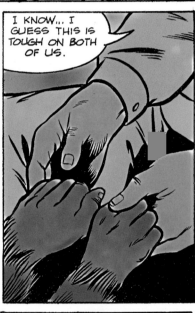

I KNOW... I GUESS THIS IS TOUGH ON BOTH OF US.

VERY TOUGH.

TELL YOU WHAT, THOUGH. I'M WILLING TO GIVE IT ANOTHER TRY, IF YOU ARE.

YES, TRY!

TRY VERY HARD!

RIGHT DOM? WE'LL SHOW 'EM!

THEN I'LL BUY THAT *YACHT* I NEED!

IGN'RANT *PEONS*... SO I BUY MYS'LF A FEW LUXURIES... S'NO REASON TO DEPOSE ME... *PEON* PEASANTS... I'LL SHOW 'EM!

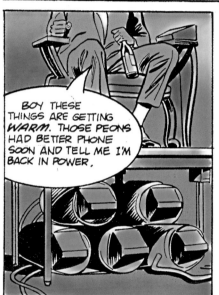

BOY THESE THINGS ARE GETTING *WARM*. THOSE PEONS HAD BETTER PHONE SOON AND TELL ME I'M BACK IN POWER.

OR I'LL DO SOMETHIN' *DRASTIC!*

AN' I *WILL*, TOO!

ATOMIC DEVICES PRIMED

LESSEE... THE *RED* SWITCH DIS'ARMS THE BOMBS... AND THE *RED* SETS 'EM OFF IN THREE MINUTES...

OR IS IT THE *OTHER* WAY AROUND? I FORGET.

POOOF!

HEY!

... MONKEY SHOT ME... GAS MAKIN' ME... LESS TRY THE *RED* SWITCH...

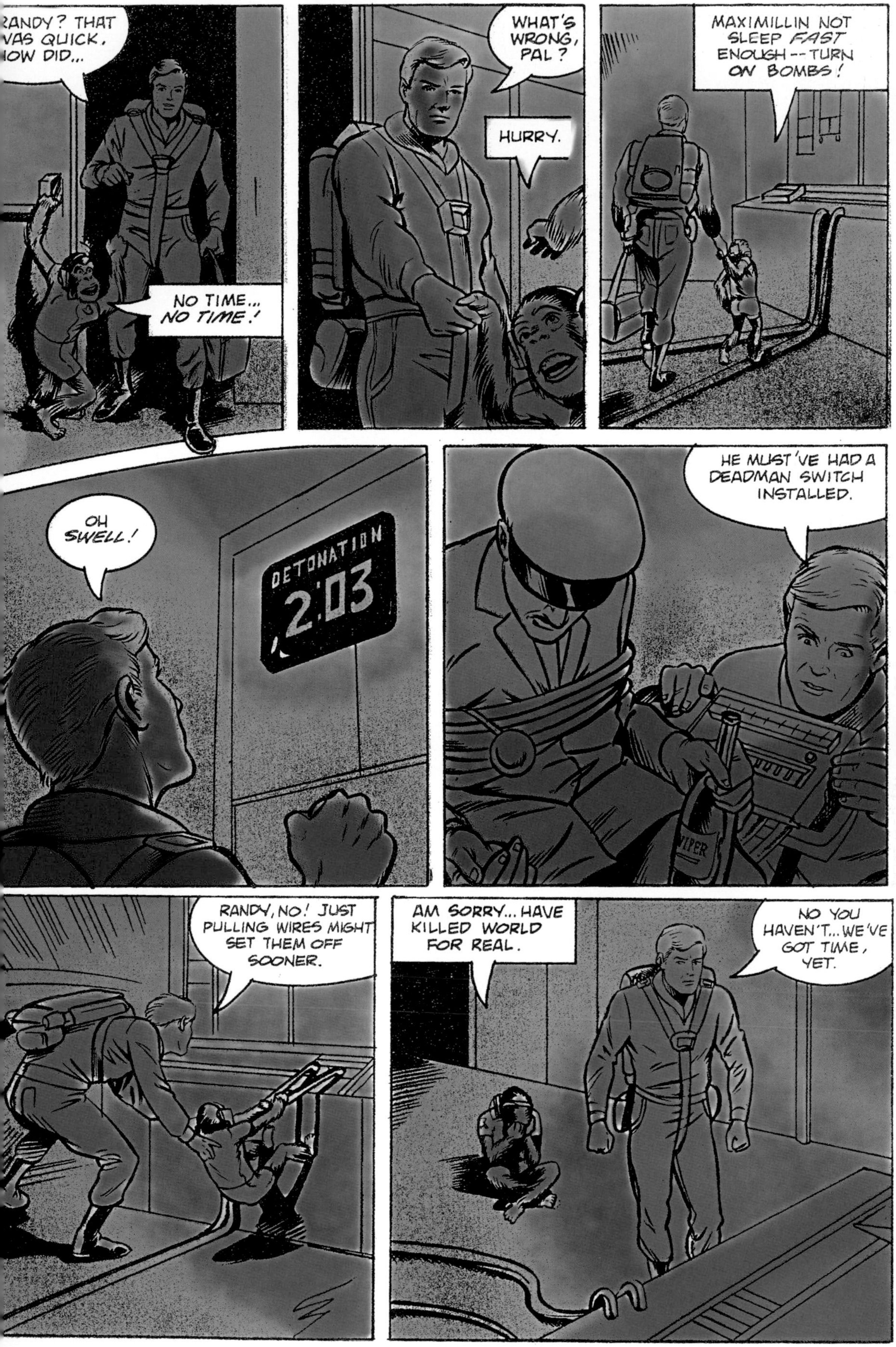
RANDY? THAT WAS QUICK. HOW DID...
NO TIME... NO TIME!
WHAT'S WRONG, PAL?
HURRY.
MAXIMILLIN NOT SLEEP FAST ENOUGH -- TURN ON BOMBS!
OH SWELL!
DETONATION
2:03
HE MUST'VE HAD A DEADMAN SWITCH INSTALLED.
VIPER
RANDY, NO! JUST PULLING WIRES MIGHT SET THEM OFF SOONER.
AM SORRY... HAVE KILLED WORLD FOR REAL.
NO YOU HAVEN'T... WE'VE GOT TIME, YET.

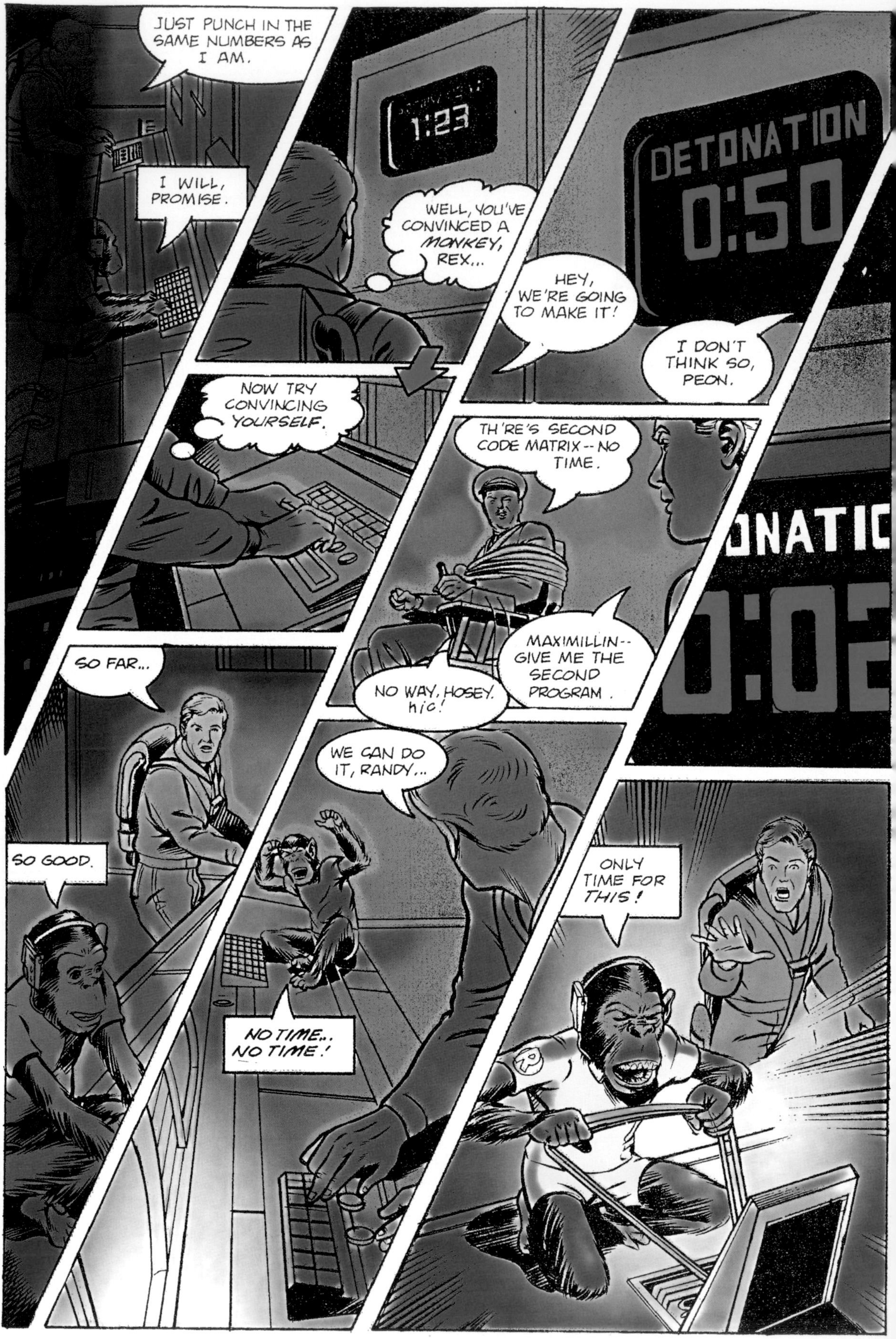
JUST PUNCH IN THE SAME NUMBERS AS I AM.
I WILL, PROMISE.
1:23
WELL, YOU'VE CONVINCED A MONKEY, REX...
DETONATION
0:50
HEY, WE'RE GOING TO MAKE IT!
I DON'T THINK SO, PEON.
NOW TRY CONVINCING YOURSELF.
TH'RE'S SECOND CODE MATRIX -- NO TIME.
ONATIC
0:02
MAXIMILLIN-- GIVE ME THE SECOND PROGRAM.
NO WAY, HOSEY. hic!
SO FAR...
SO GOOD.
WE CAN DO IT, RANDY...
NO TIME.. NO TIME!
ONLY TIME FOR THIS!

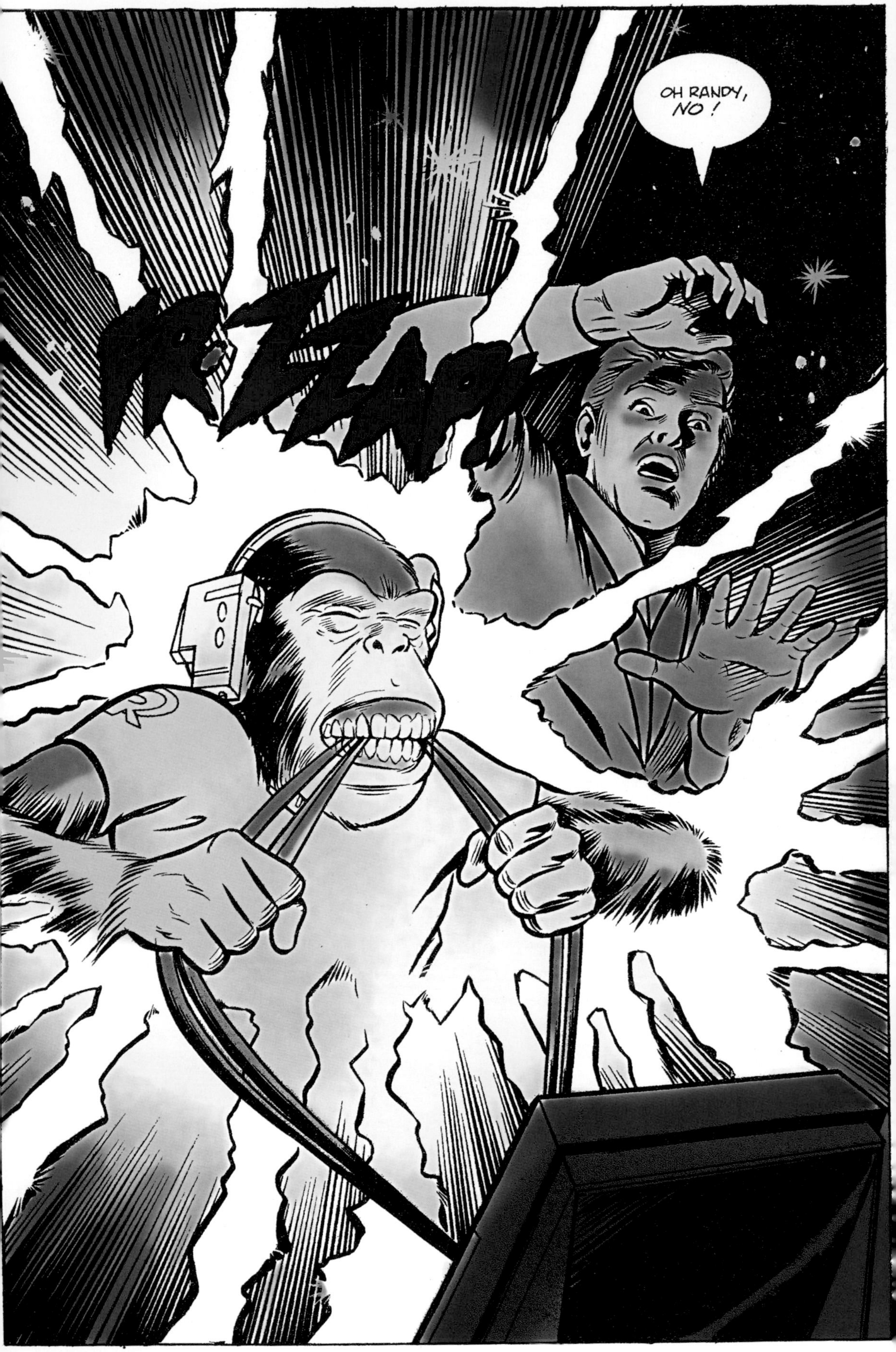
OH RANDY,
NO!

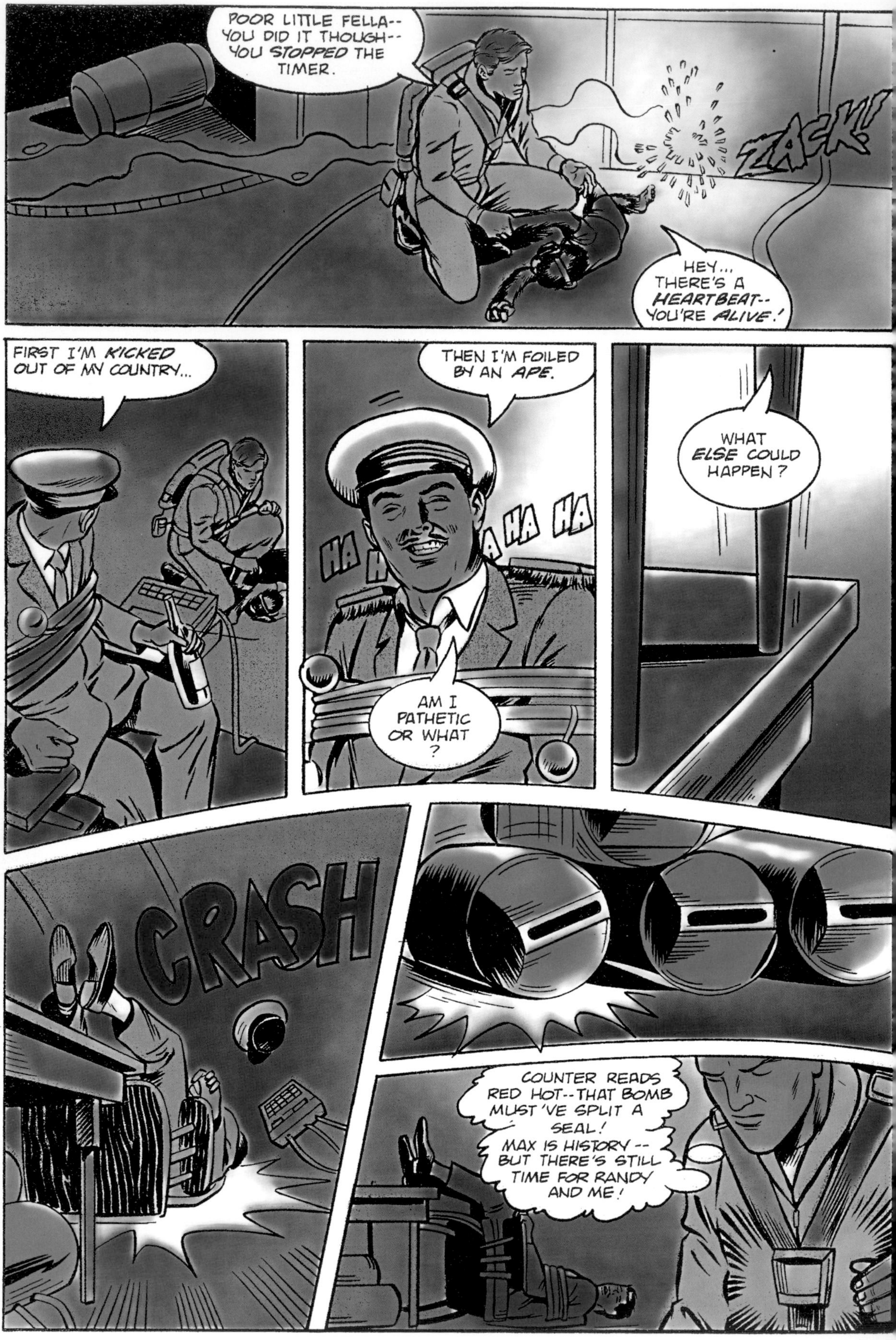
POOR LITTLE FELLA-- YOU DID IT THOUGH-- YOU STOPPED THE TIMER.
ZACK!
HEY... THERE'S A HEARTBEAT-- YOU'RE ALIVE!
FIRST I'M KICKED OUT OF MY COUNTRY...
THEN I'M FOILED BY AN APE.
HA HA HA HA HA
AM I PATHETIC OR WHAT ?
WHAT ELSE COULD HAPPEN ?
CRASH
COUNTER READS RED HOT--THAT BOMB MUST'VE SPLIT A SEAL!
MAX IS HISTORY -- BUT THERE'S STILL TIME FOR RANDY AND ME!

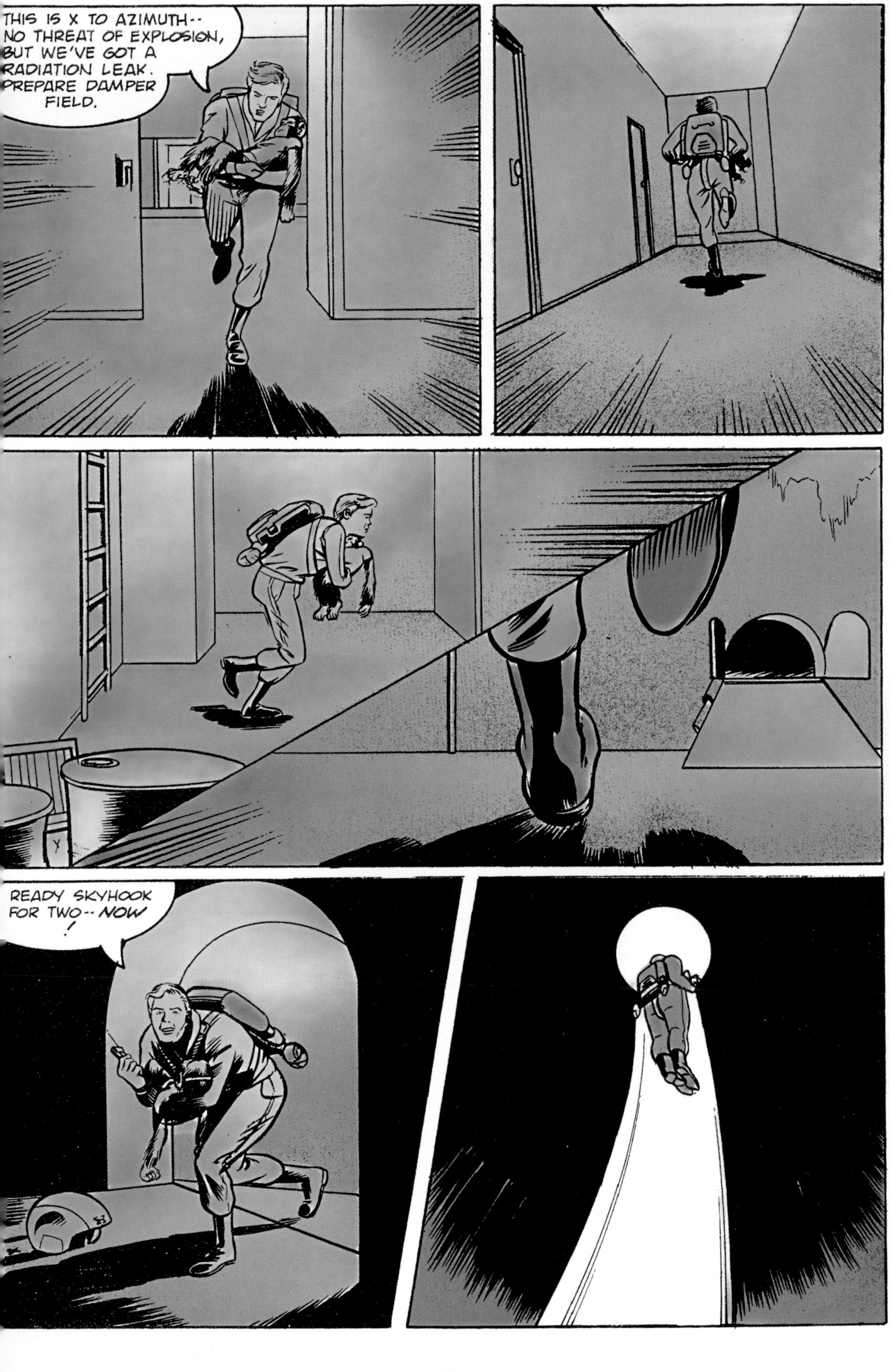
THIS IS X TO AZIMUTH-- NO THREAT OF EXPLOSION, BUT WE'VE GOT A RADIATION LEAK. PREPARE DAMPER FIELD.
READY SKYHOOK FOR TWO-- NOW!

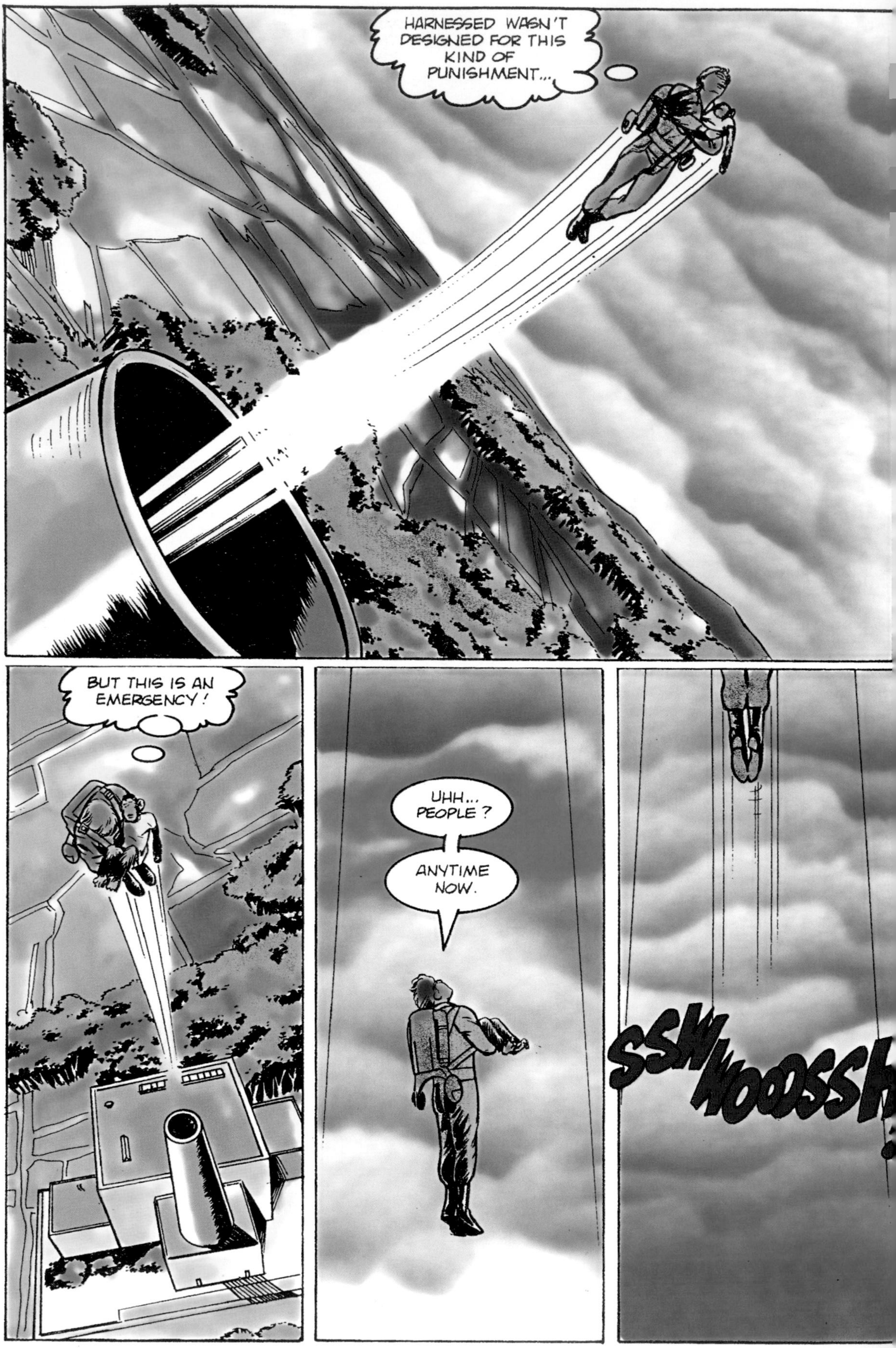
HARNESSED WASN'T DESIGNED FOR THIS KIND OF PUNISHMENT...
BUT THIS IS AN EMERGENCY!
UHH... PEOPLE?
ANYTIME NOW.
SSWHOOSSH

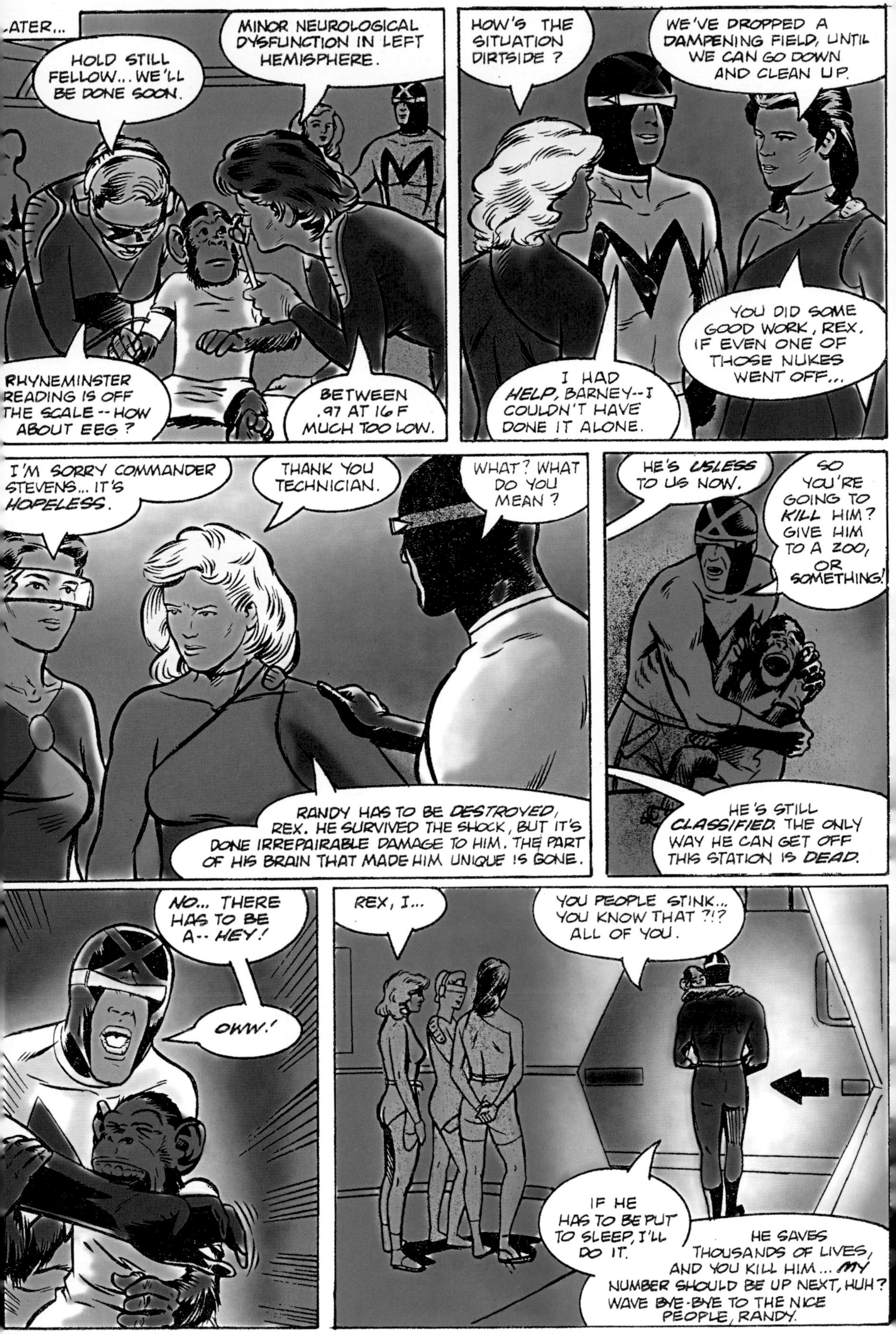

LATER...
HOLD STILL FELLOW... WE'LL BE DONE SOON.
MINOR NEUROLOGICAL DYSFUNCTION IN LEFT HEMISPHERE.
RHYNEMINSTER READING IS OFF THE SCALE -- HOW ABOUT EEG?
BETWEEN .97 AT 16F MUCH TOO LOW.
HOW'S THE SITUATION DIRTSIDE?
WE'VE DROPPED A DAMPENING FIELD, UNTIL WE CAN GO DOWN AND CLEAN UP.
YOU DID SOME GOOD WORK, REX. IF EVEN ONE OF THOSE NUKES WENT OFF...
I HAD HELP, BARNEY-- I COULDN'T HAVE DONE IT ALONE.
I'M SORRY COMMANDER STEVENS... IT'S HOPELESS.
THANK YOU TECHNICIAN.
WHAT? WHAT DO YOU MEAN?
RANDY HAS TO BE DESTROYED, REX. HE SURVIVED THE SHOCK, BUT IT'S DONE IRREPAIRABLE DAMAGE TO HIM. THE PART OF HIS BRAIN THAT MADE HIM UNIQUE IS GONE.
HE'S USLESS TO US NOW.
SO YOU'RE GOING TO KILL HIM? GIVE HIM TO A ZOO, OR SOMETHING!
HE'S STILL CLASSIFIED. THE ONLY WAY HE CAN GET OFF THIS STATION IS DEAD.
NO... THERE HAS TO BE A-- HEY!
OWW!
REX, I...
YOU PEOPLE STINK... YOU KNOW THAT ?!?
ALL OF YOU.
IF HE HAS TO BE PUT TO SLEEP, I'LL DO IT.
HE SAVES THOUSANDS OF LIVES, AND YOU KILL HIM... MY NUMBER SHOULD BE UP NEXT, HUH? WAVE BYE-BYE TO THE NICE PEOPLE, RANDY.

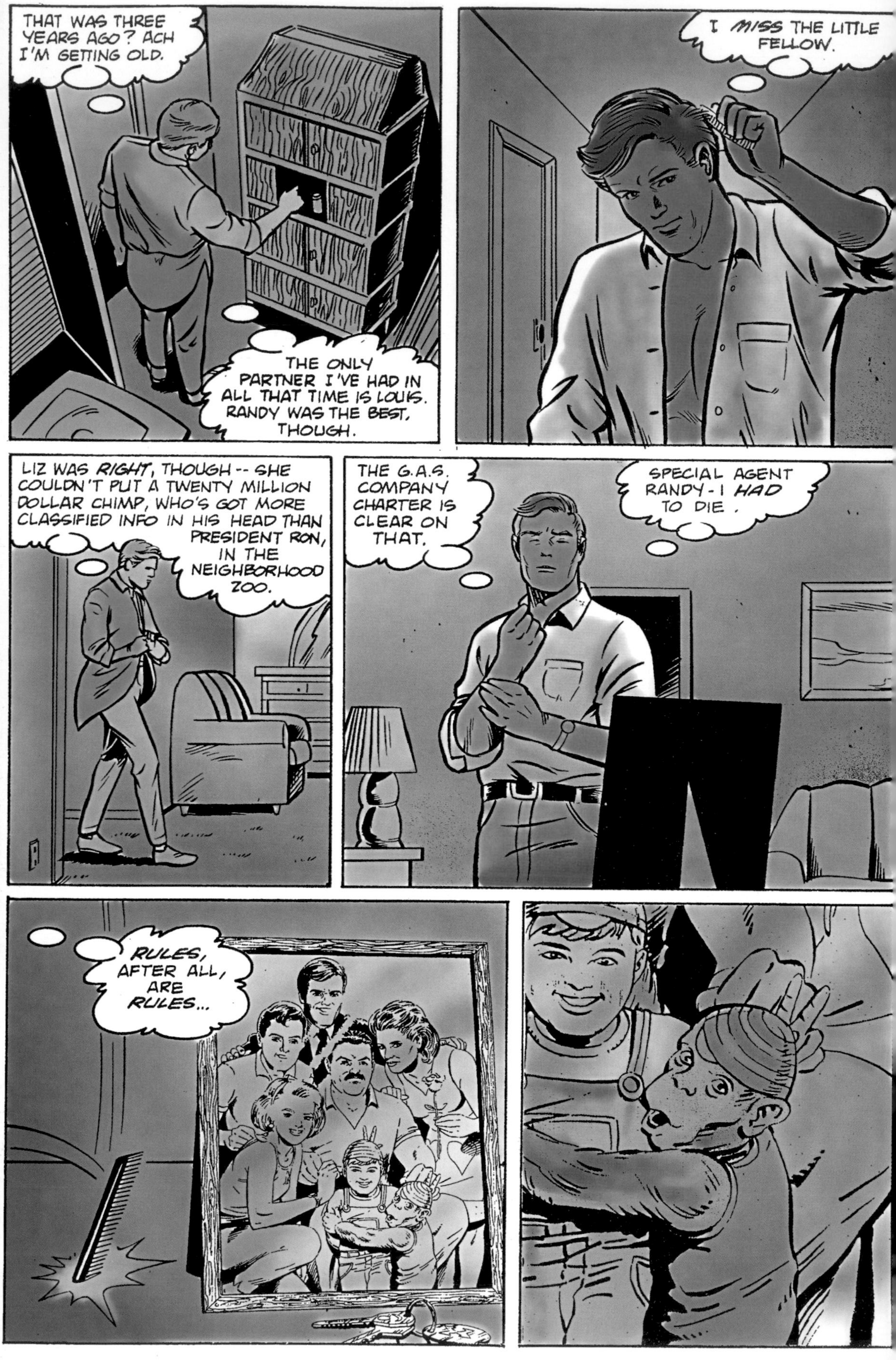
THAT WAS THREE YEARS AGO? ACH I'M GETTING OLD.
THE ONLY PARTNER I'VE HAD IN ALL THAT TIME IS LOUIS. RANDY WAS THE BEST, THOUGH.
I MISS THE LITTLE FELLOW.
LIZ WAS RIGHT, THOUGH -- SHE COULDN'T PUT A TWENTY MILLION DOLLAR CHIMP, WHO'S GOT MORE CLASSIFIED INFO IN HIS HEAD THAN PRESIDENT RON, IN THE NEIGHBORHOOD ZOO.
THE G.A.S. COMPANY CHARTER IS CLEAR ON THAT.
SPECIAL AGENT RANDY - I HAD TO DIE.
RULES, AFTER ALL, ARE RULES...

Racer X #2

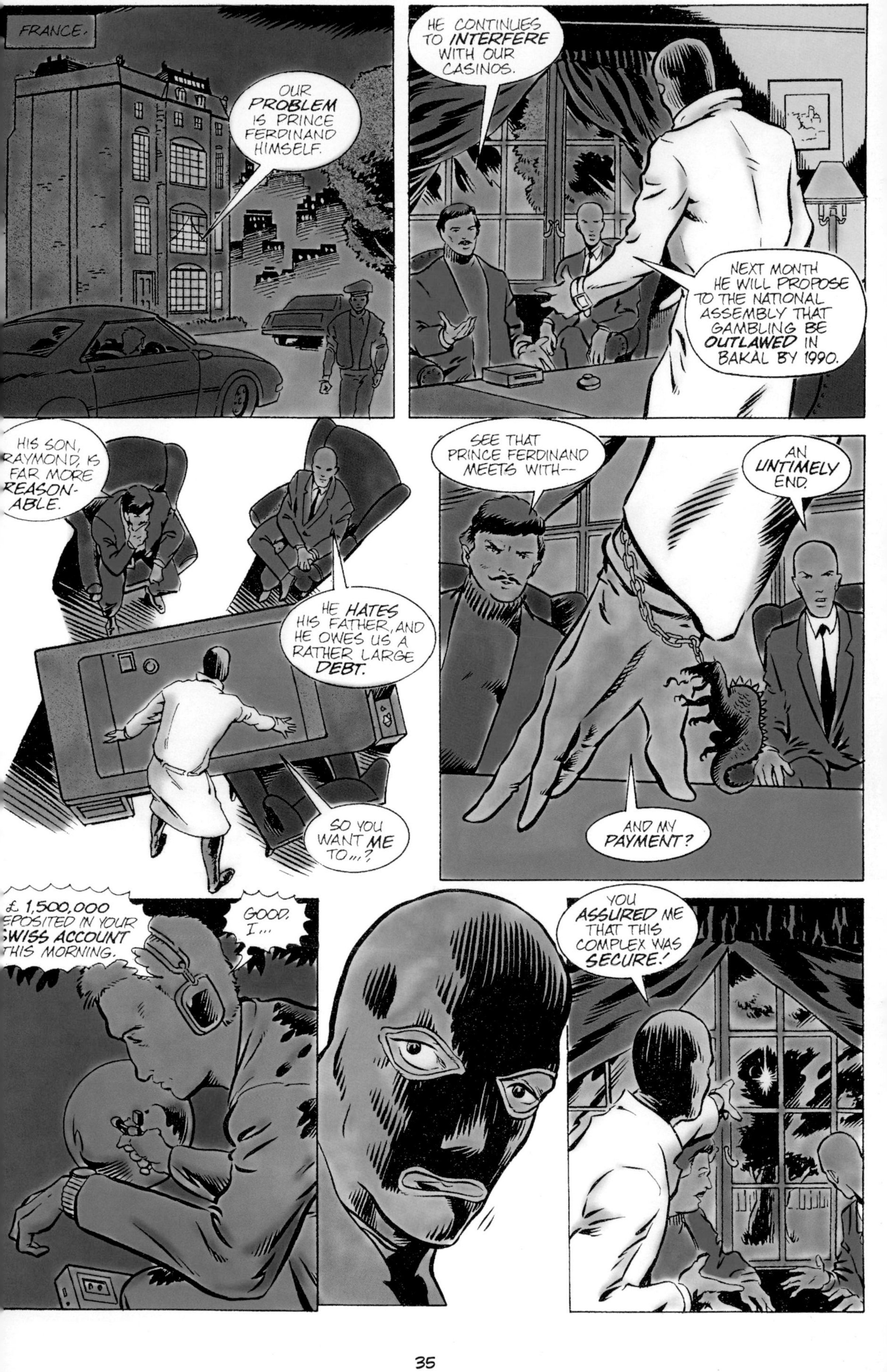
FRANCE.
OUR PROBLEM IS PRINCE FERDINAND HIMSELF.
HE CONTINUES TO INTERFERE WITH OUR CASINOS.
NEXT MONTH HE WILL PROPOSE TO THE NATIONAL ASSEMBLY THAT GAMBLING BE OUTLAWED IN BAKAL BY 1990.
HIS SON, RAYMOND, IS FAR MORE REASON-ABLE.
HE HATES HIS FATHER, AND HE OWES US A RATHER LARGE DEBT.
SO YOU WANT ME TO...?
SEE THAT PRINCE FERDINAND MEETS WITH--
AN UNTIMELY END.
AND MY PAYMENT?
£ 1,500,000 DEPOSITED IN YOUR SWISS ACCOUNT THIS MORNING.
GOOD. I...
YOU ASSURED ME THAT THIS COMPLEX WAS SECURE!

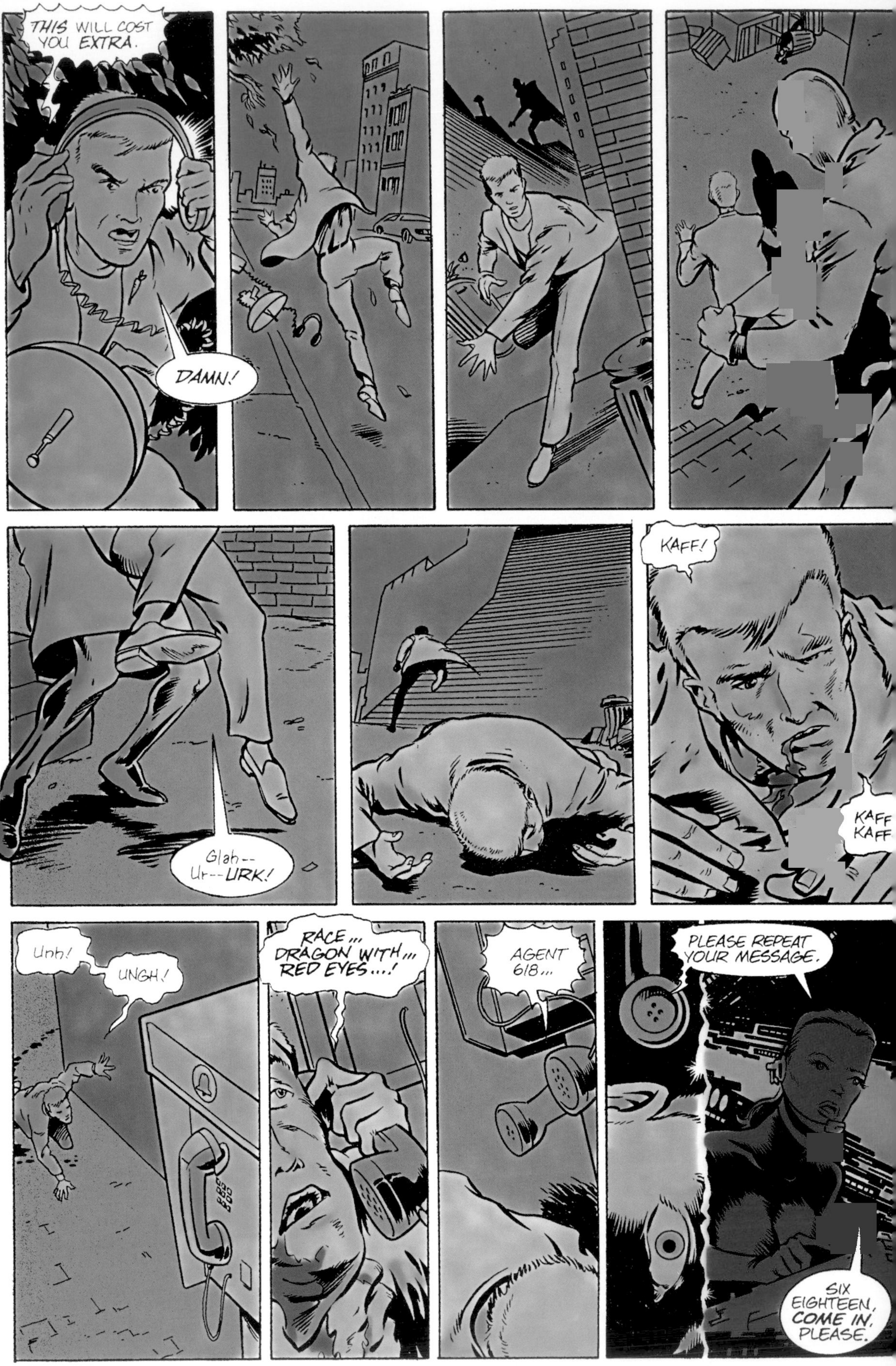
THIS WILL COST YOU EXTRA.
DAMN!
Glah-- Ur--URK!
KAFF!
KAFF KAFF
Unh!
UNGH!
RACE... DRAGON WITH... RED EYES....!
AGENT 618...
PLEASE REPEAT YOUR MESSAGE.
SIX EIGHTEEN, COME IN, PLEASE.

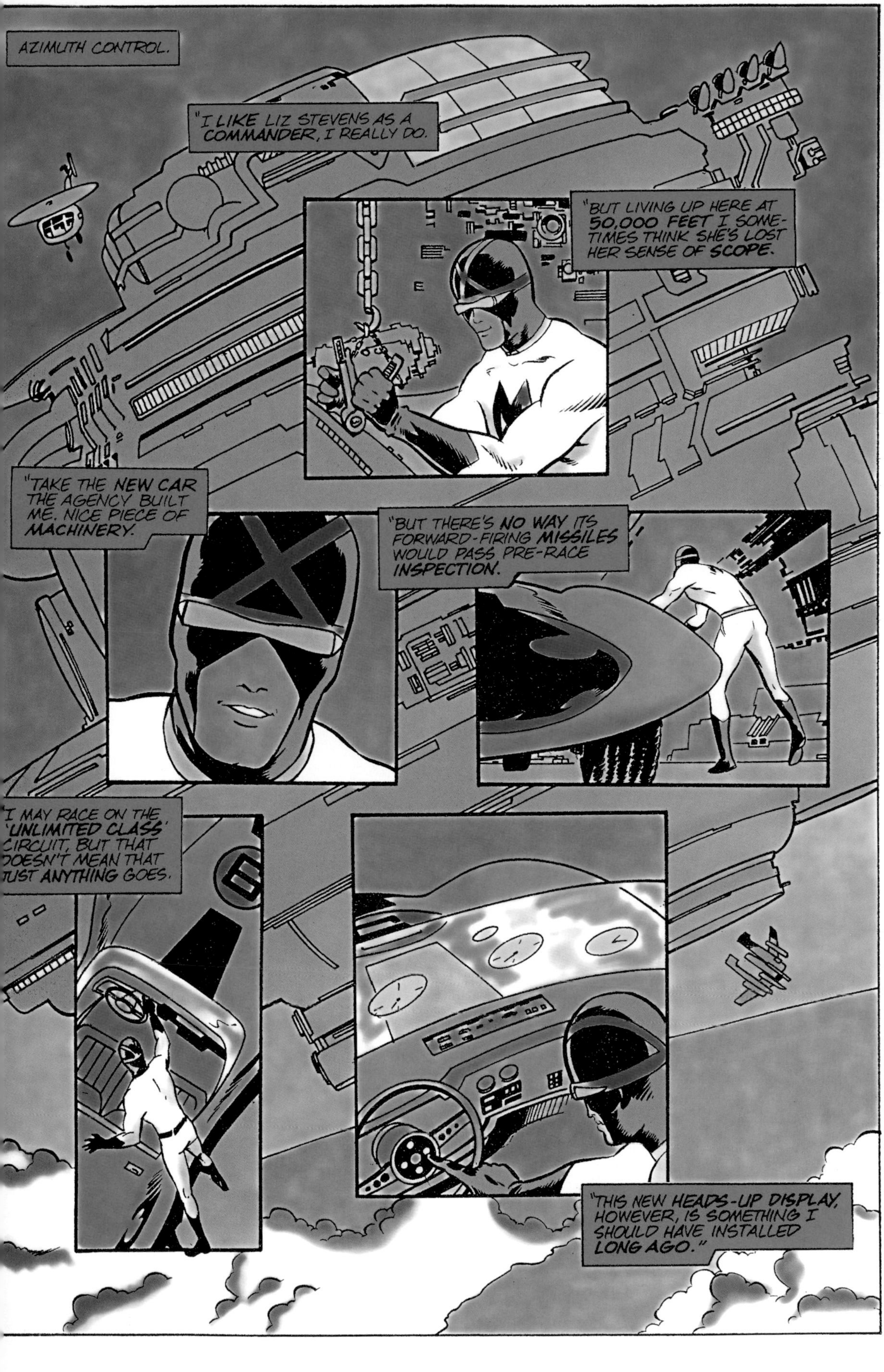
AZIMUTH CONTROL.
"I LIKE LIZ STEVENS AS A COMMANDER, I REALLY DO.
"BUT LIVING UP HERE AT 50,000 FEET I SOMETIMES THINK SHE'S LOST HER SENSE OF SCOPE.
"TAKE THE NEW CAR THE AGENCY BUILT ME. NICE PIECE OF MACHINERY.
"BUT THERE'S NO WAY ITS FORWARD-FIRING MISSILES WOULD PASS PRE-RACE INSPECTION.
"I MAY RACE ON THE 'UNLIMITED CLASS' CIRCUIT, BUT THAT DOESN'T MEAN THAT JUST ANYTHING GOES.
"THIS NEW HEADS-UP DISPLAY, HOWEVER, IS SOMETHING I SHOULD HAVE INSTALLED LONG AGO."

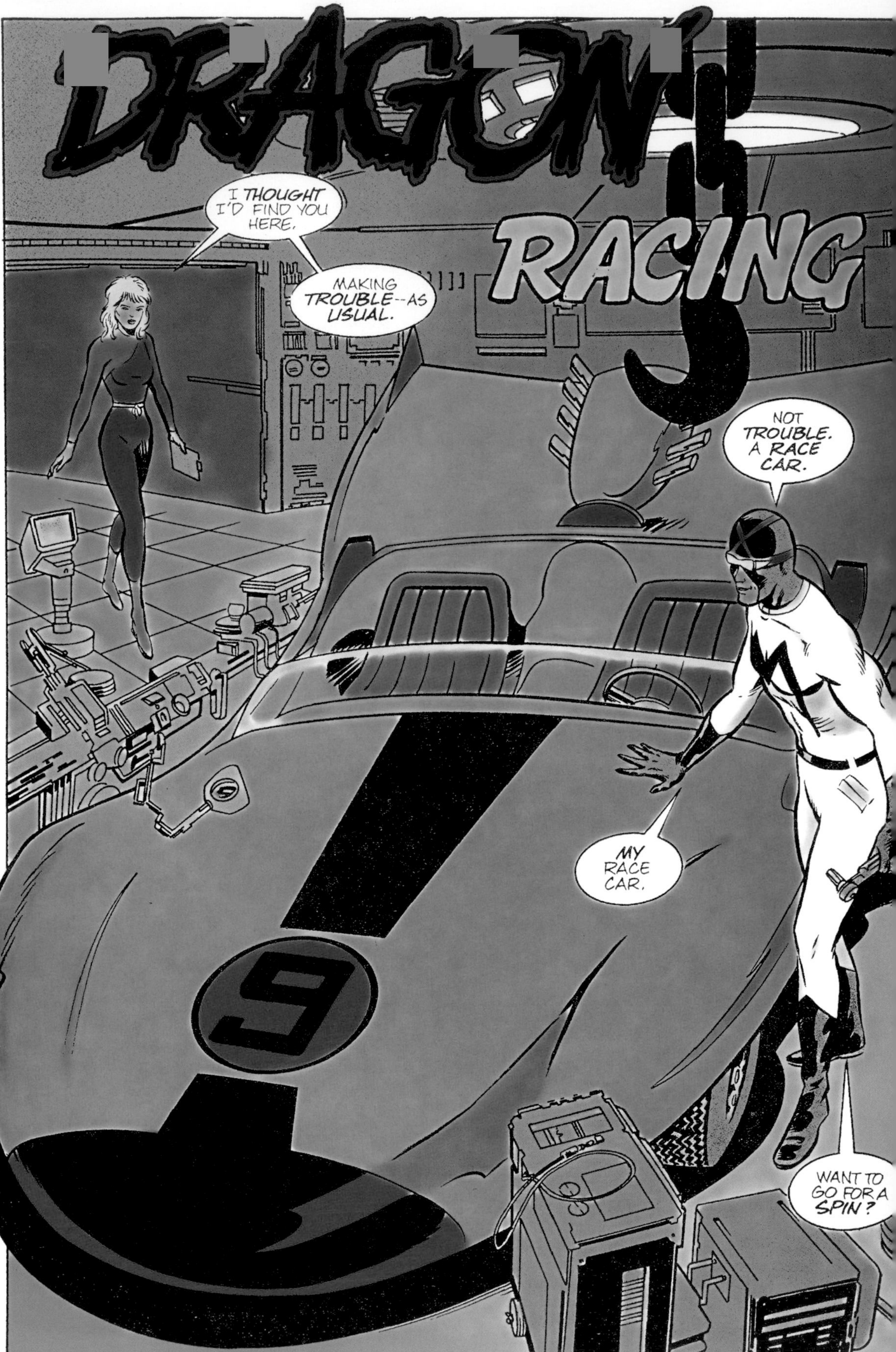
DRAGON
RACING
I THOUGHT I'D FIND YOU HERE.
MAKING TROUBLE--AS USUAL.
NOT TROUBLE. A RACE CAR.
MY RACE CAR.
WANT TO GO FOR A SPIN?

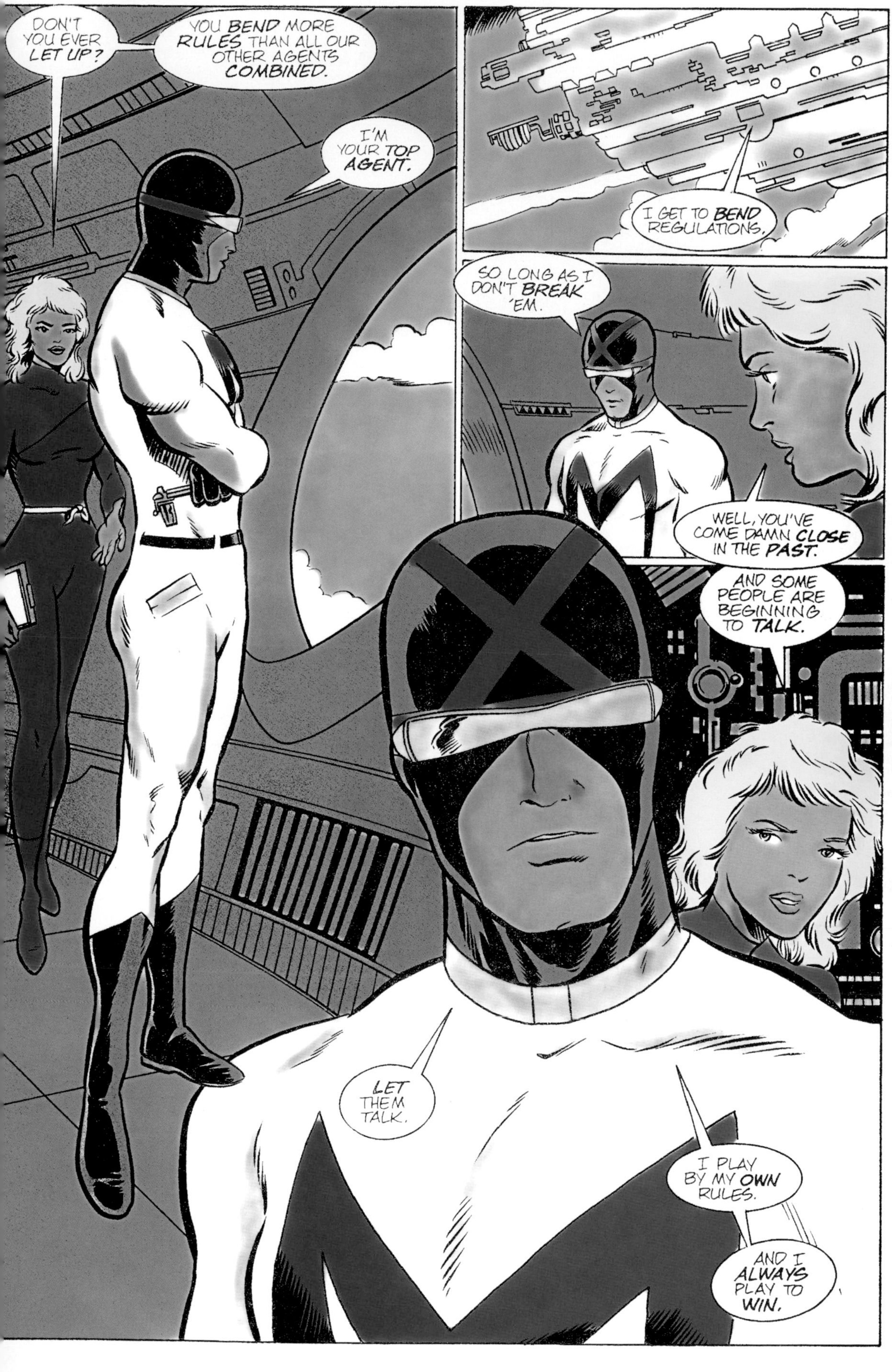
DON'T YOU EVER LET UP?
YOU BEND MORE RULES THAN ALL OUR OTHER AGENTS COMBINED.
I'M YOUR TOP AGENT.
I GET TO BEND REGULATIONS,
SO LONG AS I DON'T BREAK 'EM.
WELL, YOU'VE COME DAMN CLOSE IN THE PAST.
AND SOME PEOPLE ARE BEGINNING TO TALK.
LET THEM TALK.
I PLAY BY MY OWN RULES.
AND I ALWAYS PLAY TO WIN.

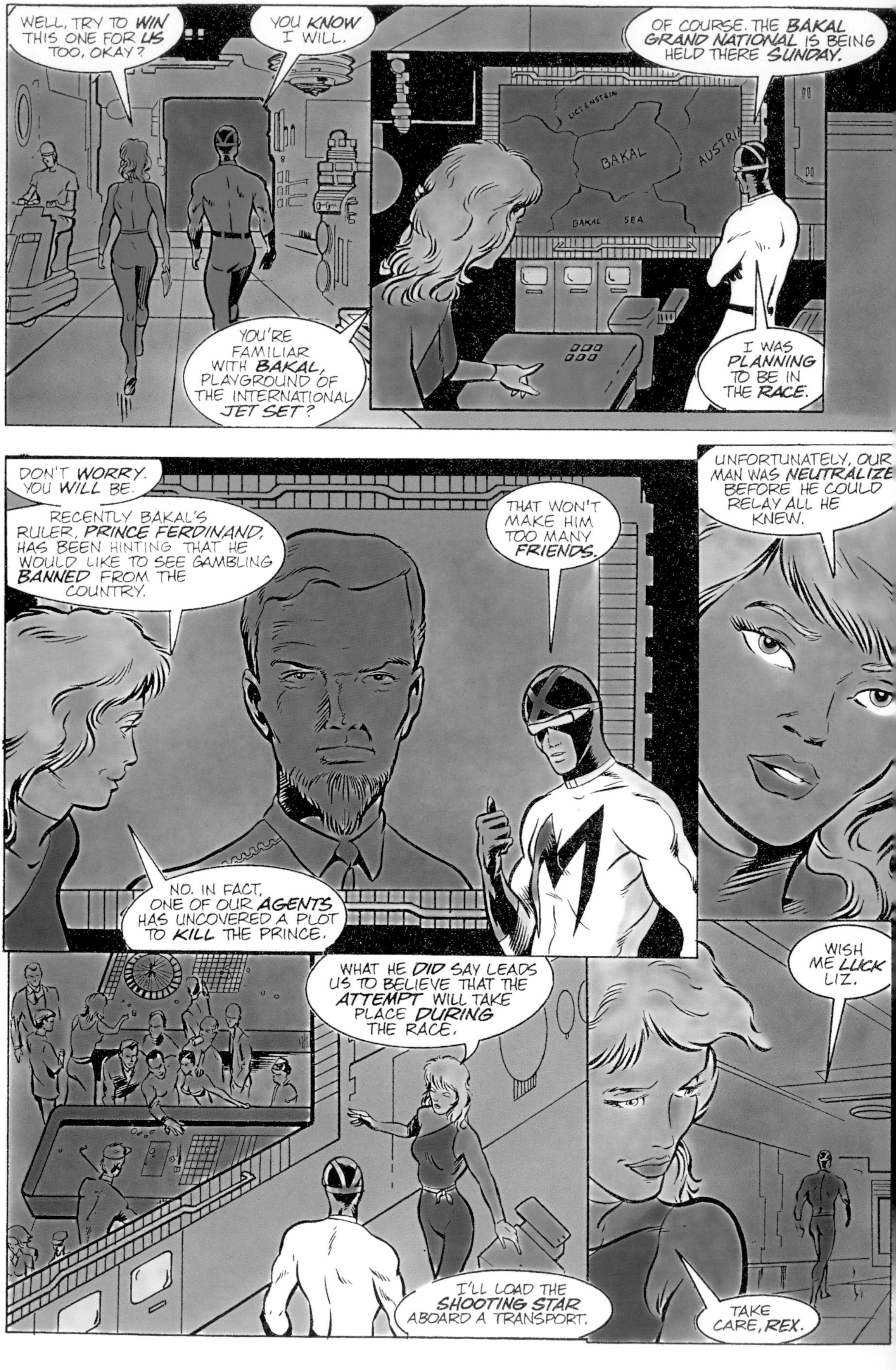

WELL, TRY TO WIN THIS ONE FOR US TOO, OKAY?
YOU KNOW I WILL.
YOU'RE FAMILIAR WITH BAKAL, PLAYGROUND OF THE INTERNATIONAL JET SET?
OF COURSE. THE BAKAL GRAND NATIONAL IS BEING HELD THERE SUNDAY.
LICTENSTEIN
BAKAL
AUSTRIA
BAKAL SEA
I WAS PLANNING TO BE IN THE RACE.
DON'T WORRY. YOU WILL BE.
RECENTLY BAKAL'S RULER, PRINCE FERDINAND, HAS BEEN HINTING THAT HE WOULD LIKE TO SEE GAMBLING BANNED FROM THE COUNTRY.
THAT WON'T MAKE HIM TOO MANY FRIENDS.
NO. IN FACT, ONE OF OUR AGENTS HAS UNCOVERED A PLOT TO KILL THE PRINCE.
UNFORTUNATELY, OUR MAN WAS NEUTRALIZE BEFORE HE COULD RELAY ALL HE KNEW.
WHAT HE DID SAY LEADS US TO BELIEVE THAT THE ATTEMPT WILL TAKE PLACE DURING THE RACE.
I'LL LOAD THE SHOOTING STAR ABOARD A TRANSPORT.
WISH ME LUCK LIZ.
TAKE CARE, REX.

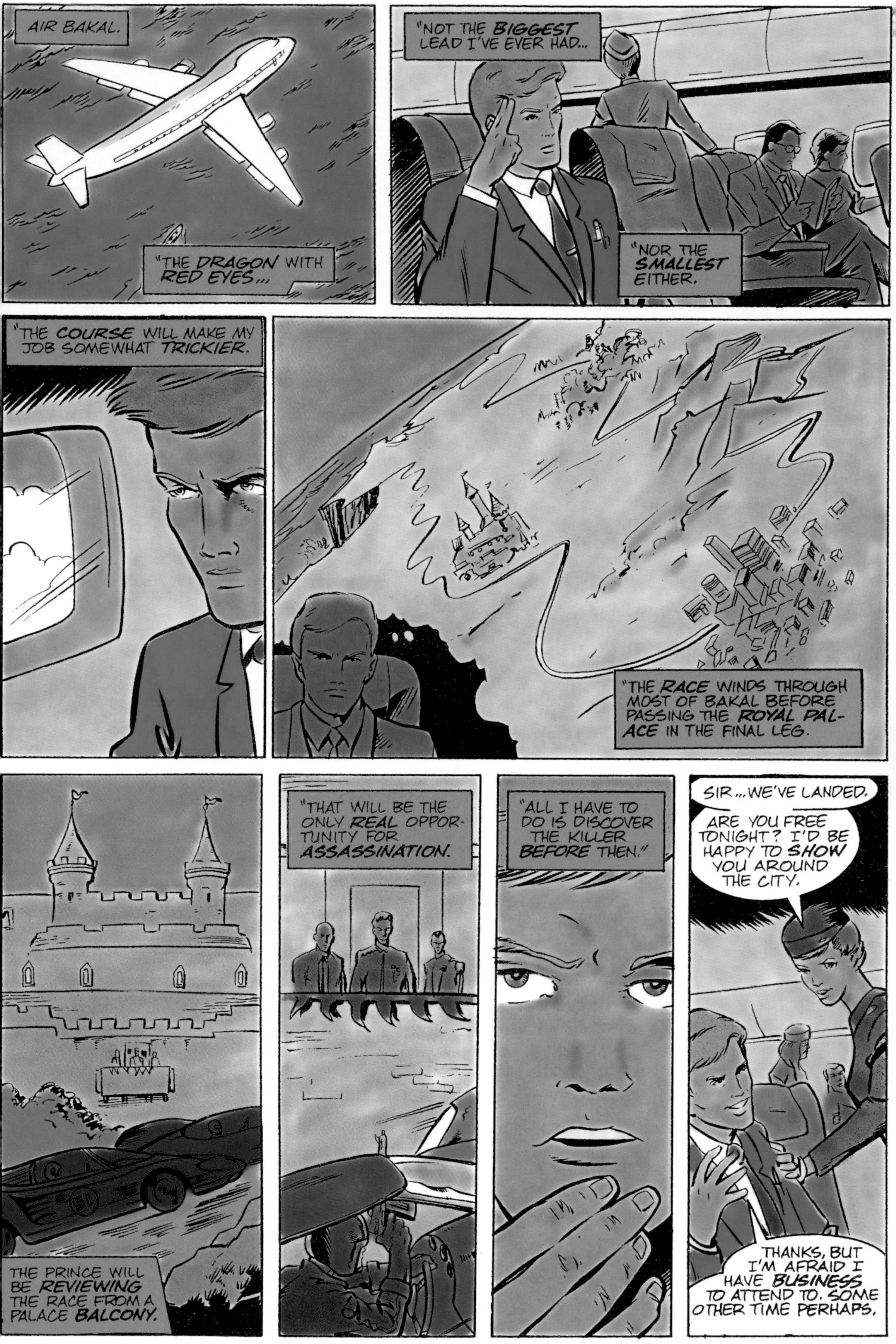
AIR BAKAL.
"THE DRAGON WITH RED EYES...
"NOT THE BIGGEST LEAD I'VE EVER HAD...
"NOR THE SMALLEST EITHER.
"THE COURSE WILL MAKE MY JOB SOMEWHAT TRICKIER.
"THE RACE WINDS THROUGH MOST OF BAKAL BEFORE PASSING THE ROYAL PALACE IN THE FINAL LEG.
THE PRINCE WILL BE REVIEWING THE RACE FROM A PALACE BALCONY.
"THAT WILL BE THE ONLY REAL OPPORTUNITY FOR ASSASSINATION.
"ALL I HAVE TO DO IS DISCOVER THE KILLER BEFORE THEN."
SIR... WE'VE LANDED.
ARE YOU FREE TONIGHT? I'D BE HAPPY TO SHOW YOU AROUND THE CITY.
THANKS, BUT I'M AFRAID I HAVE BUSINESS TO ATTEND TO. SOME OTHER TIME PERHAPS.

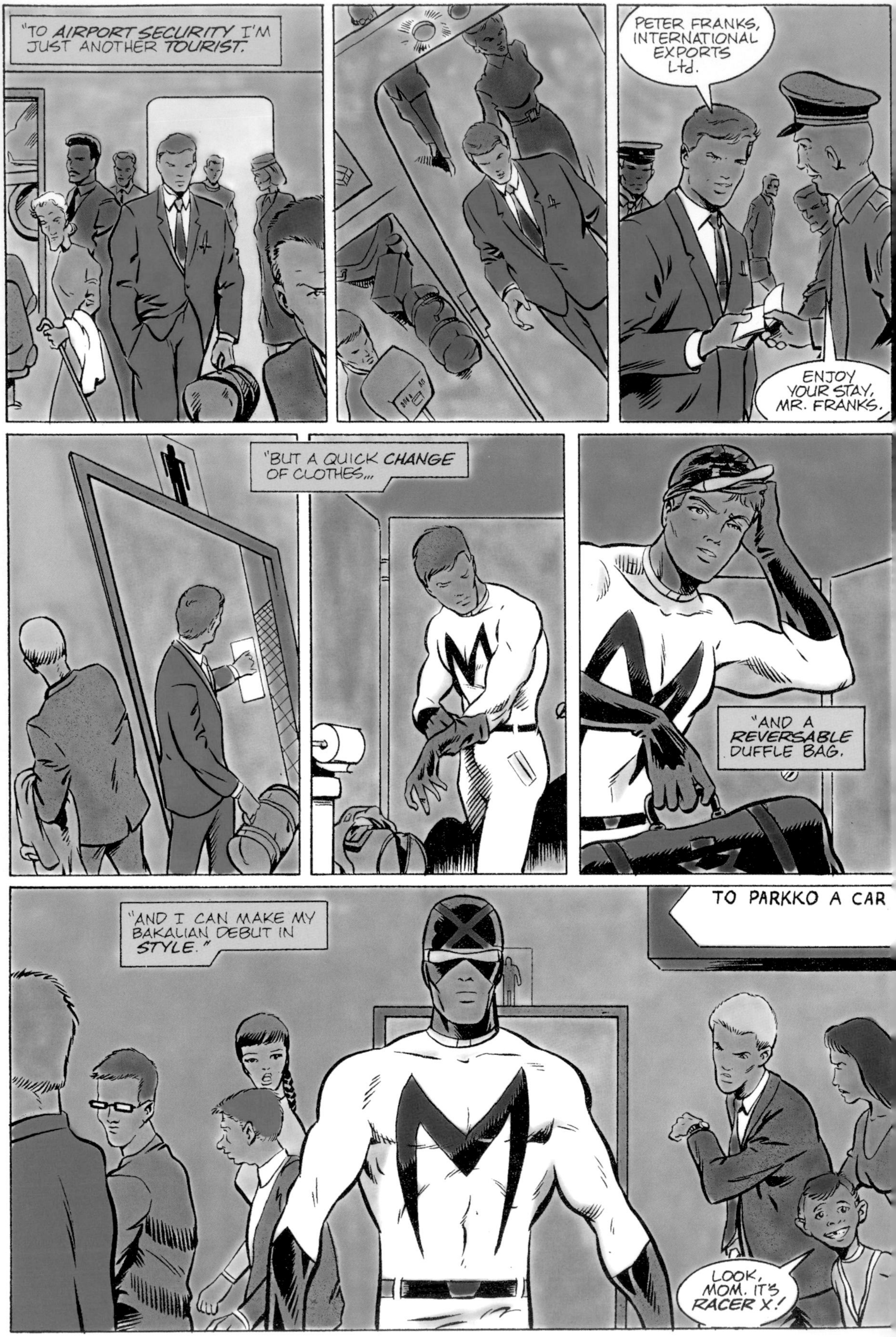
"TO AIRPORT SECURITY I'M JUST ANOTHER TOURIST.
PETER FRANKS, INTERNATIONAL EXPORTS Ltd.
ENJOY YOUR STAY, MR. FRANKS.
"BUT A QUICK CHANGE OF CLOTHES...
"AND A REVERSABLE DUFFLE BAG.
"AND I CAN MAKE MY BAKALIAN DEBUT IN STYLE."
TO PARKKO A CAR
LOOK, MOM. IT'S RACER X!

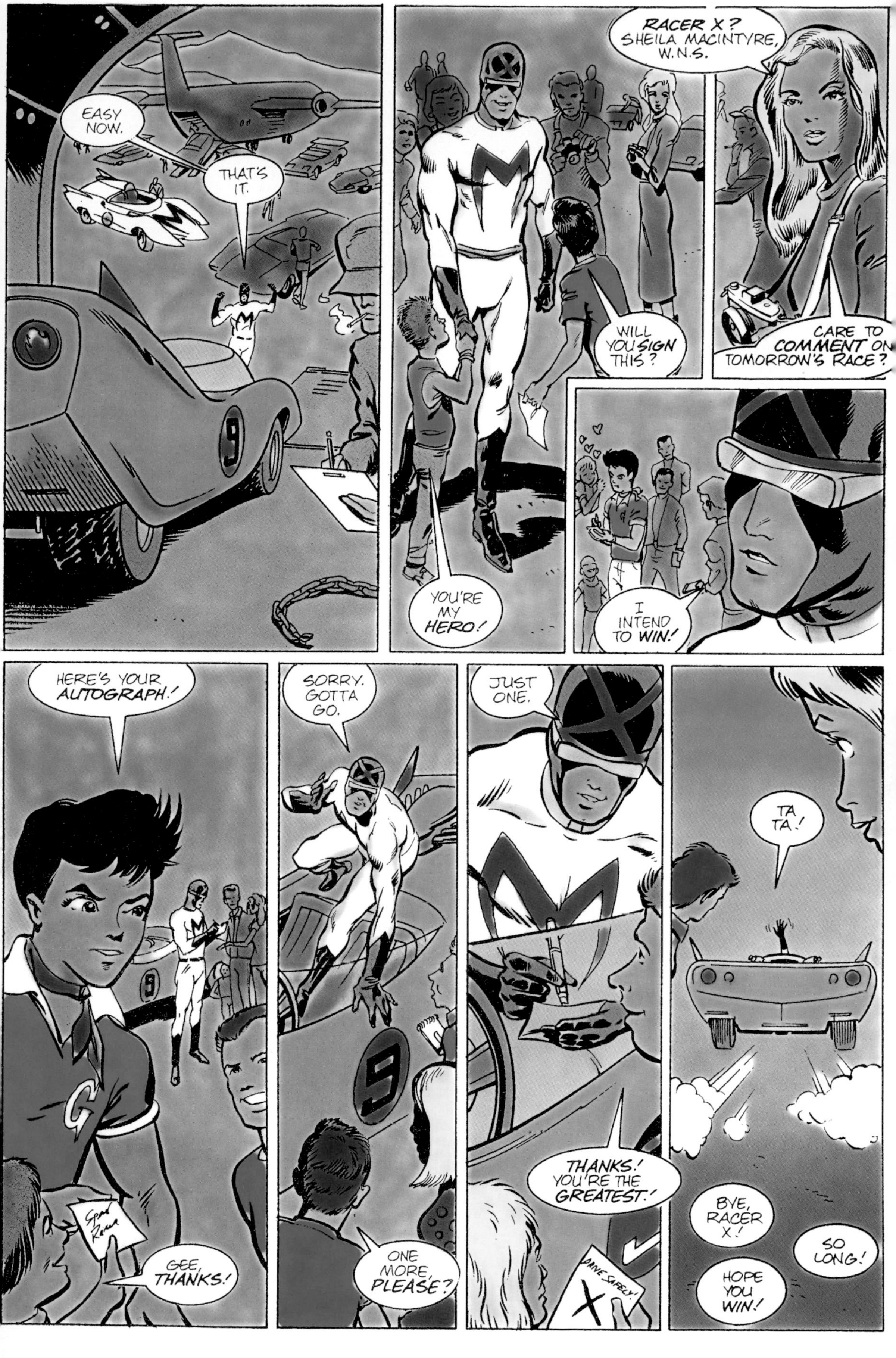
EASY NOW.
THAT'S IT.
RACER X? SHEILA MACINTYRE, W.N.S.
WILL YOU SIGN THIS?
YOU'RE MY HERO!
CARE TO COMMENT ON TOMORROW'S RACE?
I INTEND TO WIN!
HERE'S YOUR AUTOGRAPH!
GEE, THANKS!
SORRY. GOTTA GO.
ONE MORE, PLEASE?
JUST ONE.
THANKS! YOU'RE THE GREATEST!
TA TA!
BYE, RACER X!
SO LONG!
HOPE YOU WIN!

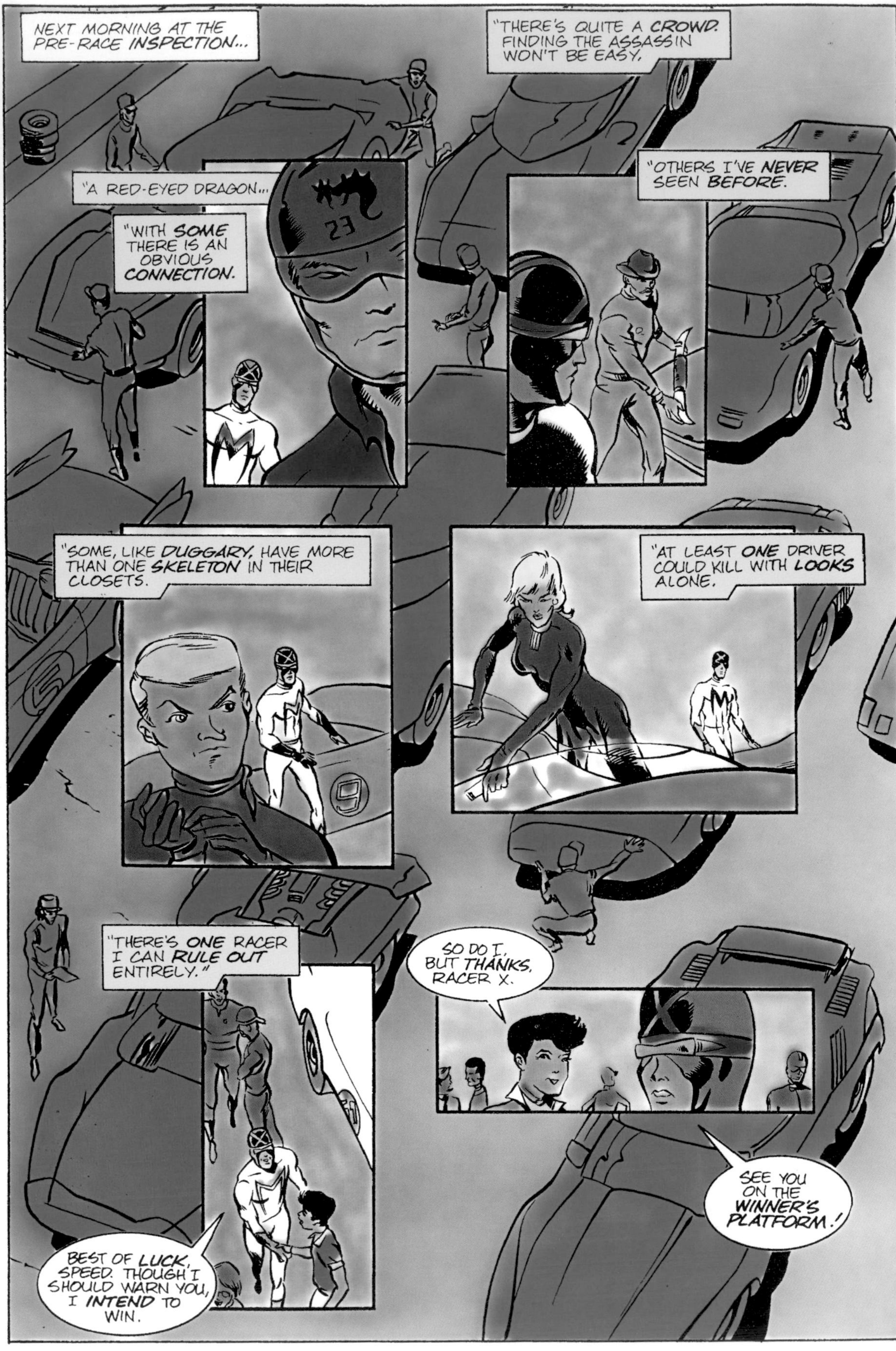
NEXT MORNING AT THE PRE-RACE INSPECTION...
"THERE'S QUITE A CROWD. FINDING THE ASSASSIN WON'T BE EASY.
"A RED-EYED DRAGON...
"WITH SOME THERE IS AN OBVIOUS CONNECTION.
"OTHERS I'VE NEVER SEEN BEFORE.
"SOME, LIKE DUGGARY, HAVE MORE THAN ONE SKELETON IN THEIR CLOSETS.
"AT LEAST ONE DRIVER COULD KILL WITH LOOKS ALONE.
"THERE'S ONE RACER I CAN RULE OUT ENTIRELY."
BEST OF LUCK, SPEED. THOUGH I SHOULD WARN YOU, I INTEND TO WIN.
SO DO I, BUT THANKS, RACER X.
SEE YOU ON THE WINNER'S PLATFORM!

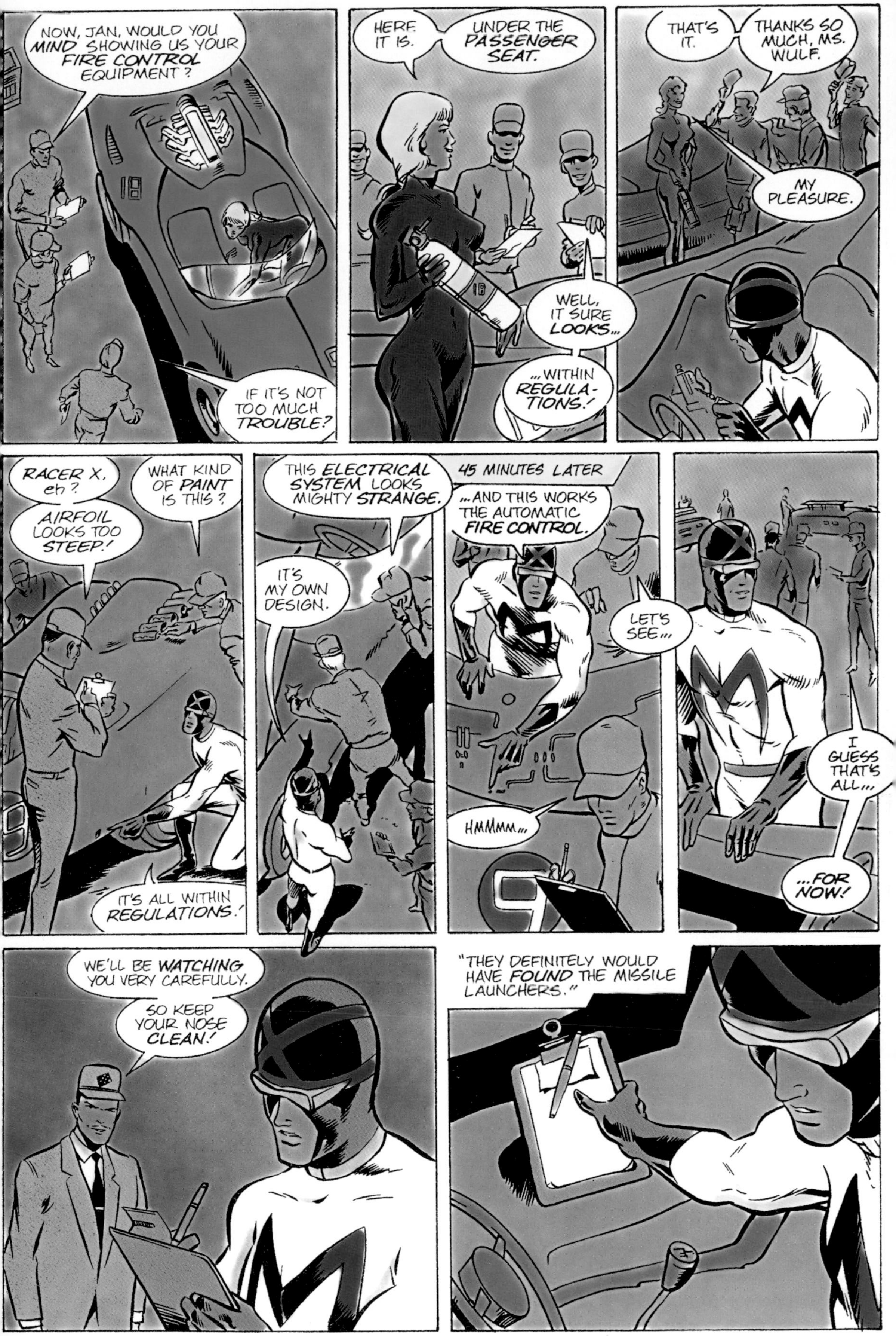
NOW, JAN, WOULD YOU MIND SHOWING US YOUR FIRE CONTROL EQUIPMENT?
IF IT'S NOT TOO MUCH TROUBLE?
HERE IT IS.
UNDER THE PASSENGER SEAT.
WELL, IT SURE LOOKS...
...WITHIN REGULA-TIONS.!
THAT'S IT.
THANKS SO MUCH, MS. WULF.
MY PLEASURE.
RACER X, eh?
AIRFOIL LOOKS TOO STEEP.!
WHAT KIND OF PAINT IS THIS?
IT'S ALL WITHIN REGULATIONS.!
THIS ELECTRICAL SYSTEM LOOKS MIGHTY STRANGE.
IT'S MY OWN DESIGN.
45 MINUTES LATER
...AND THIS WORKS THE AUTOMATIC FIRE CONTROL.
LET'S SEE...
HMMMM...
I GUESS THAT'S ALL...
...FOR NOW!
WE'LL BE WATCHING YOU VERY CAREFULLY.
SO KEEP YOUR NOSE CLEAN.!
"THEY DEFINITELY WOULD HAVE FOUND THE MISSILE LAUNCHERS."

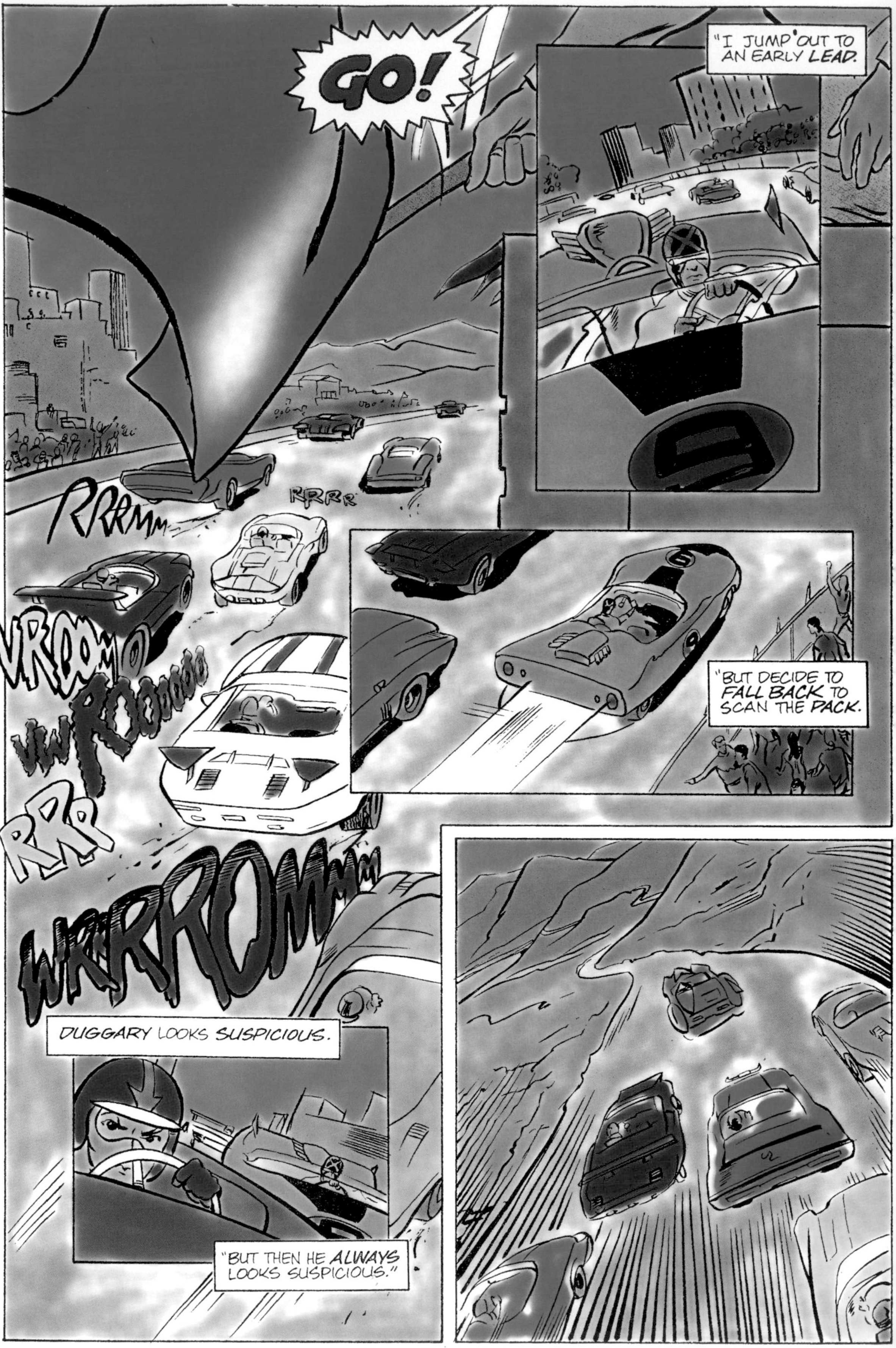
GO!
"I JUMP OUT TO AN EARLY LEAD.
RRRMMM
RRRR
VROOM
VWROOOOOO
RRR
WRRROMMMM
"BUT DECIDE TO FALL BACK TO SCAN THE PACK.
DUGGARY LOOKS SUSPICIOUS.
"BUT THEN HE ALWAYS LOOKS SUSPICIOUS."

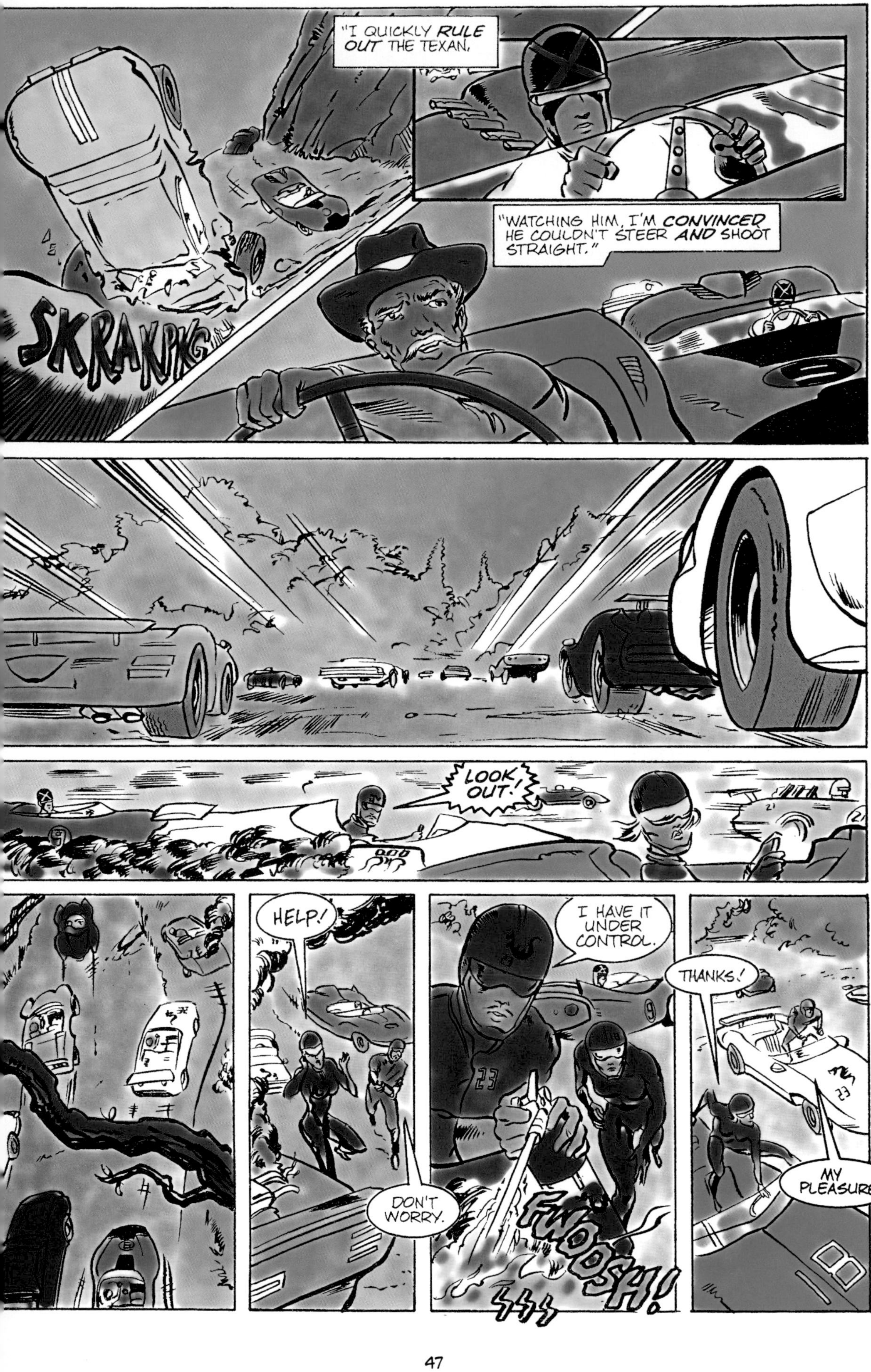
"I QUICKLY RULE OUT THE TEXAN.
SKRAKPKG
"WATCHING HIM, I'M CONVINCED HE COULDN'T STEER AND SHOOT STRAIGHT."
LOOK OUT!
HELP!
DON'T WORRY.
I HAVE IT UNDER CONTROL.
FWOOSH!
THANKS!
MY PLEASURE.

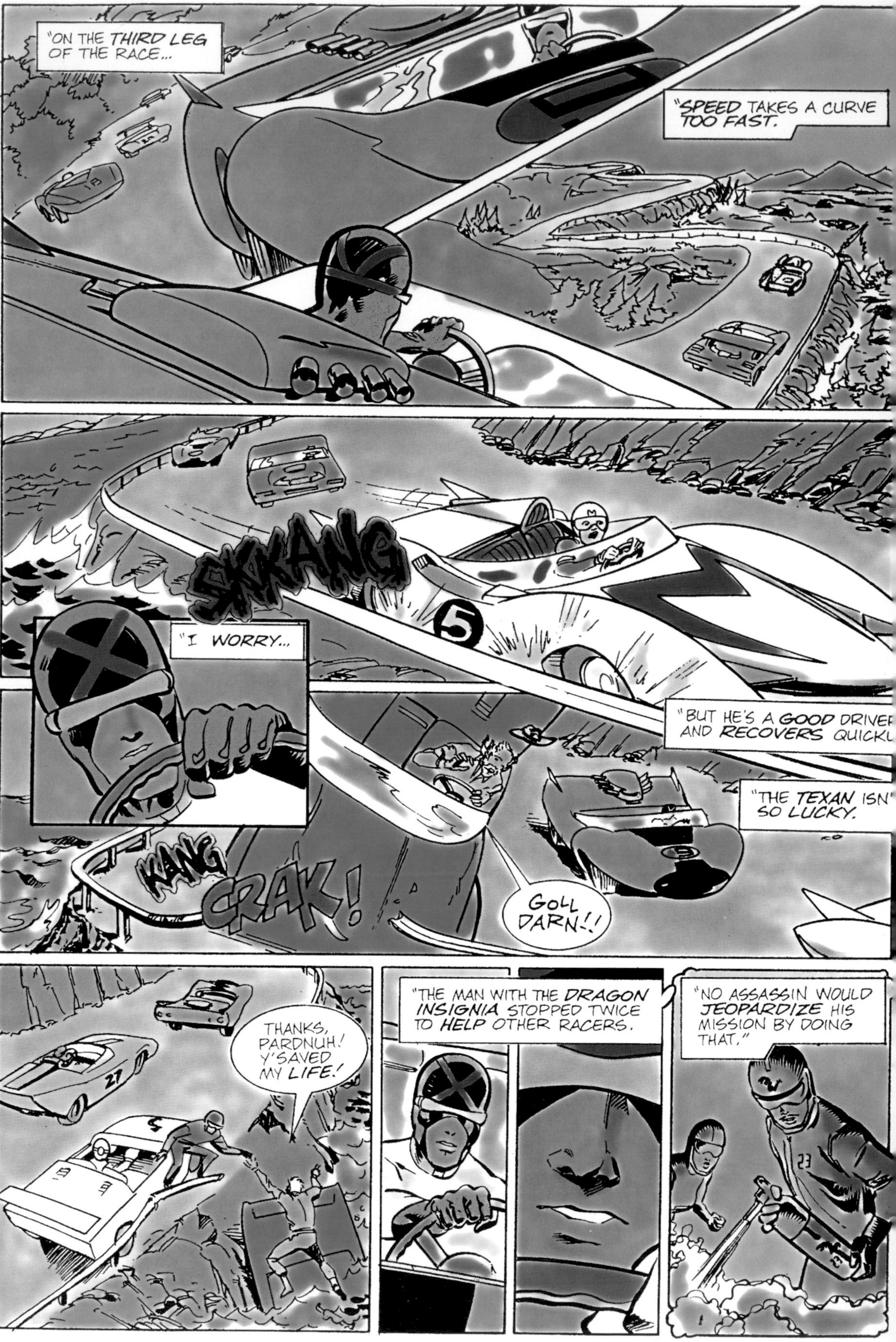
"ON THE THIRD LEG OF THE RACE...
"SPEED TAKES A CURVE TOO FAST.
SKKANG
"I WORRY...
"BUT HE'S A GOOD DRIVE
AND RECOVERS QUICKL
"THE TEXAN ISN
SO LUCKY.
KANG
CRAK!
GOLL DARN!!
THANKS, PARDNUH! Y'SAVED MY LIFE!
"THE MAN WITH THE DRAGON INSIGNIA STOPPED TWICE TO HELP OTHER RACERS.
"NO ASSASSIN WOULD JEOPARDIZE HIS MISSION BY DOING THAT."

"THEN IT *HITS* ME.

"WHY DIDN'T SHE USE HER *OWN* FIRE EXTINGUISHER?"

"MAYBE SHE PANICKED...."

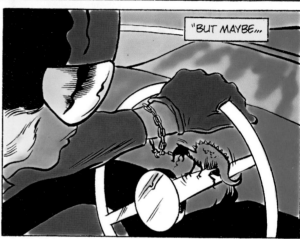

"BUT MAYBE...."

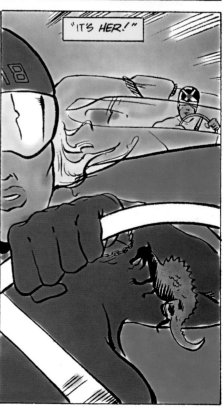

"IT'S *HER!*"

"I *WONDER* JUST WHAT SHE HAS INSIDE THAT *FIRE EXTINGUISHER*.

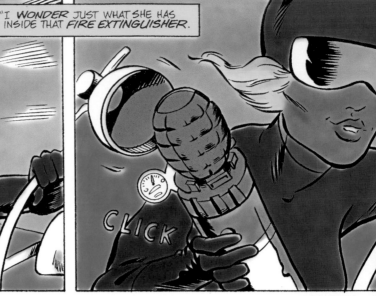

CLICK

"THE CAR THE *AGENCY* BUILT ME HAS FORWARD MOUNTED *MISSILE LAUNCHERS* AND *MACHINE GUNS*.

"THE *SHOOTING STAR* DOESN'T,

"BUT I *BUILT* THIS CAR...

CLICK

"AND I'M NOT WITHOUT *WEAPONS* OF MY *OWN*."

TW'K!

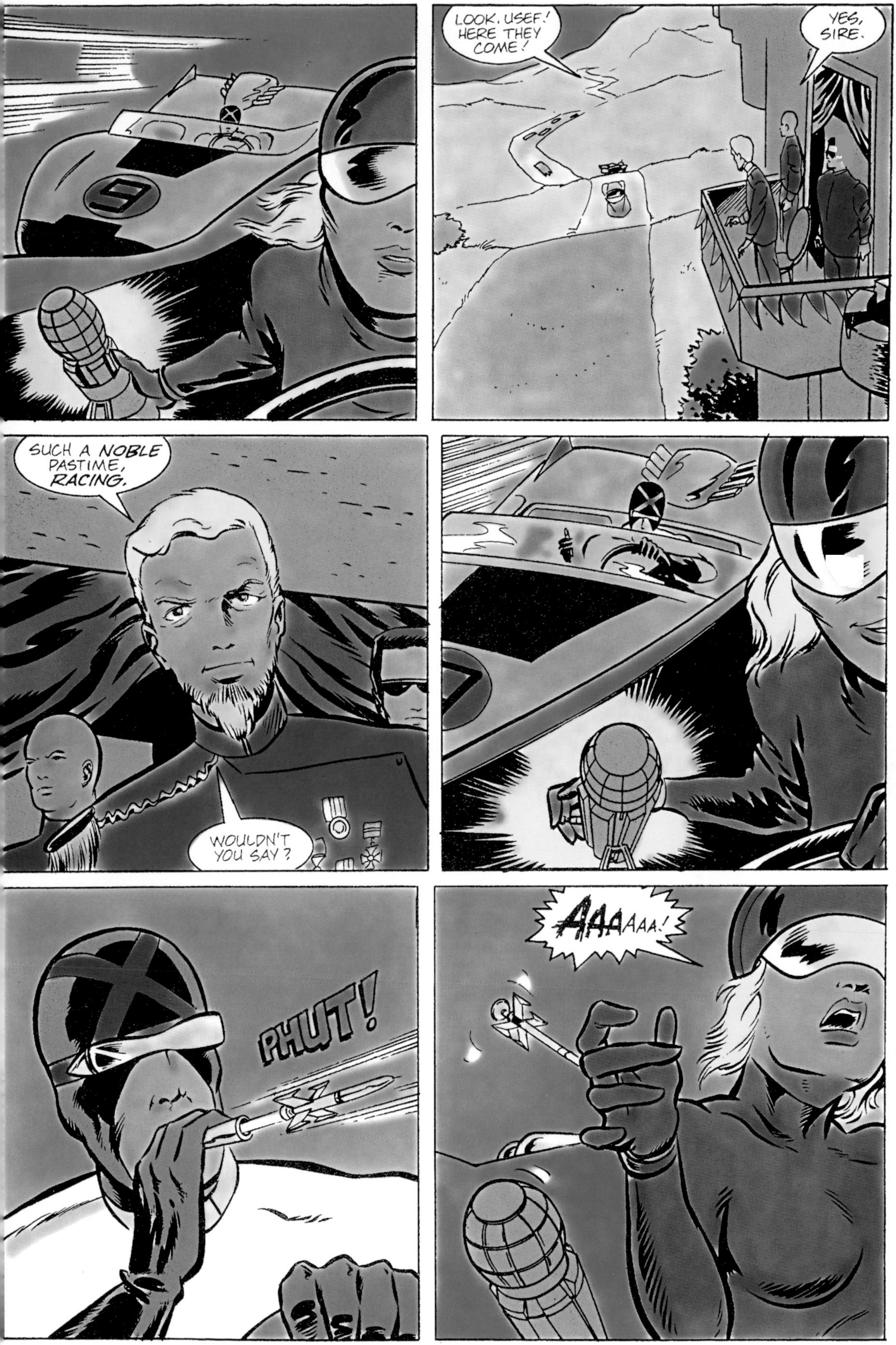
LOOK, USEF! HERE THEY COME!
YES, SIRE.
SUCH A NOBLE PASTIME, RACING.
WOULDN'T YOU SAY?
PHUT!
AAAAAA!

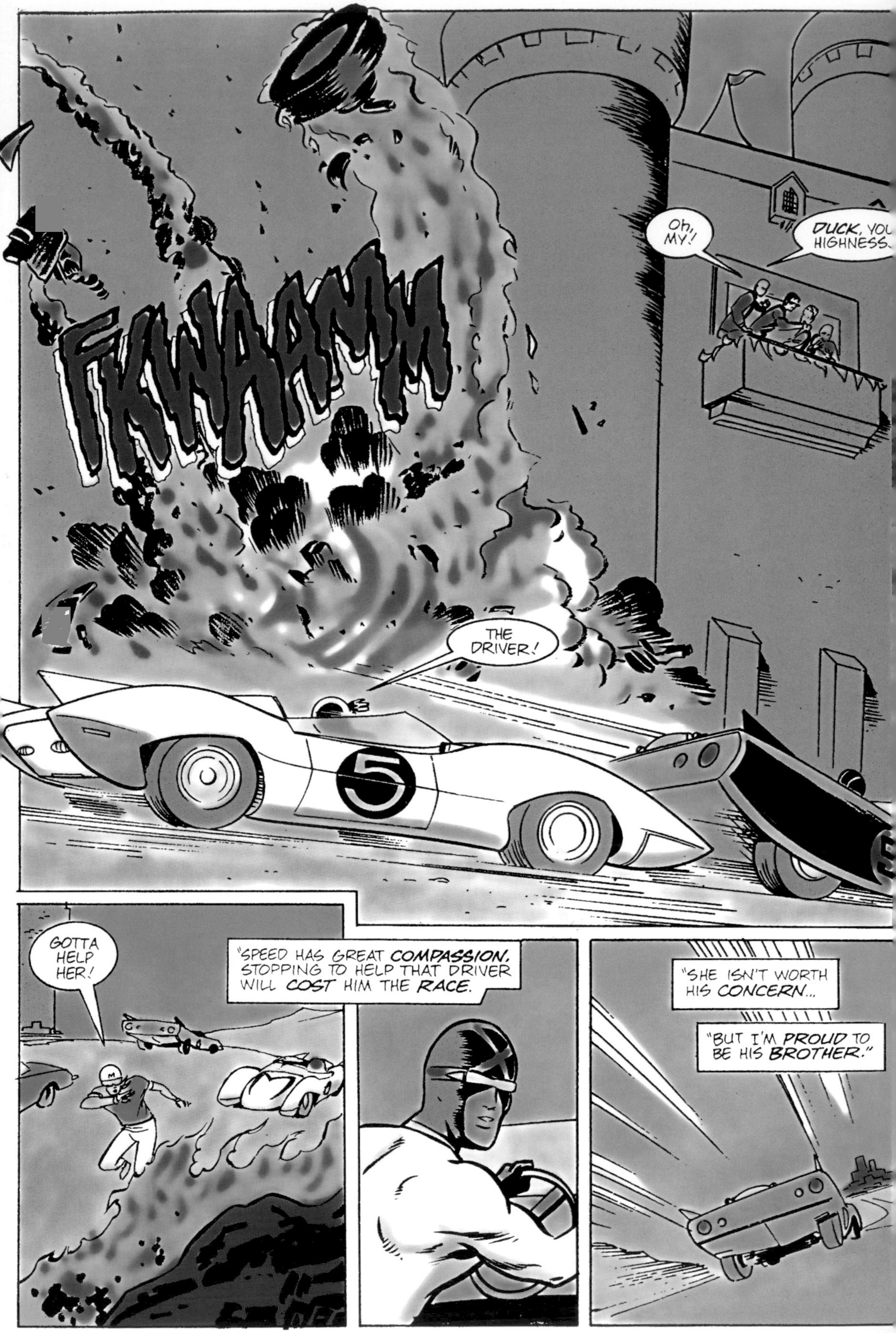
FKWAAMM
Oh, MY!
DUCK, YOU HIGHNESS.
THE DRIVER!
GOTTA HELP HER!
"SPEED HAS GREAT COMPASSION. STOPPING TO HELP THAT DRIVER WILL COST HIM THE RACE.
"SHE ISN'T WORTH HIS CONCERN...
"BUT I'M PROUD TO BE HIS BROTHER."

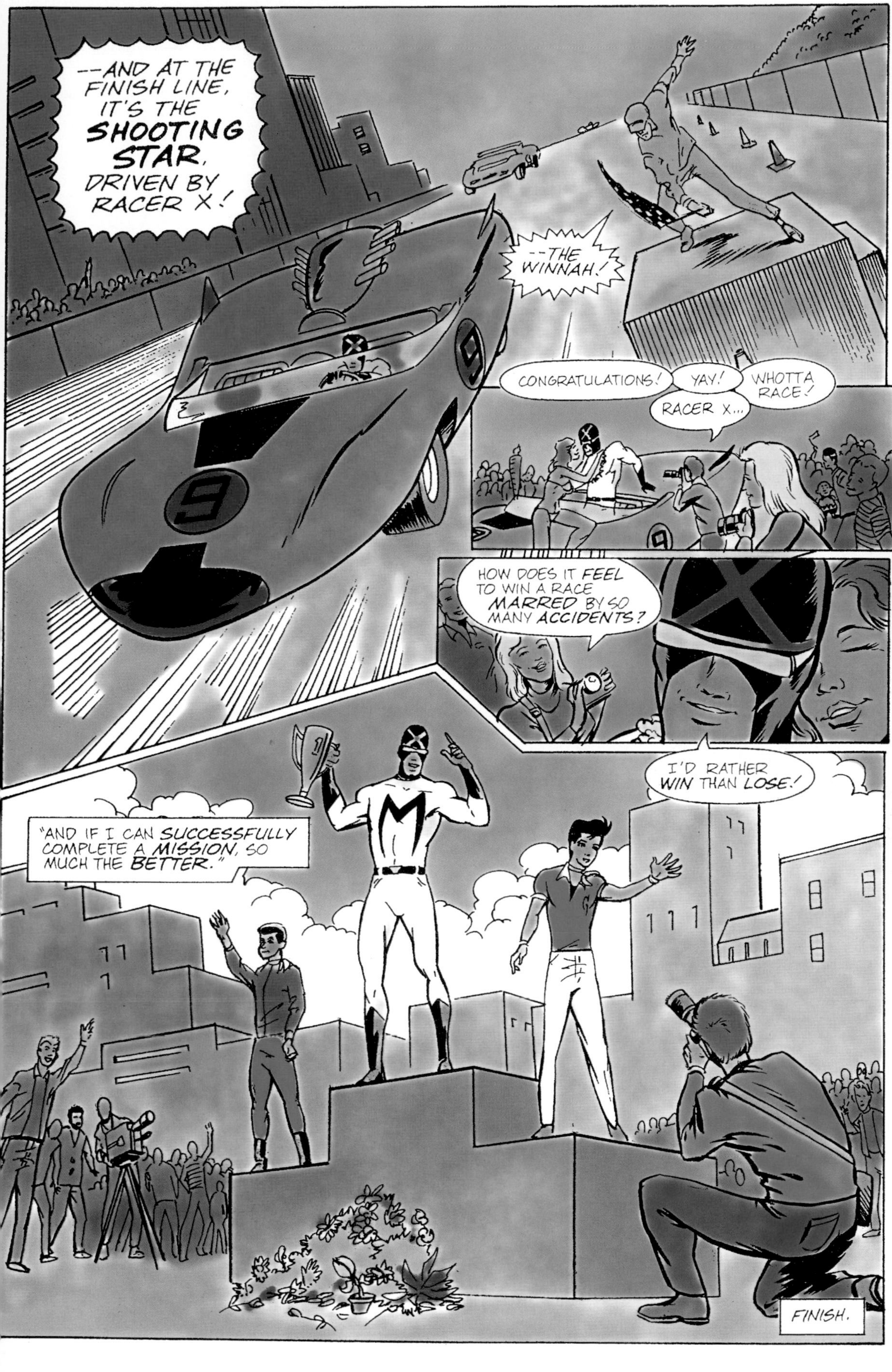
--AND AT THE FINISH LINE, IT'S THE SHOOTING STAR, DRIVEN BY RACER X!
--THE WINNAH!
CONGRATULATIONS!
YAY!
WHOTTA RACE!
RACER X...
HOW DOES IT FEEL TO WIN A RACE MARRED BY SO MANY ACCIDENTS?
I'D RATHER WIN THAN LOSE!
"AND IF I CAN SUCCESSFULLY COMPLETE A MISSION, SO MUCH THE BETTER."
FINISH.

EPILOGUE

AZIMUTH H.Q.

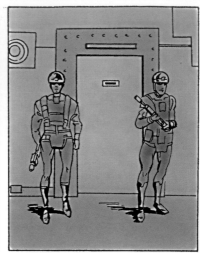

THEY SHALL BURN IN THE *HELL* OF UPSIDE-DOWN SINNERS....

SHI TALWIN.....!

eh?

ANOTHER *TRICK?* GIVE UP, CURS.!

I WILL TELL YOU *NOTHING!*

NO TRICKS, TALWIN!

I OFFER FREEDOM!

FOLLOW MY DIRECTIONS AND I ASSURE YOU....

...YOU WILL BE *FREE!*

AND RACER X SHALL **DIE!**

NEXT ISSUE: TROUBLE IN AZIMUTH CONTROL AND RACER X FACES DEATH IN—*THE ALPINE GAMBIT!*

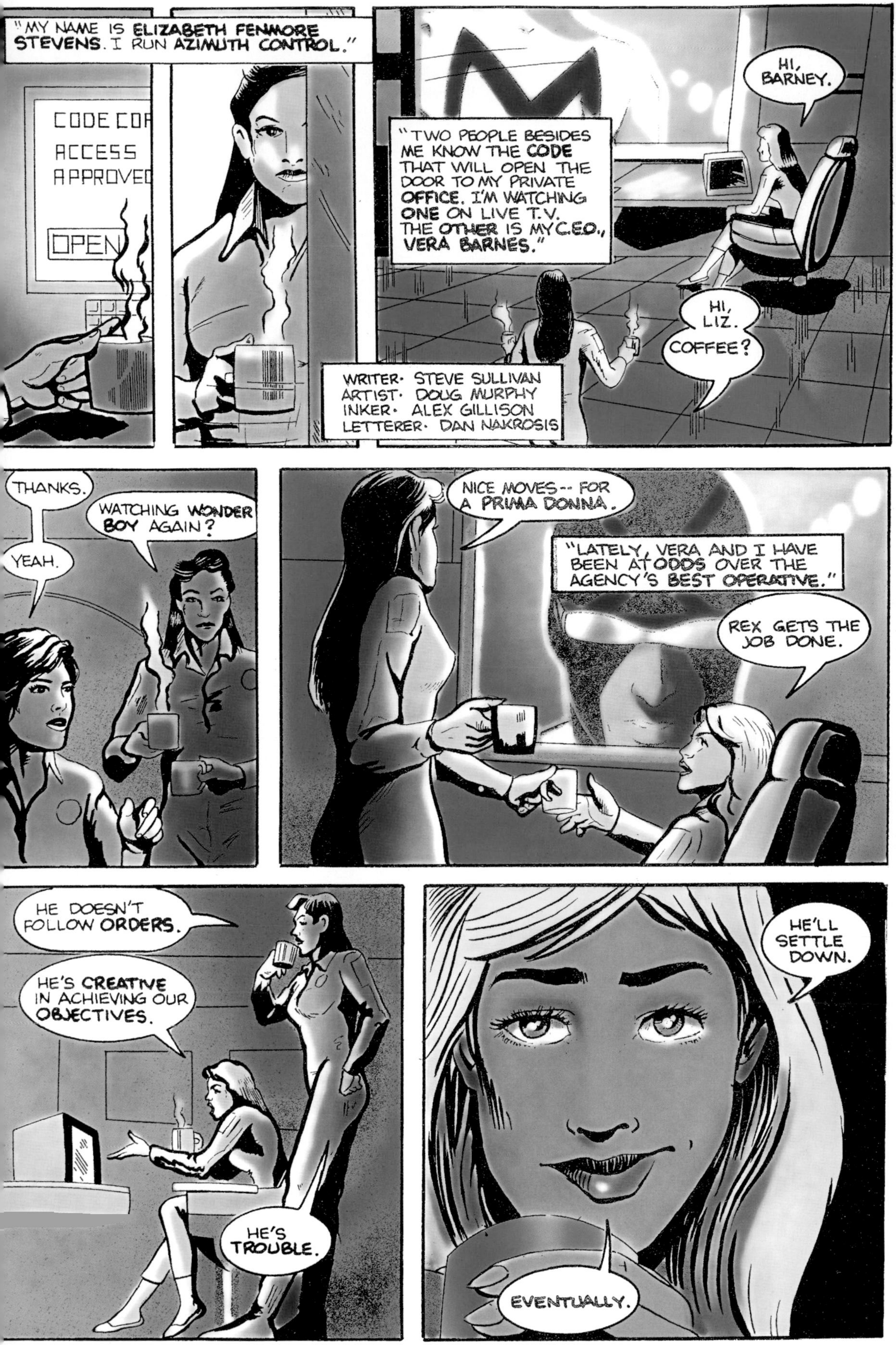
"MY NAME IS ELIZABETH FENMORE STEVENS. I RUN AZIMUTH CONTROL."
ACCESS
OPEN
"TWO PEOPLE BESIDES ME KNOW THE CODE THAT WILL OPEN THE DOOR TO MY PRIVATE OFFICE. I'M WATCHING ONE ON LIVE T.V. THE OTHER IS MY C.E.O., VERA BARNES."
HI, BARNEY.
HI, LIZ.
COFFEE?
WRITER· STEVE SULLIVAN
ARTIST· DOUG MURPHY
INKER· ALEX GILLISON
LETTERER· DAN NAKROSIS
THANKS.
WATCHING WONDER BOY AGAIN?
YEAH.
NICE MOVES-- FOR A PRIMA DONNA.
"LATELY, VERA AND I HAVE BEEN AT ODDS OVER THE AGENCY'S BEST OPERATIVE."
REX GETS THE JOB DONE.
HE DOESN'T FOLLOW ORDERS.
HE'S CREATIVE IN ACHIEVING OUR OBJECTIVES.
HE'S TROUBLE.
HE'LL SETTLE DOWN.
EVENTUALLY.

"MY STATION RUNS **SMOOTHLY**, EVERYONE PULLING FOR THE **SAME TEAM**.."

HE'S WON AGAIN.

WAY TO GO!

HOW MANY IS THAT THIS YEAR?

A **CREDIT** TO THE AGENCY.

ANOTHER VICTORY FOR WORLD **PEACE** AND SECURITY.

ANOTHER BOOST FOR REX RACER'S EGO, YOU MEAN.

PARDON ME?

I SAID, RACER X IS A **GLORY HOUND**.

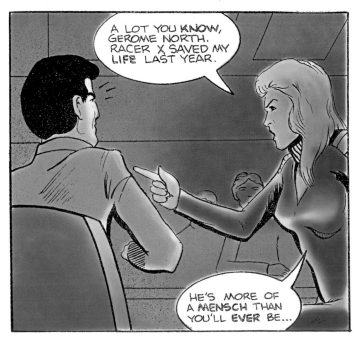

A LOT YOU KNOW, GEROME NORTH. RACER X SAVED MY LIFE LAST YEAR.

HE'S MORE OF A **MENSCH** THAN YOU'LL EVER BE...

...JERRY.

NO NEED TO GET **NASTY**.

CATCH YOU LATER.

WITCH.

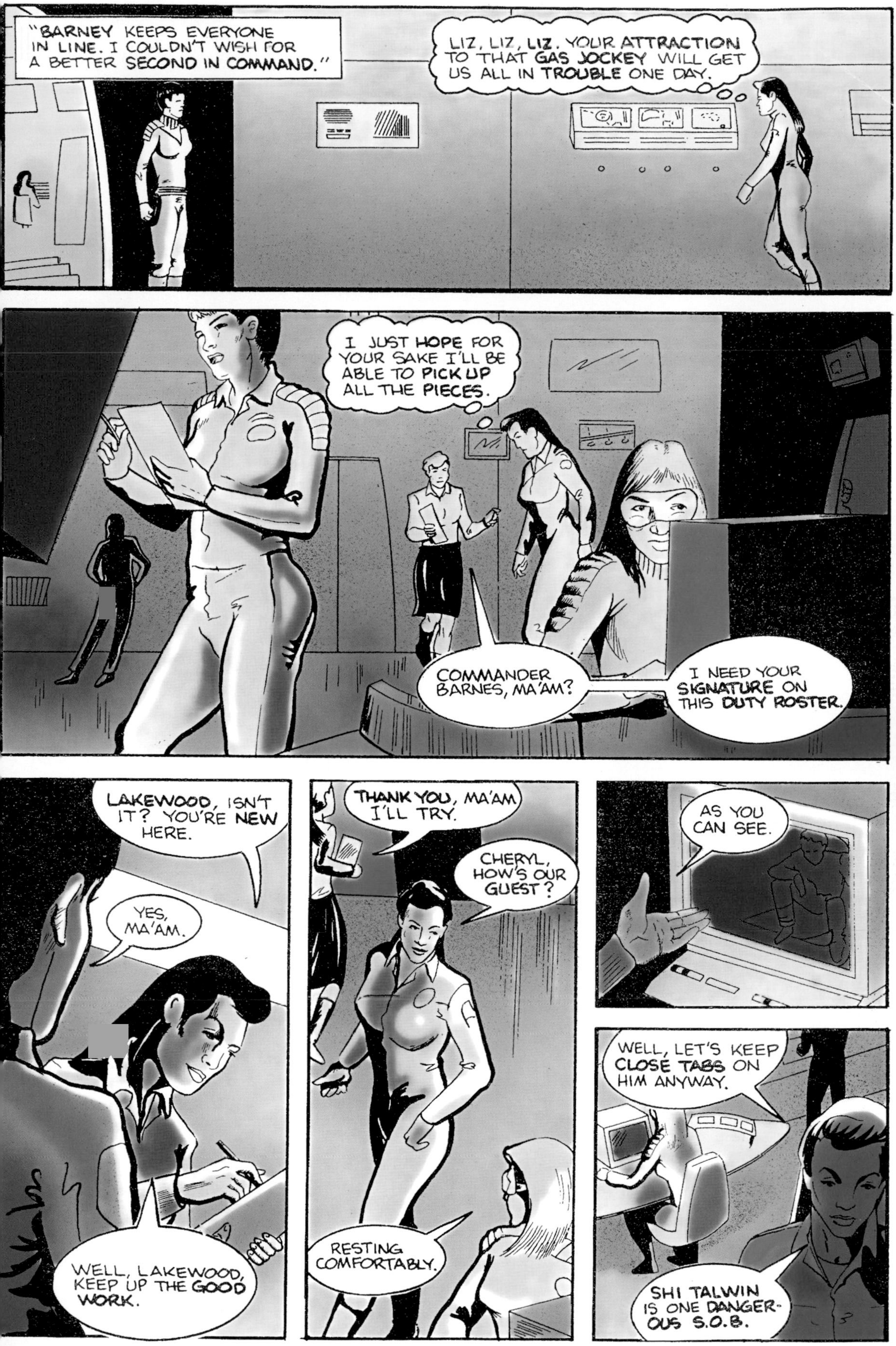
"BARNEY KEEPS EVERYONE IN LINE. I COULDN'T WISH FOR A BETTER SECOND IN COMMAND."
LIZ, LIZ, LIZ. YOUR ATTRACTION TO THAT GAS JOCKEY WILL GET US ALL IN TROUBLE ONE DAY.
I JUST HOPE FOR YOUR SAKE I'LL BE ABLE TO PICK UP ALL THE PIECES.
COMMANDER BARNES, MA'AM?
I NEED YOUR SIGNATURE ON THIS DUTY ROSTER.
LAKEWOOD, ISN'T IT? YOU'RE NEW HERE.
YES, MA'AM.
WELL, LAKEWOOD, KEEP UP THE GOOD WORK.
THANK YOU, MA'AM I'LL TRY.
CHERYL, HOW'S OUR GUEST?
RESTING COMFORTABLY.
AS YOU CAN SEE.
WELL, LET'S KEEP CLOSE TABS ON HIM ANYWAY.
SHI TALWIN IS ONE DANGER-OUS S.O.B.

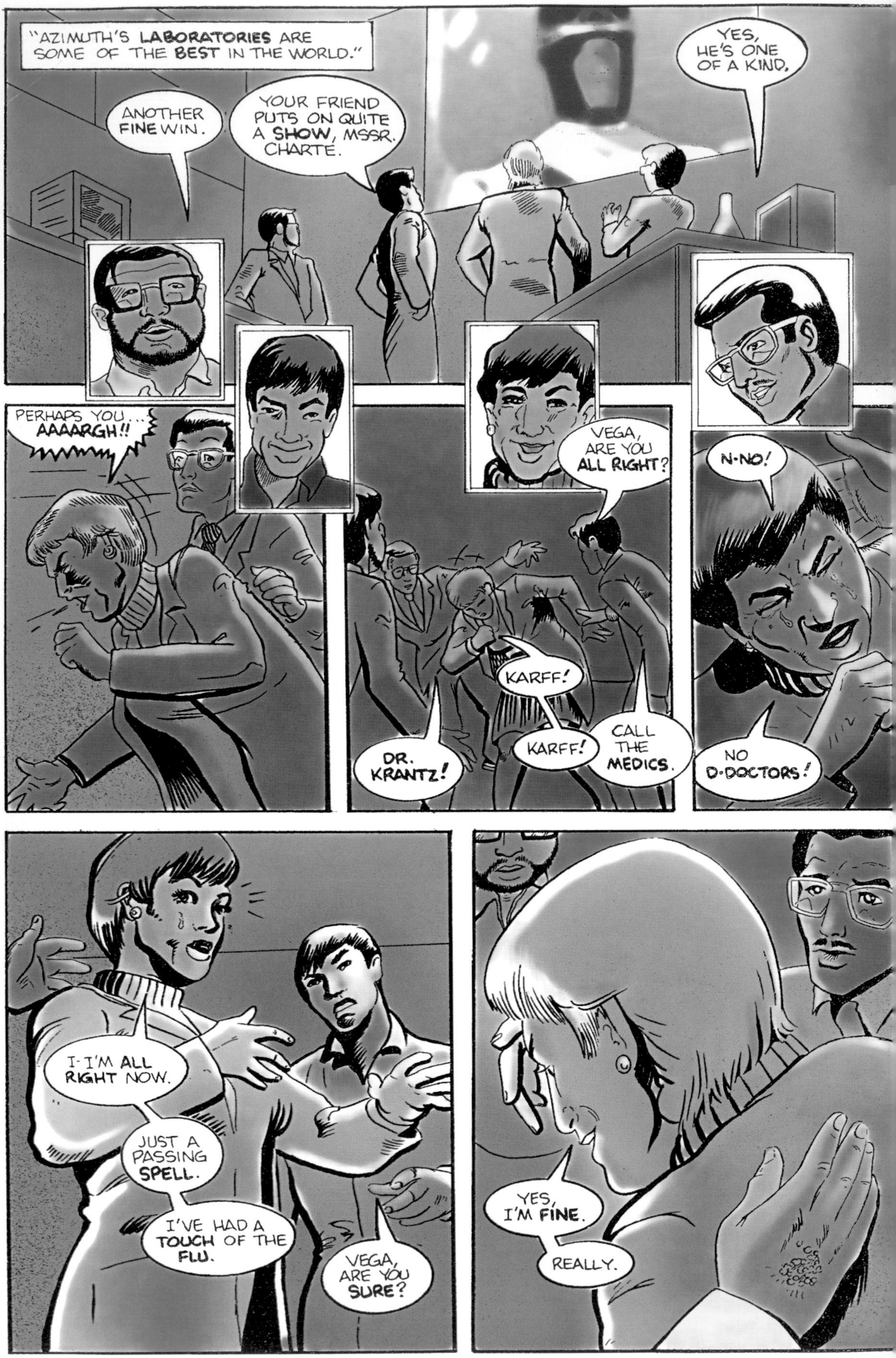
"AZIMUTH'S LABORATORIES ARE SOME OF THE BEST IN THE WORLD."
ANOTHER FINE WIN.
YOUR FRIEND PUTS ON QUITE A SHOW, MSSR. CHARTE.
YES, HE'S ONE OF A KIND.
PERHAPS YOU... AAAARGH!!
VEGA, ARE YOU ALL RIGHT?
DR. KRANTZ!
KARFF!
KARFF!
CALL THE MEDICS.
N-NO!
NO D-DOCTORS!
I-I'M ALL RIGHT NOW.
JUST A PASSING SPELL.
I'VE HAD A TOUCH OF THE FLU.
VEGA, ARE YOU SURE?
YES, I'M FINE.
REALLY.

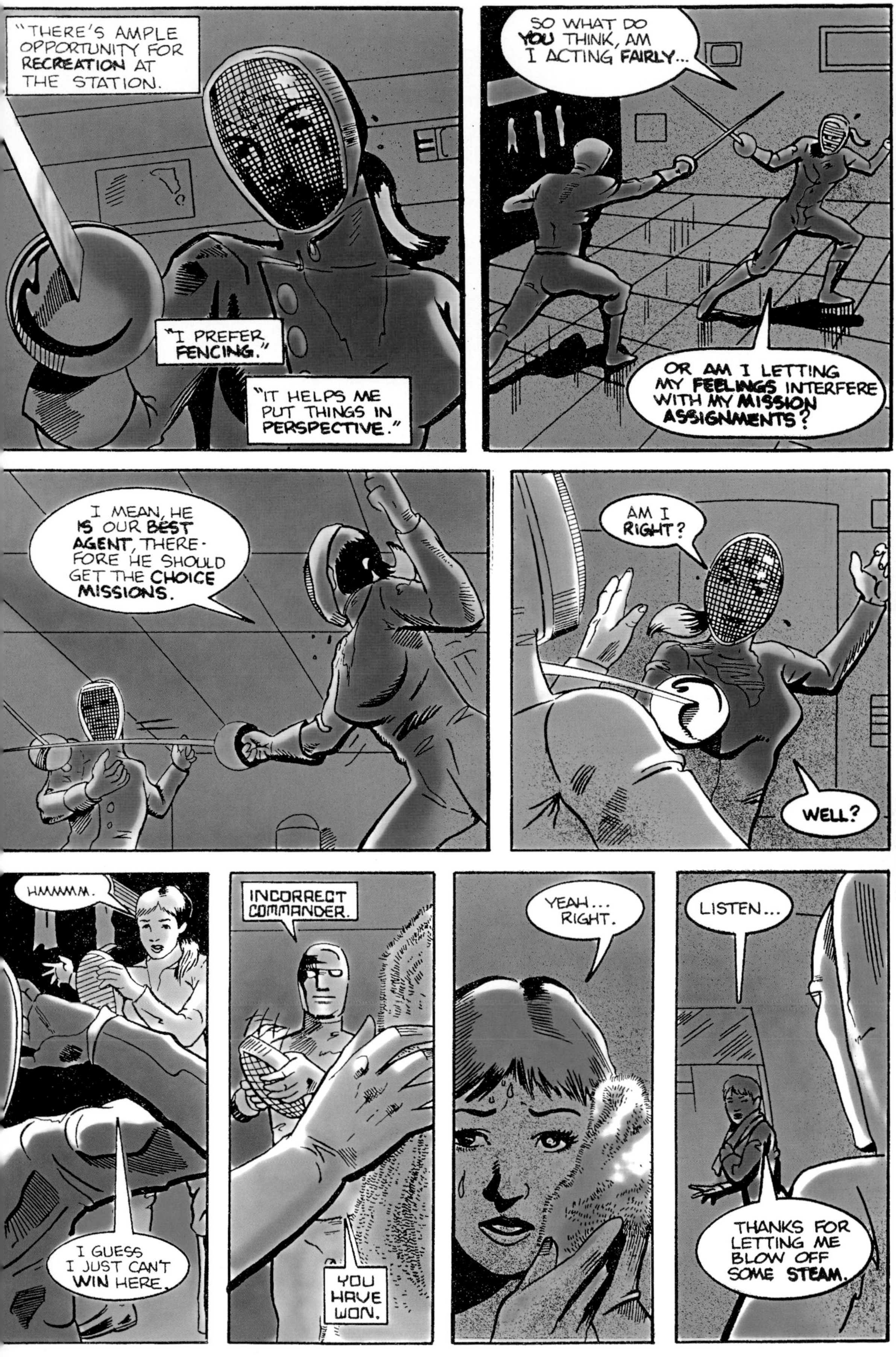
"THERE'S AMPLE OPPORTUNITY FOR RECREATION AT THE STATION.
"I PREFER FENCING."
"IT HELPS ME PUT THINGS IN PERSPECTIVE."
SO WHAT DO YOU THINK, AM I ACTING FAIRLY...
OR AM I LETTING MY FEELINGS INTERFERE WITH MY MISSION ASSIGNMENTS?
I MEAN, HE IS OUR BEST AGENT, THERE-FORE HE SHOULD GET THE CHOICE MISSIONS.
AM I RIGHT?
WELL?
HMMMM.
I GUESS I JUST CAN'T WIN HERE.
INCORRECT COMMANDER.
YOU HAVE WON.
YEAH... RIGHT.
LISTEN...
THANKS FOR LETTING ME BLOW OFF SOME STEAM.

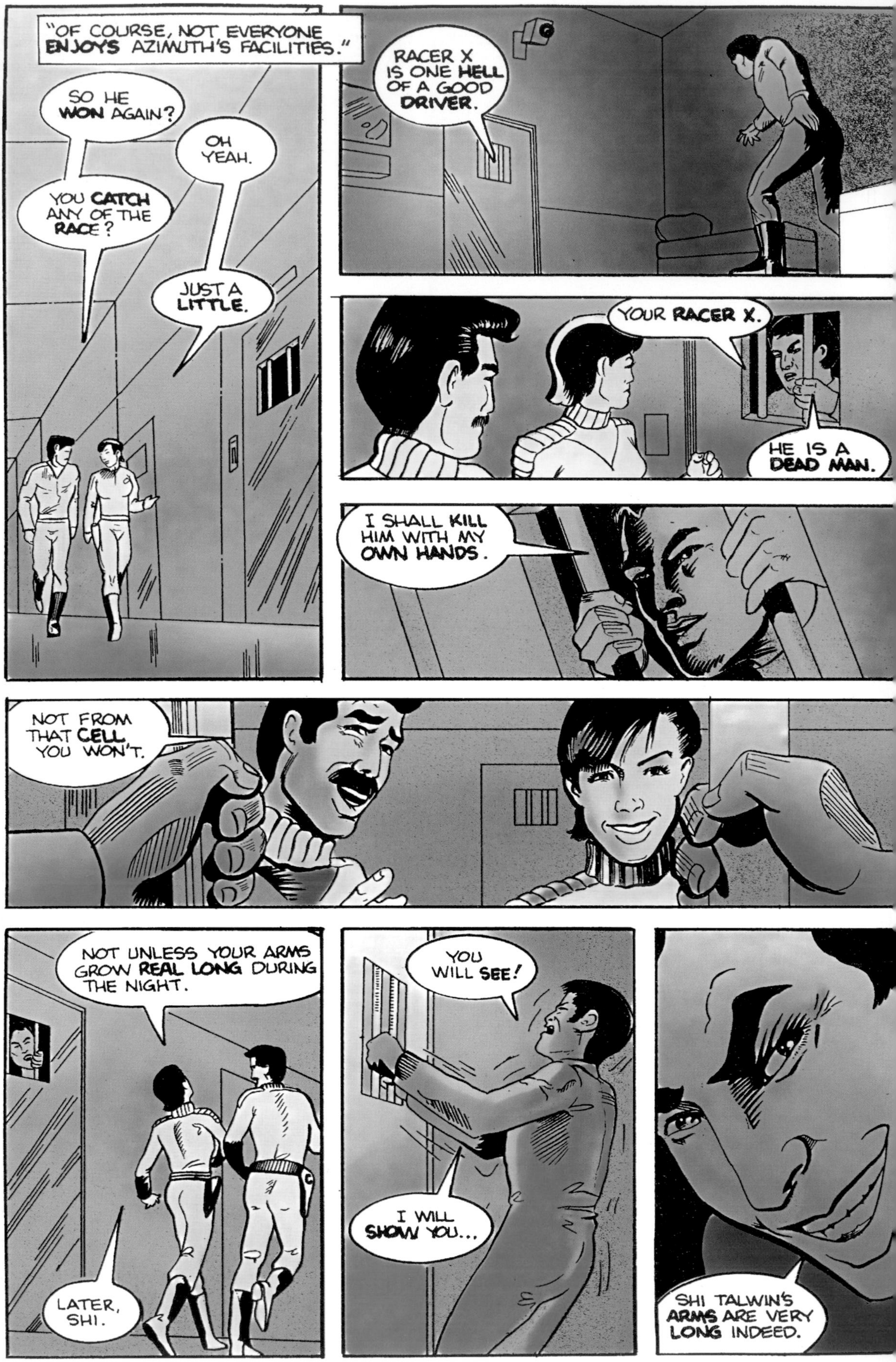
"OF COURSE, NOT EVERYONE ENJOYS AZIMUTH'S FACILITIES."
SO HE WON AGAIN?
OH YEAH.
YOU CATCH ANY OF THE RACE?
JUST A LITTLE.
RACER X IS ONE HELL OF A GOOD DRIVER.
YOUR RACER X.
HE IS A DEAD MAN.
I SHALL KILL HIM WITH MY OWN HANDS.
NOT FROM THAT CELL YOU WON'T.
NOT UNLESS YOUR ARMS GROW REAL LONG DURING THE NIGHT.
LATER, SHI.
YOU WILL SEE!
I WILL SHOW YOU...
SHI TALWIN'S ARMS ARE VERY LONG INDEED.

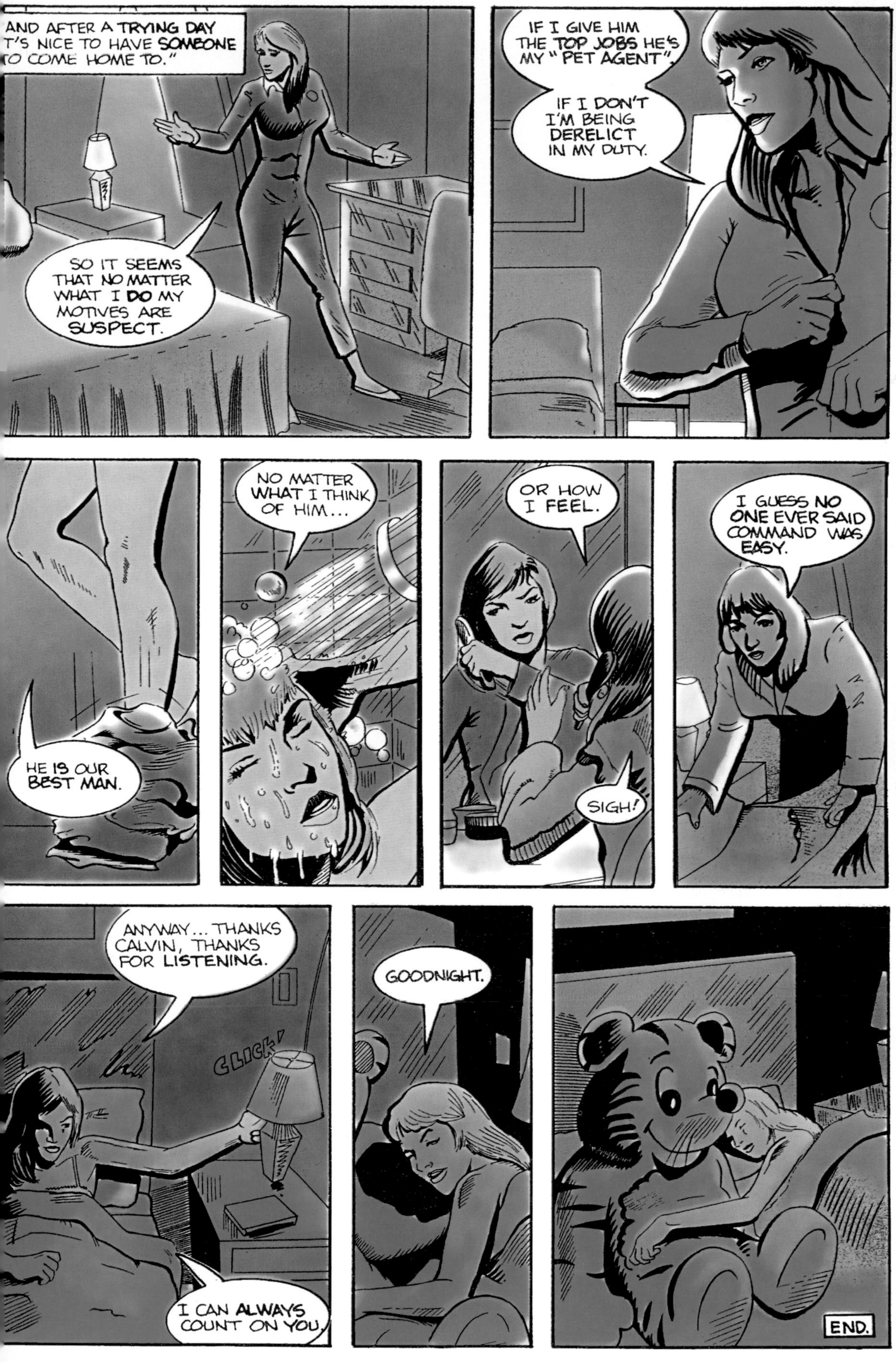
AND AFTER A TRYING DAY
T'S NICE TO HAVE SOMEONE
TO COME HOME TO."
SO IT SEEMS THAT NO MATTER WHAT I DO MY MOTIVES ARE SUSPECT.
IF I GIVE HIM THE TOP JOBS HE'S MY "PET AGENT".
IF I DON'T I'M BEING DERELICT IN MY DUTY.
HE IS OUR BEST MAN.
NO MATTER WHAT I THINK OF HIM...
OR HOW I FEEL.
SIGH!
I GUESS NO ONE EVER SAID COMMAND WAS EASY.
ANYWAY... THANKS CALVIN, THANKS FOR LISTENING.
CLICK!
I CAN ALWAYS COUNT ON YOU.
GOODNIGHT.
END.

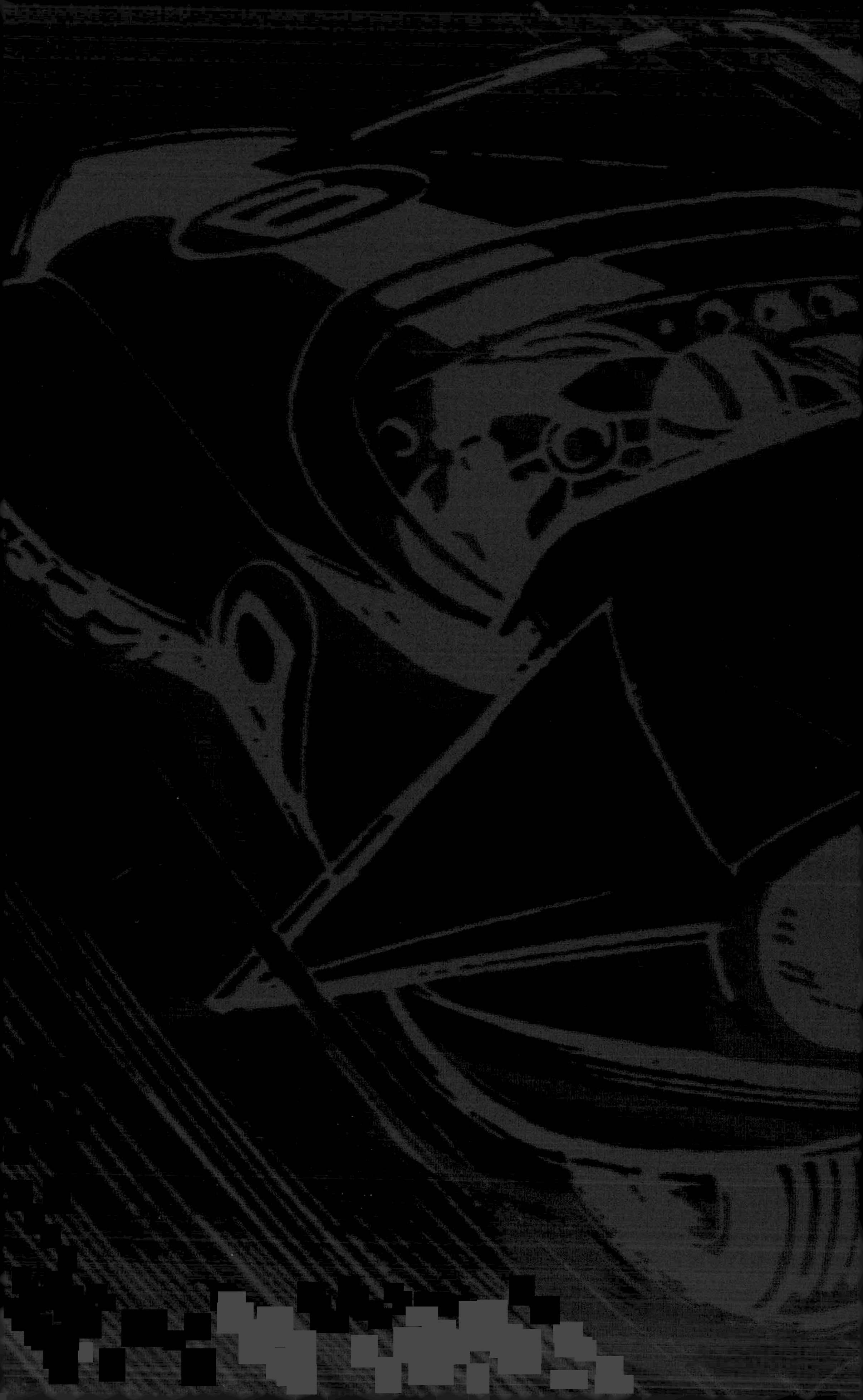

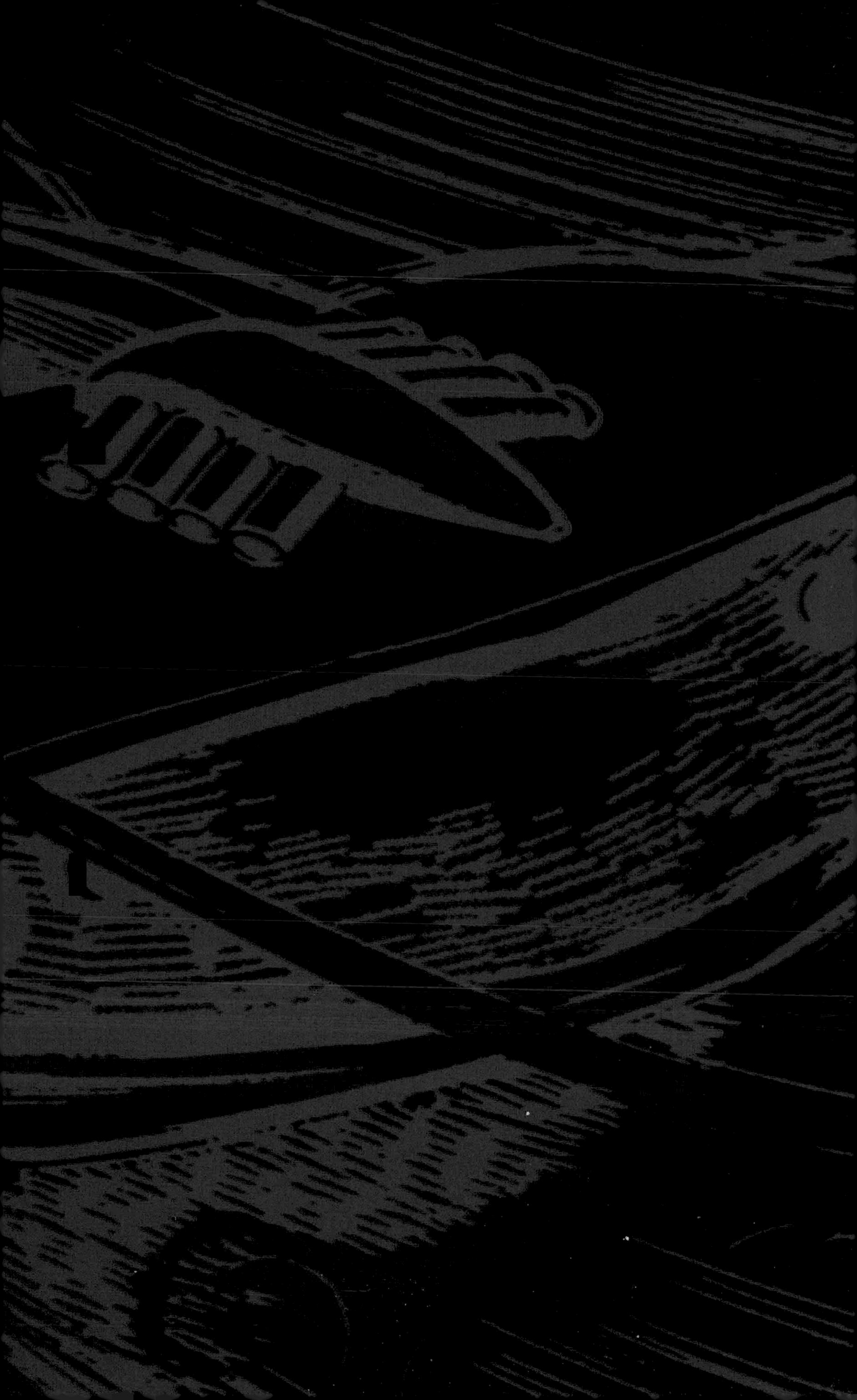

Racer X #3

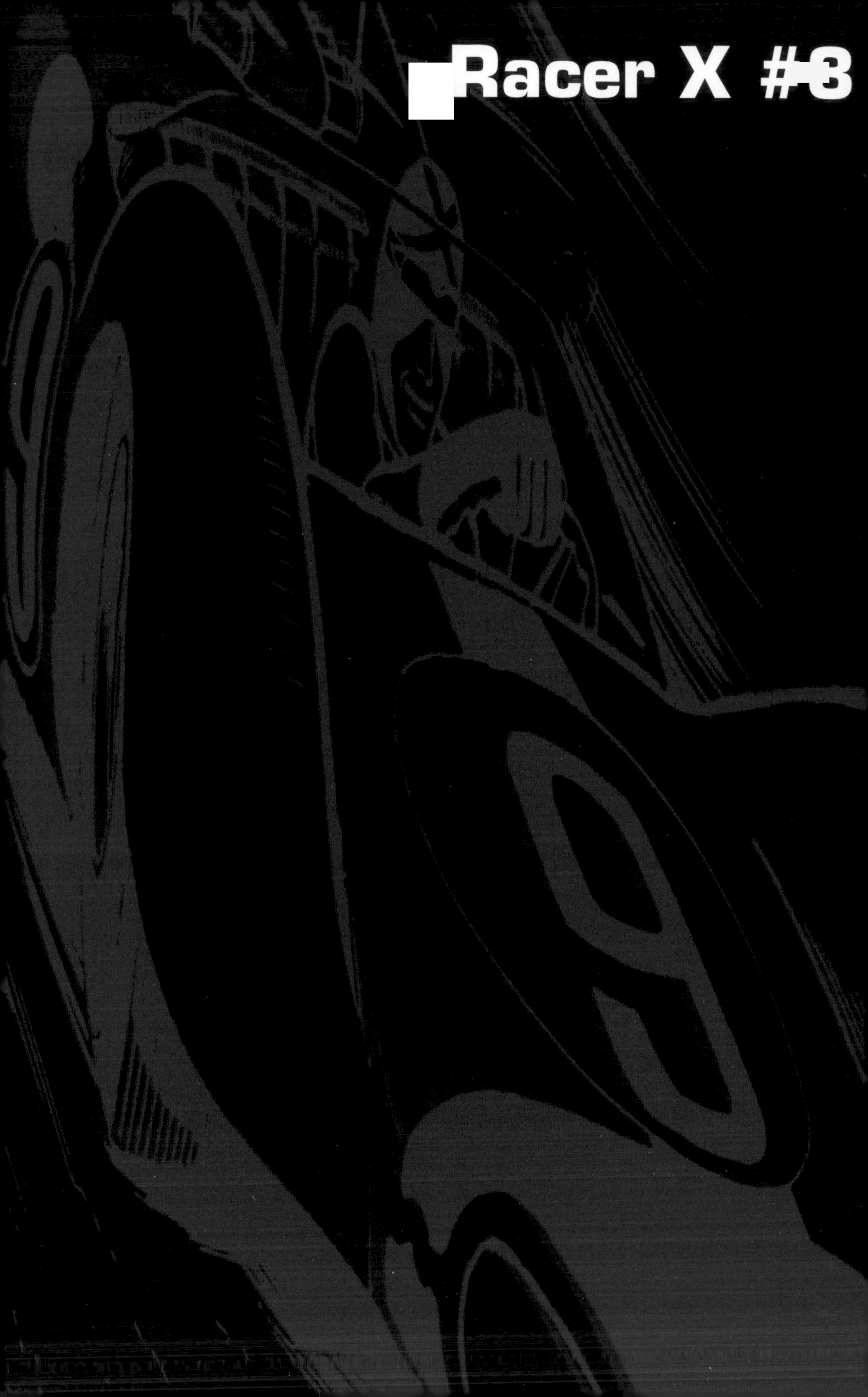

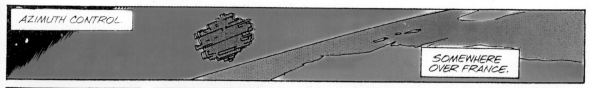

AZIMUTH CONTROL.

SOMEWHERE OVER FRANCE.

SHI TALWIN...

SO, AT LAST YOU APPEAR.

OUR TIME HAS NEARLY COME.

YOU KNOW WHAT TO DO?

YES.

SOON, VERY SOON...

RACER X WILL DIE!

OKAY, TALWIN...

YOU READY?

OH, YES.

QUITE READY.

LIZ, WAIT UP.

VERA-- HOW'S THE *PRISONER TRASFER* SHAPING UP?

SO FAR, SO GOOD.

HOW'S YOUR *PET AGENT?*

I HEAR HE'S OFF *RACING* AGAIN.

HE'S *NOT* MY "PET AGENT."

AFTERNOON, COMMANDER.

OH, HI, JERRY.

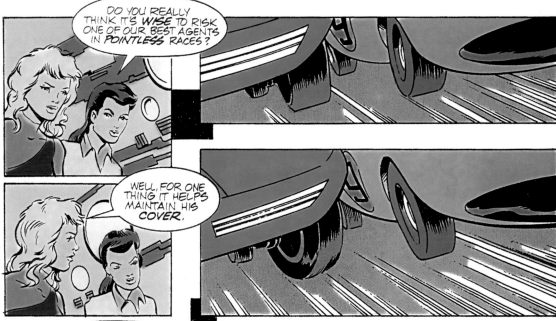

DO YOU REALLY THINK IT'S *WISE* TO RISK ONE OF OUR BEST AGENTS IN *POINTLESS* RACES?

WELL, FOR ONE THING IT HELPS MAINTAIN HIS *COVER.*

FOR ANOTHER, I *COULDN'T* STOP HIM IF I *TRIED.*

BESIDES...

THUNK

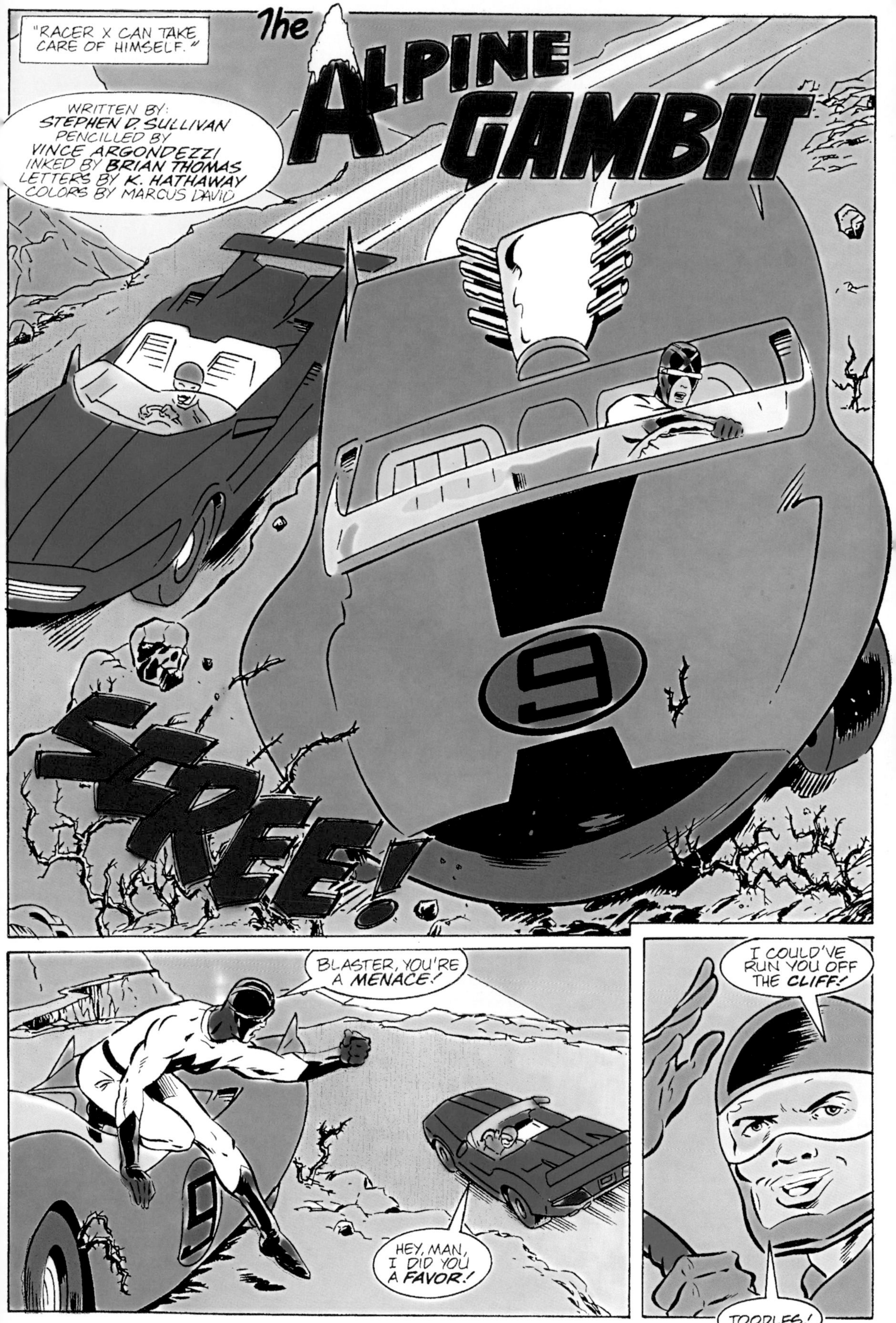
"RACER X CAN TAKE CARE OF HIMSELF."
The ALPINE GAMBIT
WRITTEN BY: STEPHEN D. SULLIVAN PENCILLED BY VINCE ARGONDEZZI INKED BY BRIAN THOMAS LETTERS BY K. HATHAWAY COLORS BY MARCUS DAVID
SCREE!
BLASTER, YOU'RE A MENACE!
HEY, MAN, I DID YOU A FAVOR!
I COULD'VE RUN YOU OFF THE CLIFF!
TOODLES!

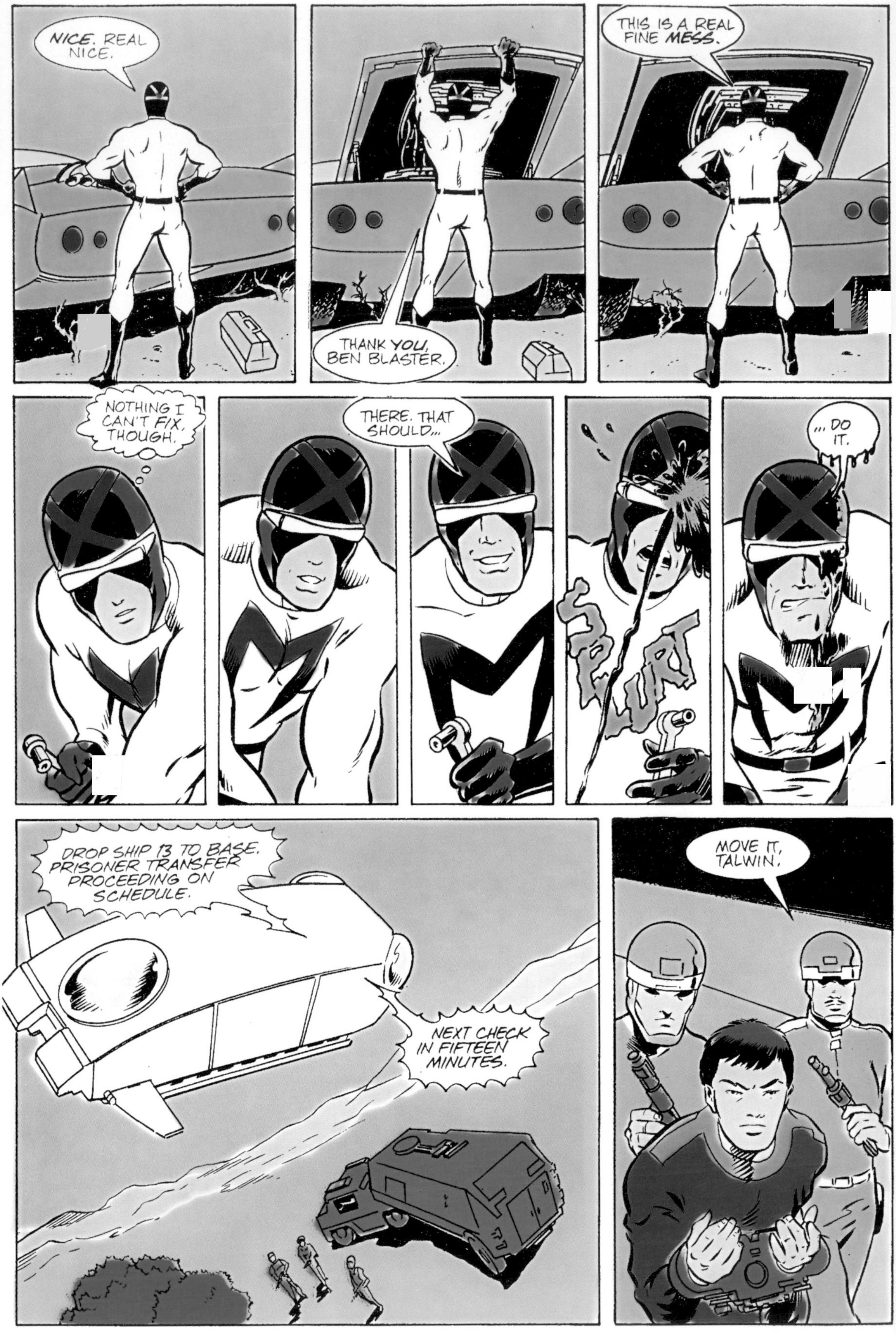
NICE. REAL NICE.
THANK YOU, BEN BLASTER.
THIS IS A REAL FINE MESS.
NOTHING I CAN'T FIX, THOUGH.
THERE. THAT SHOULD...
SPLURT
...DO IT.
DROP SHIP 13 TO BASE. PRISONER TRANSFER PROCEEDING ON SCHEDULE.
NEXT CHECK IN FIFTEEN MINUTES.
MOVE IT, TALWIN.

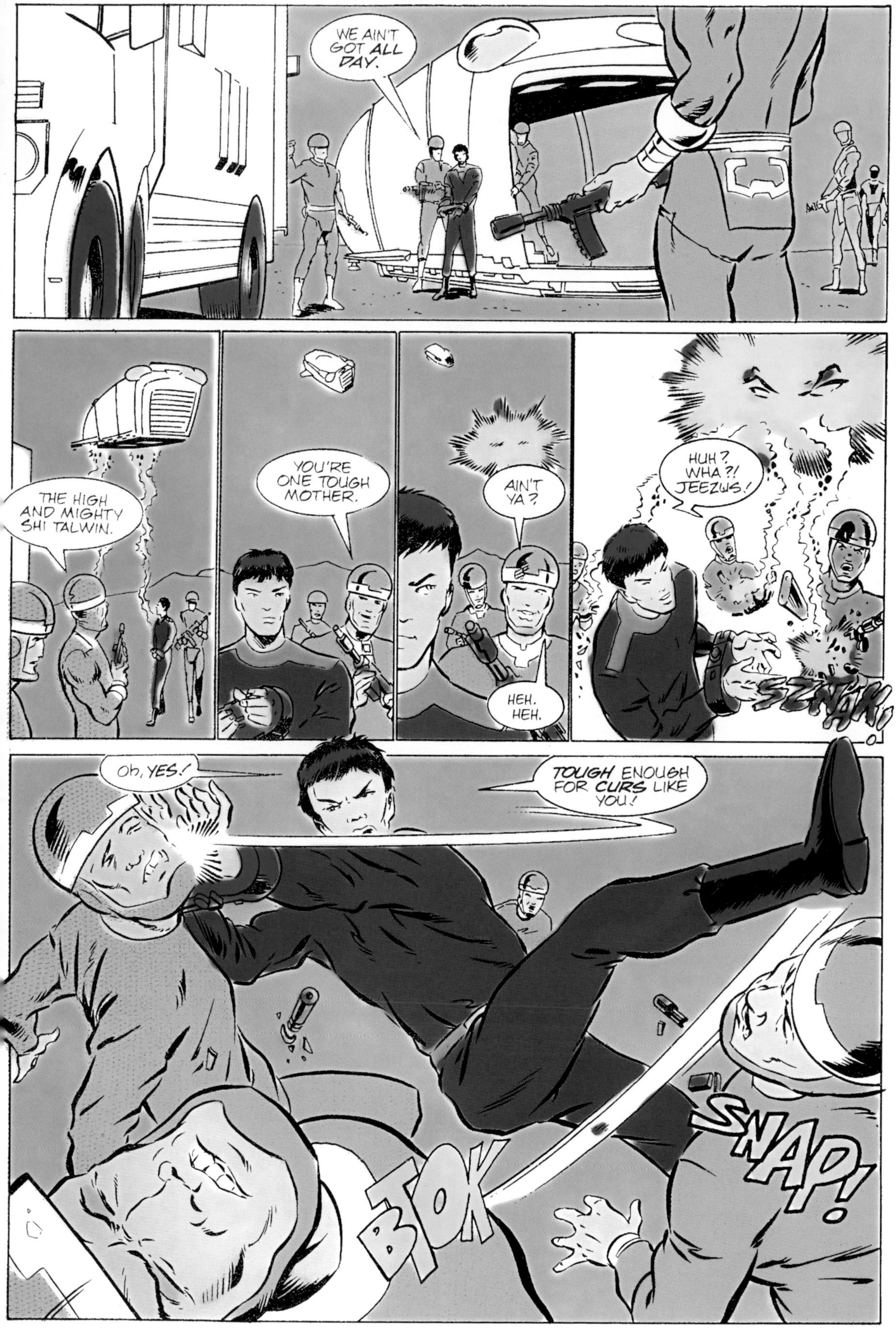

WE AIN'T GOT ALL DAY.
THE HIGH AND MIGHTY SHI TALWIN.
YOU'RE ONE TOUGH MOTHER.
AIN'T YA?
HEH. HEH.
HUH? WHA?! JEEZUS!
SZNAK!
Oh, YES!
TOUGH ENOUGH FOR CURS LIKE YOU!
BTOK
SNAP!

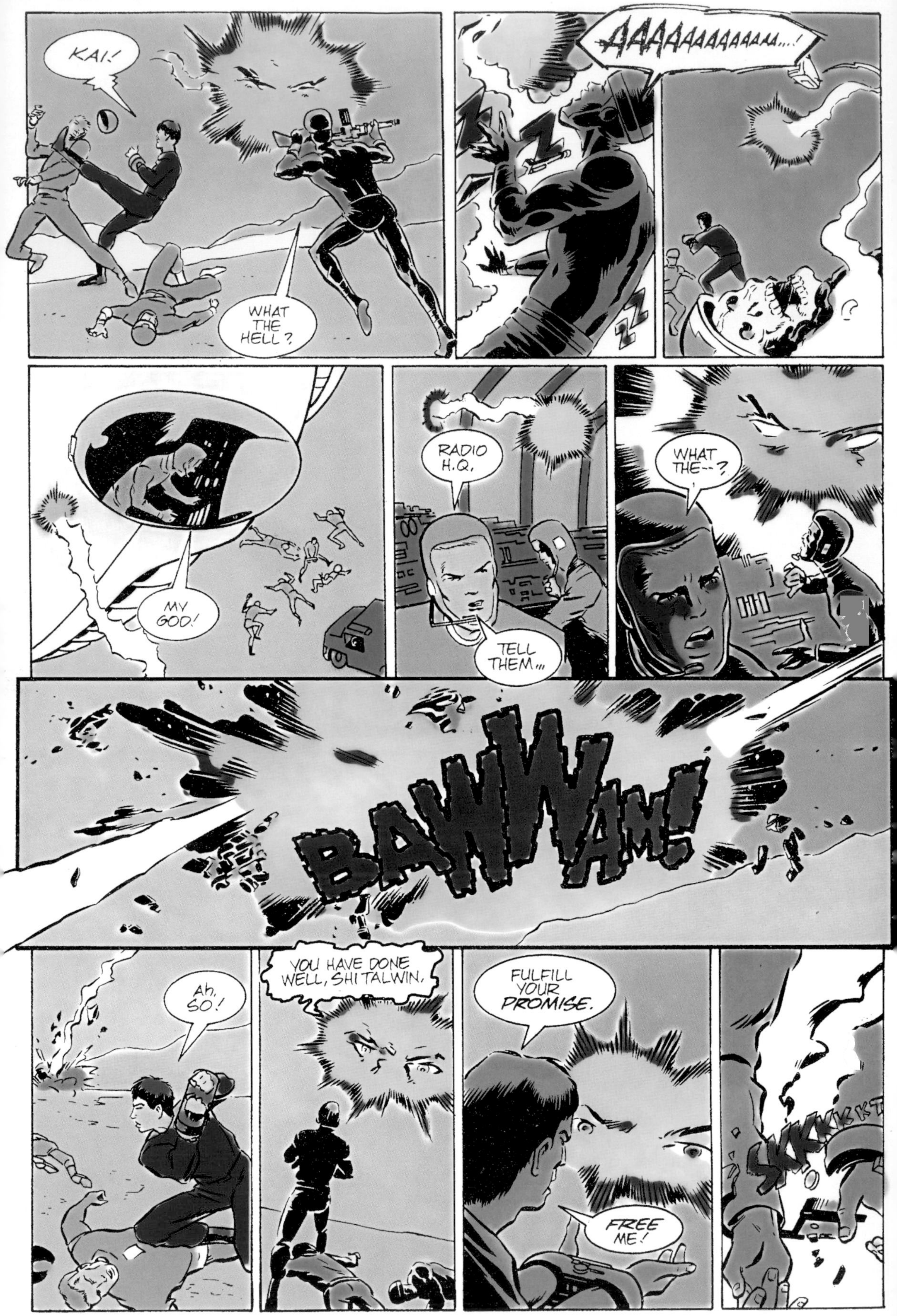
KAI!
WHAT THE HELL?
AAAAAAAAAAAA...!
MY GOD!
RADIO H.Q.
TELL THEM...
WHAT THE--?
BAWWAM!
Ah, SO!
YOU HAVE DONE WELL, SHITALWIN.
FULFILL YOUR PROMISE.
FREE ME!
SKKKKKT

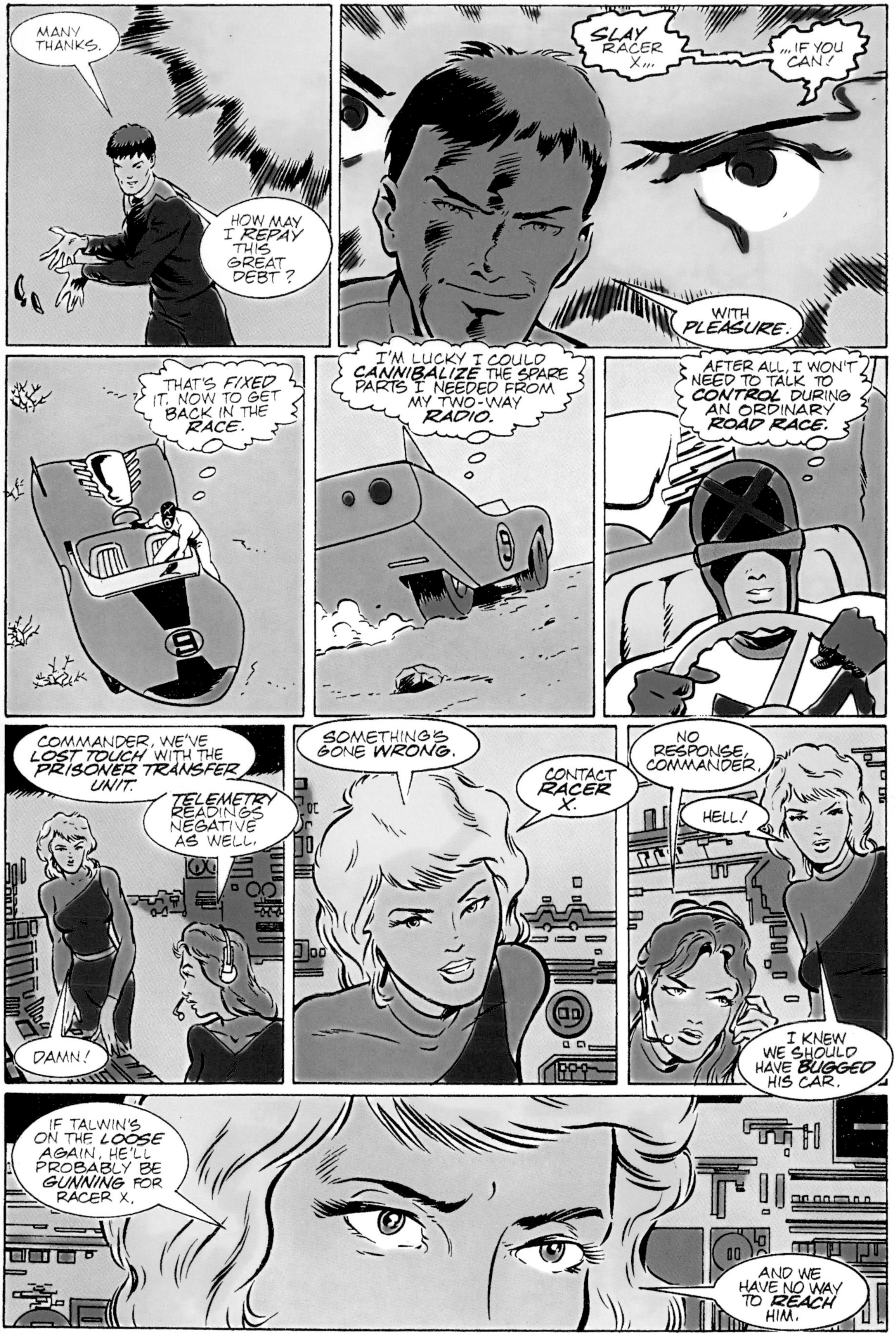

MANY THANKS.
HOW MAY I REPAY THIS GREAT DEBT?
SLAY RACER X...
...IF YOU CAN!
WITH PLEASURE.
THAT'S FIXED IT. NOW TO GET BACK IN THE RACE.
I'M LUCKY I COULD CANNIBALIZE THE SPARE PARTS I NEEDED FROM MY TWO-WAY RADIO.
AFTER ALL, I WON'T NEED TO TALK TO CONTROL DURING AN ORDINARY ROAD RACE.
COMMANDER, WE'VE LOST TOUCH WITH THE PRISONER TRANSFER UNIT.
TELEMETRY READINGS NEGATIVE AS WELL.
DAMN!
SOMETHING'S GONE WRONG.
CONTACT RACER X.
NO RESPONSE, COMMANDER.
HELL!
I KNEW WE SHOULD HAVE BUGGED HIS CAR.
IF TALWIN'S ON THE LOOSE AGAIN, HE'LL PROBABLY BE GUNNING FOR RACER X.
AND WE HAVE NO WAY TO REACH HIM.

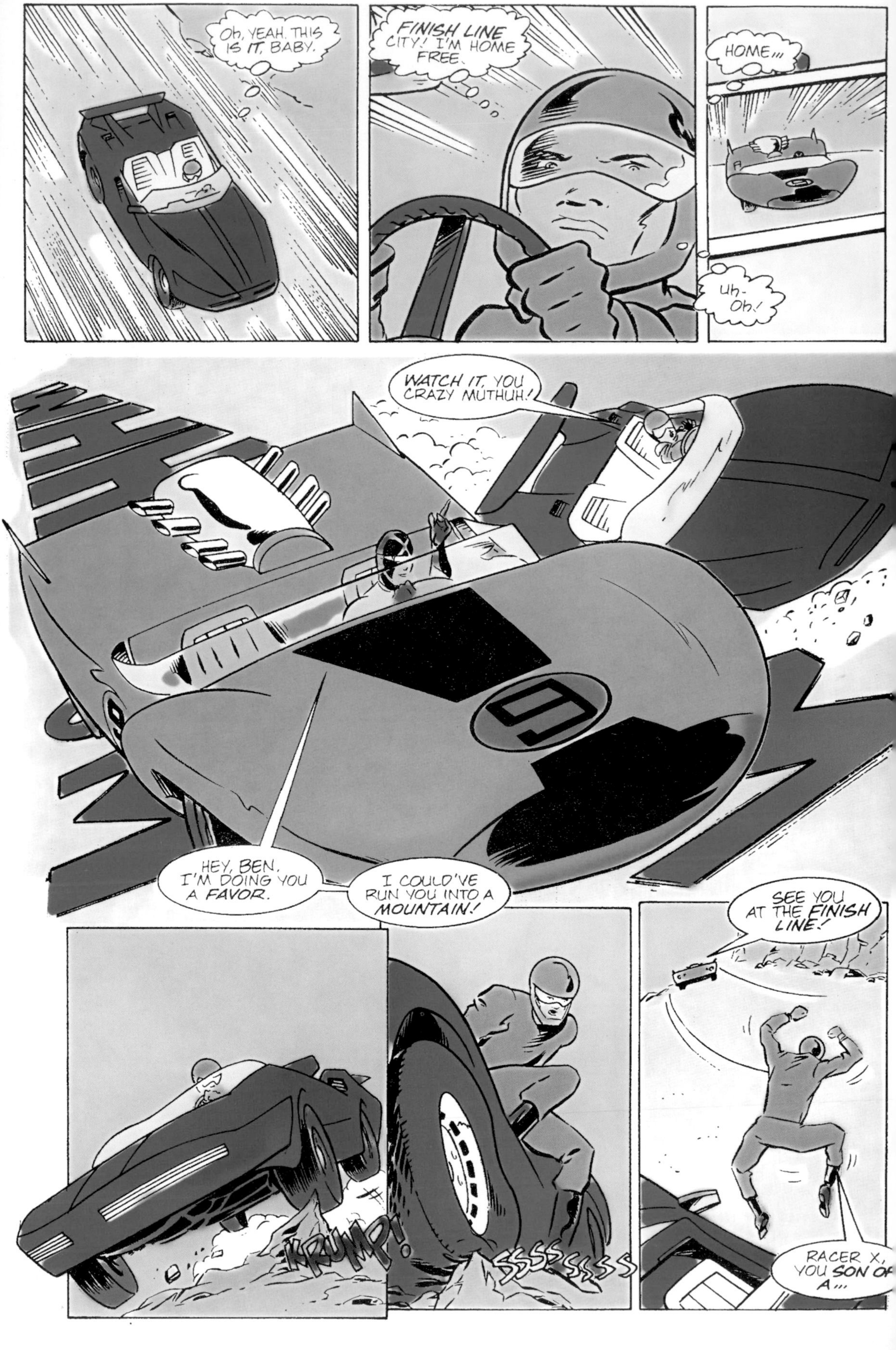

Oh, YEAH. THIS IS IT, BABY.
FINISH LINE CITY! I'M HOME FREE.
HOME...
Uh-Oh!
WATCH IT, YOU CRAZY MUTHUH!
HEY, BEN. I'M DOING YOU A FAVOR.
I COULD'VE RUN YOU INTO A MOUNTAIN!
KRUMP!
SSSSSSSSS
SEE YOU AT THE FINISH LINE!
RACER X, YOU SON OF A...

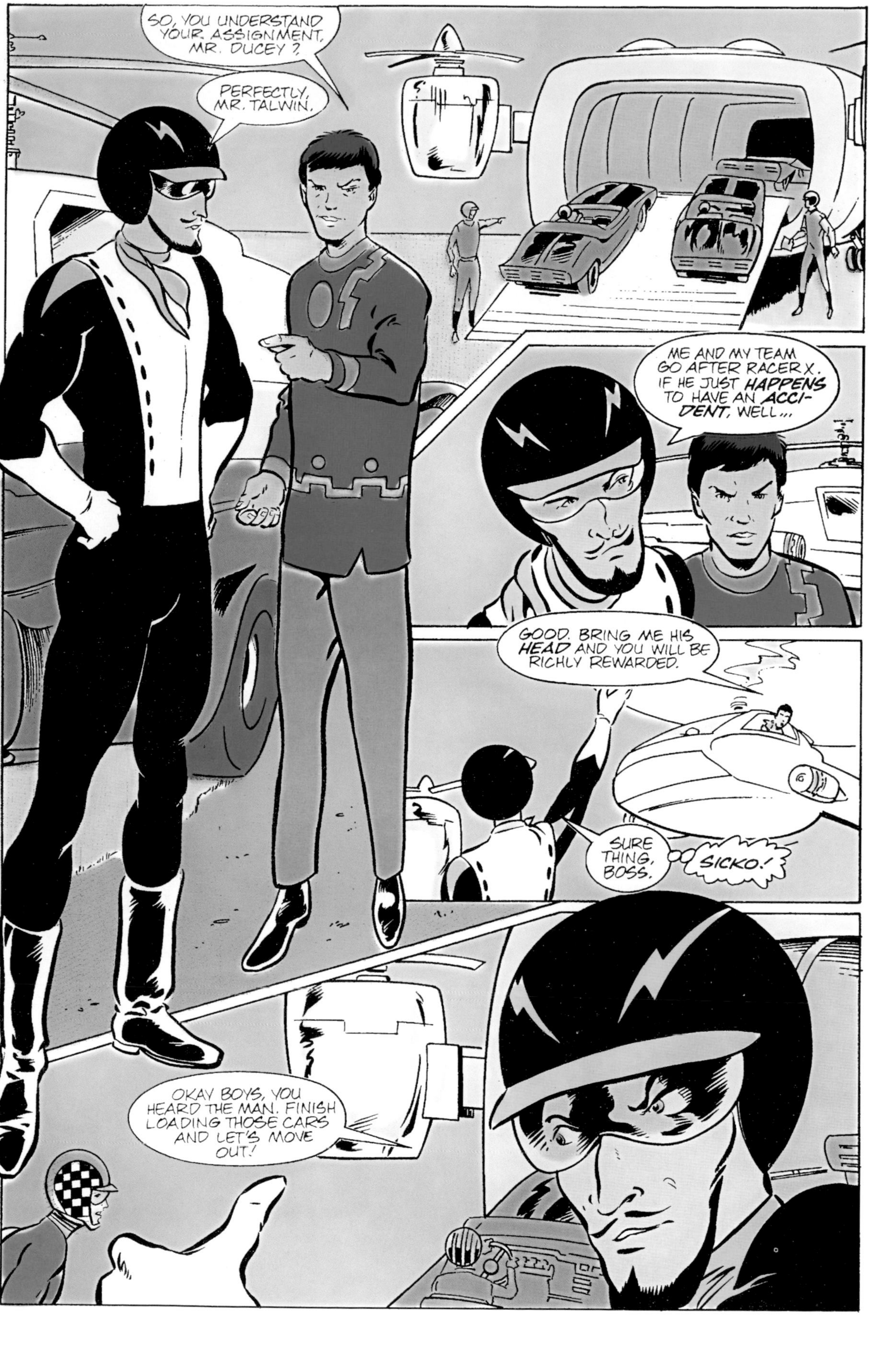
SO, YOU UNDERSTAND YOUR ASSIGNMENT, MR. DUCEY ?
PERFECTLY, MR. TALWIN.
ME AND MY TEAM GO AFTER RACER X. IF HE JUST HAPPENS TO HAVE AN ACCI-DENT, WELL...
GOOD. BRING ME HIS HEAD AND YOU WILL BE RICHLY REWARDED.
SURE THING, BOSS.
SICKO!
OKAY BOYS, YOU HEARD THE MAN. FINISH LOADING THOSE CARS AND LET'S MOVE OUT!

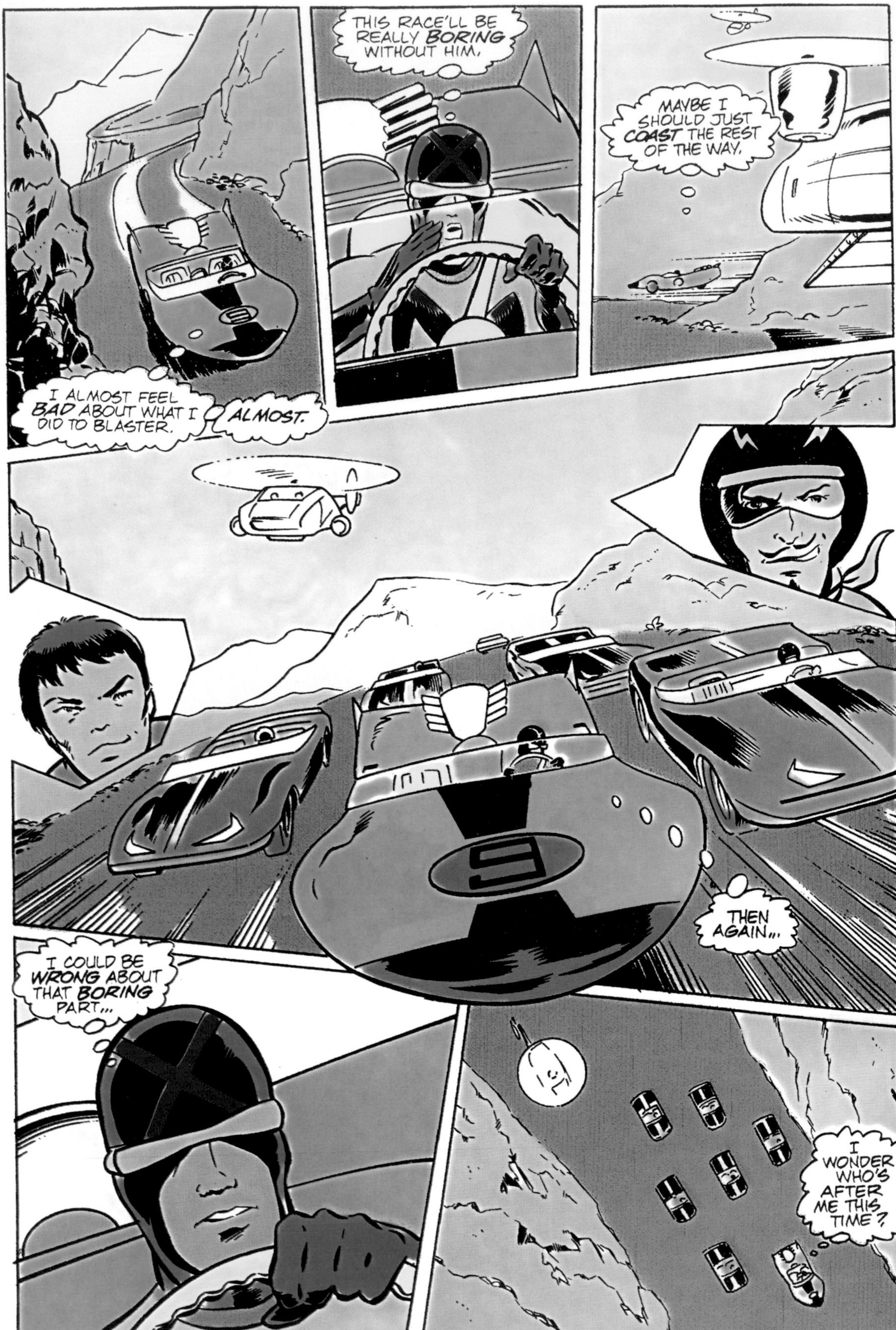
I ALMOST FEEL BAD ABOUT WHAT I DID TO BLASTER.
ALMOST.
THIS RACE'LL BE REALLY BORING WITHOUT HIM.
MAYBE I SHOULD JUST COAST THE REST OF THE WAY.
THEN AGAIN...
I COULD BE WRONG ABOUT THAT BORING PART...
I WONDER WHO'S AFTER ME THIS TIME?

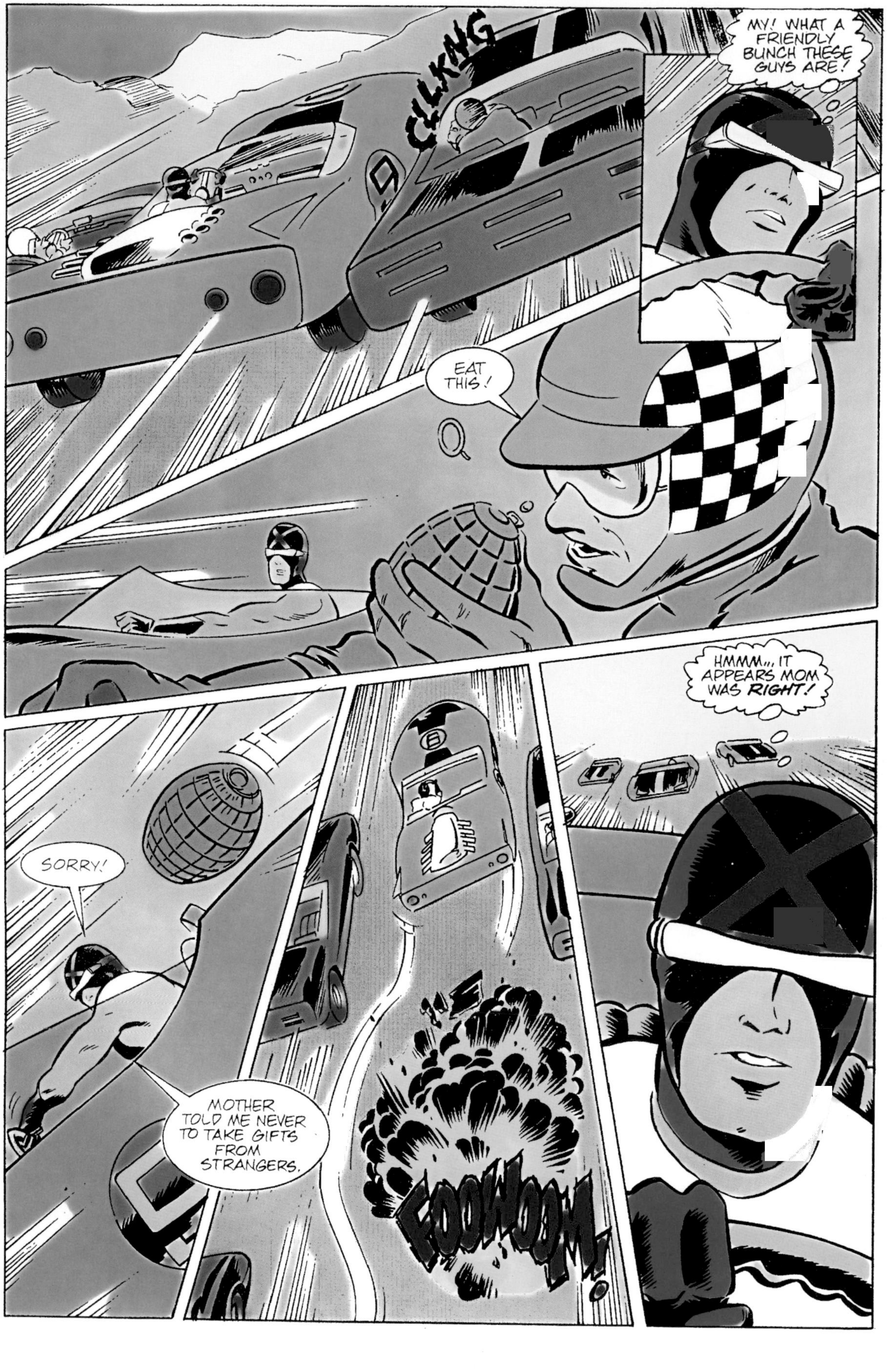
CLANG
MY! WHAT A FRIENDLY BUNCH THESE GUYS ARE!
EAT THIS!
SORRY!
MOTHER TOLD ME NEVER TO TAKE GIFTS FROM STRANGERS.
KOOWOOM!
HMMM... IT APPEARS MOM WAS RIGHT!

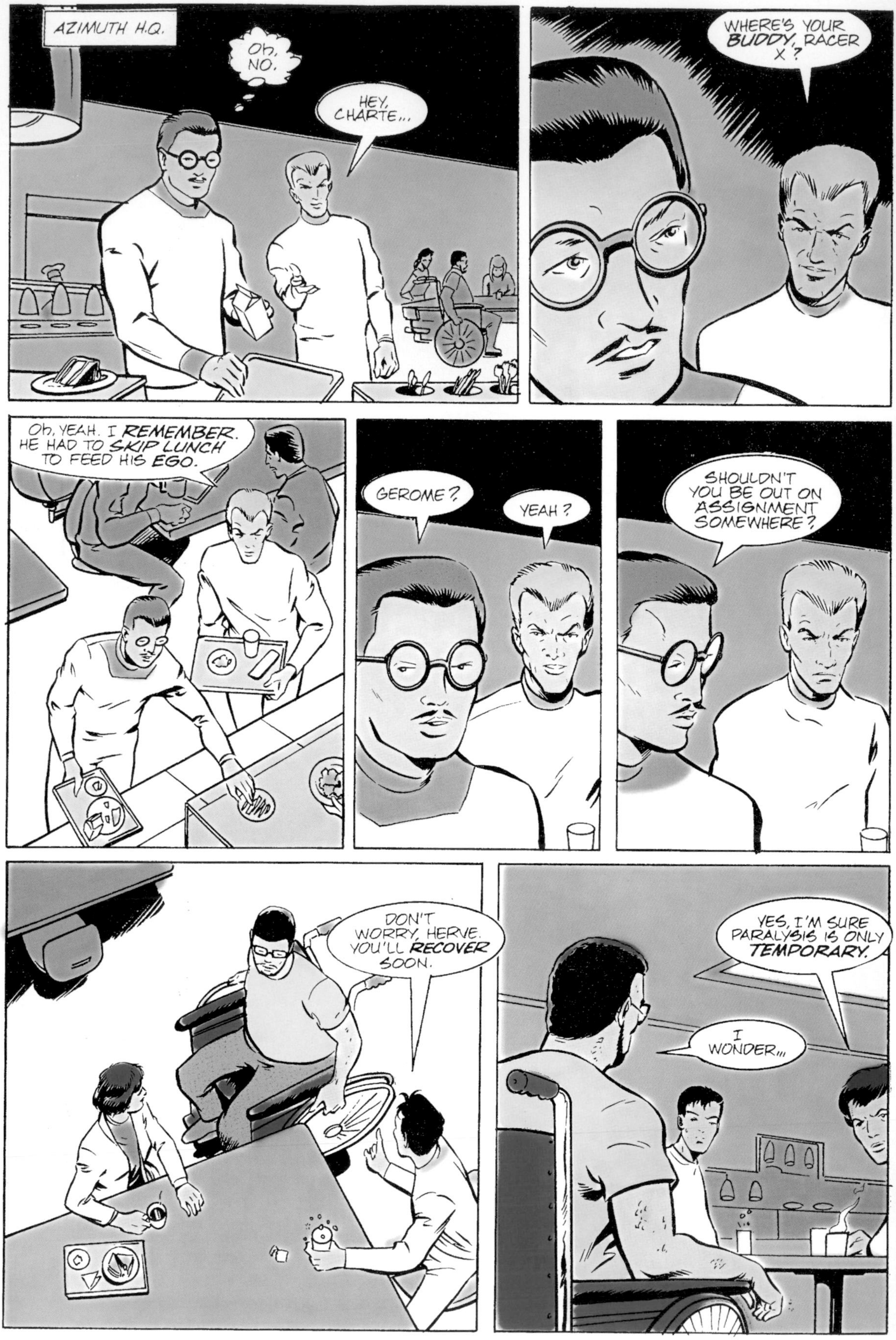
AZIMUTH H.Q.
Oh, NO.
HEY, CHARTE...
WHERE'S YOUR BUDDY, RACER X?
Oh, YEAH. I REMEMBER. HE HAD TO SKIP LUNCH TO FEED HIS EGO.
GEROME?
YEAH?
SHOULDN'T YOU BE OUT ON ASSIGNMENT SOMEWHERE?
DON'T WORRY, HERVE. YOU'LL RECOVER SOON.
YES, I'M SURE PARALYSIS IS ONLY TEMPORARY.
I WONDER...

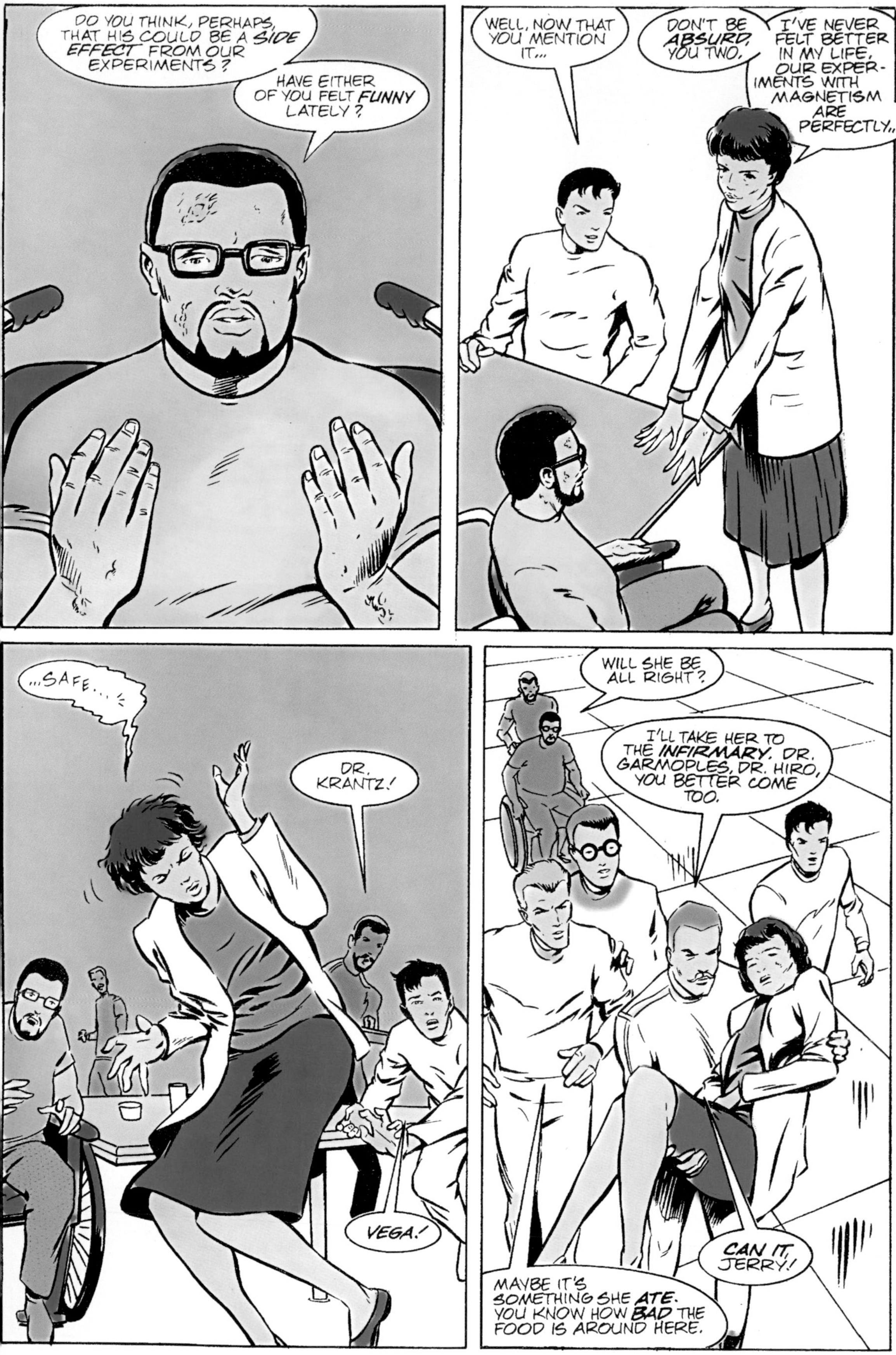
DO YOU THINK, PERHAPS, THAT HIS COULD BE A *SIDE EFFECT* FROM OUR EXPERIMENTS?
HAVE EITHER OF YOU FELT *FUNNY* LATELY?
WELL, NOW THAT YOU MENTION IT...
DON'T BE *ABSURD,* YOU TWO.
I'VE NEVER FELT BETTER IN MY LIFE. OUR EXPERIMENTS WITH MAGNETISM ARE PERFECTLY...
...SAFE...
DR. KRANTZ!
VEGA!
WILL SHE BE ALL RIGHT?
I'LL TAKE HER TO THE *INFIRMARY.* DR. GARMOPLES, DR. HIRO, YOU BETTER COME TOO.
MAYBE IT'S SOMETHING SHE *ATE.* YOU KNOW HOW *BAD* THE FOOD IS AROUND HERE.
CAN IT, JERRY!

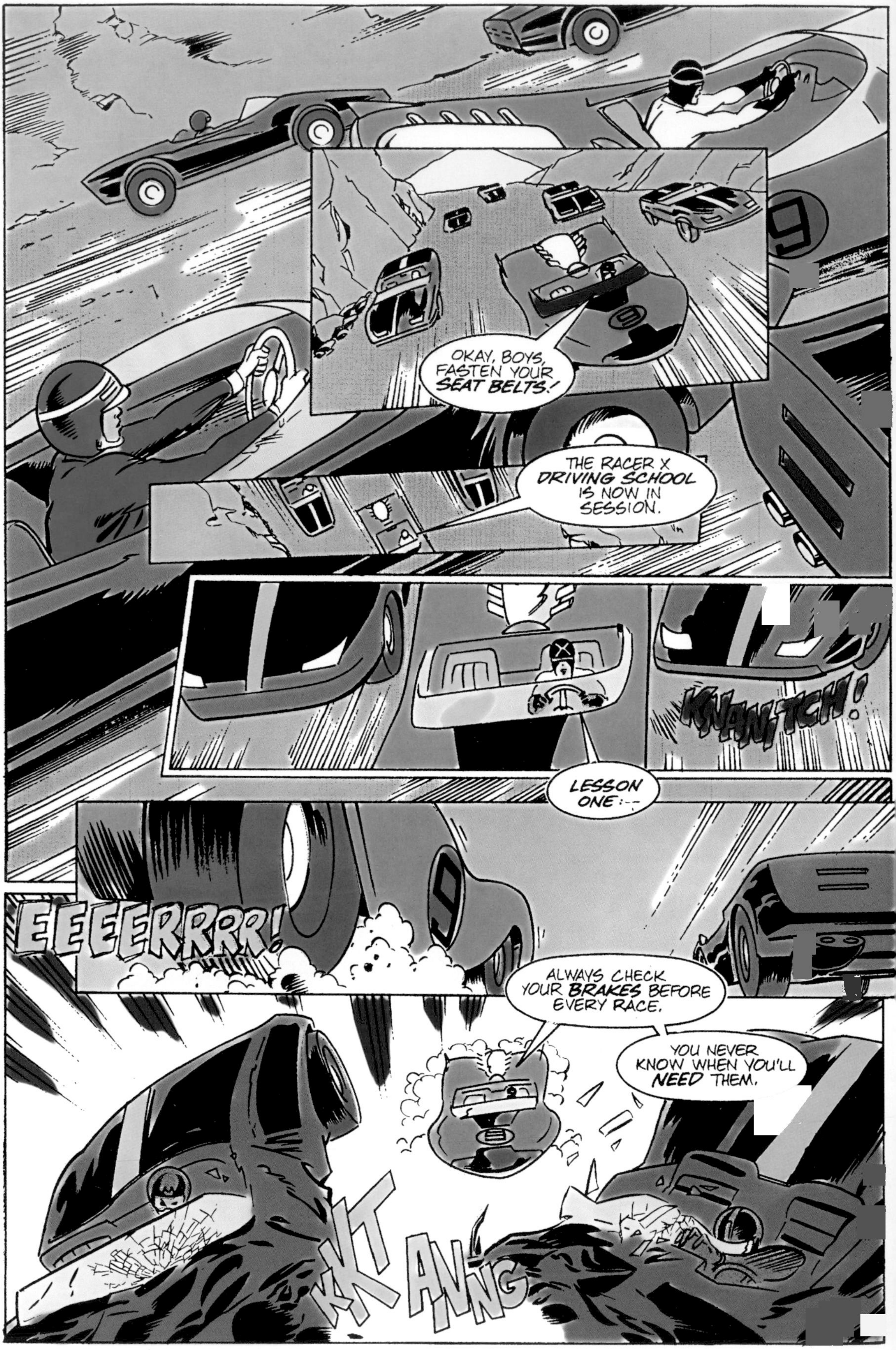
OKAY, BOYS, FASTEN YOUR SEAT BELTS!
THE RACER X DRIVING SCHOOL IS NOW IN SESSION.
KNAN TCH!
LESSON ONE:--
EEEERRRR!
ALWAYS CHECK YOUR BRAKES BEFORE EVERY RACE.
YOU NEVER KNOW WHEN YOU'LL NEED THEM.
KKT ANNG

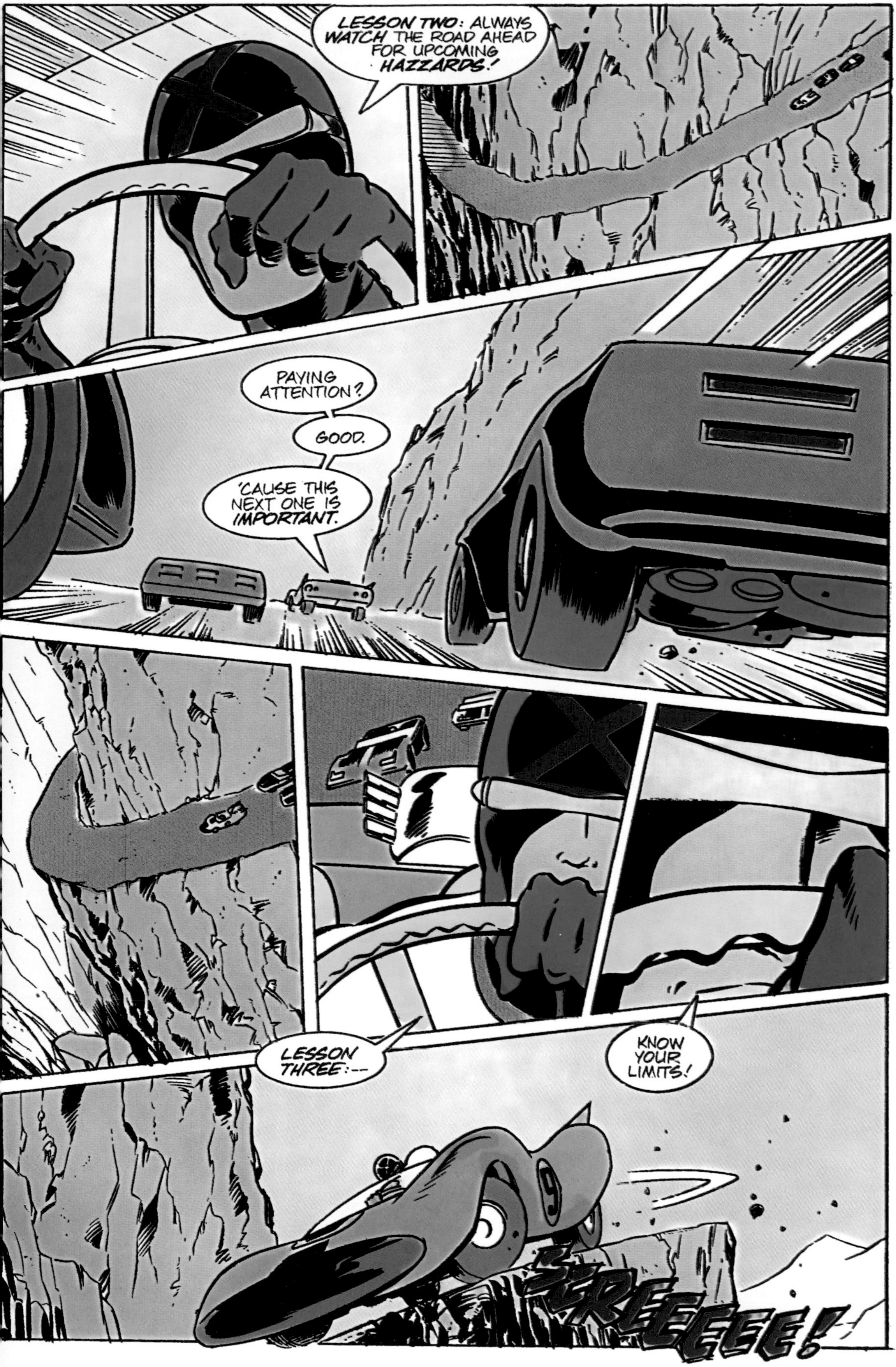
LESSON TWO: ALWAYS WATCH THE ROAD AHEAD FOR UPCOMING HAZZARDS!
PAYING ATTENTION?
GOOD.
'CAUSE THIS NEXT ONE IS IMPORTANT.
LESSON THREE:--
KNOW YOUR LIMITS!
SCREEEEEE!

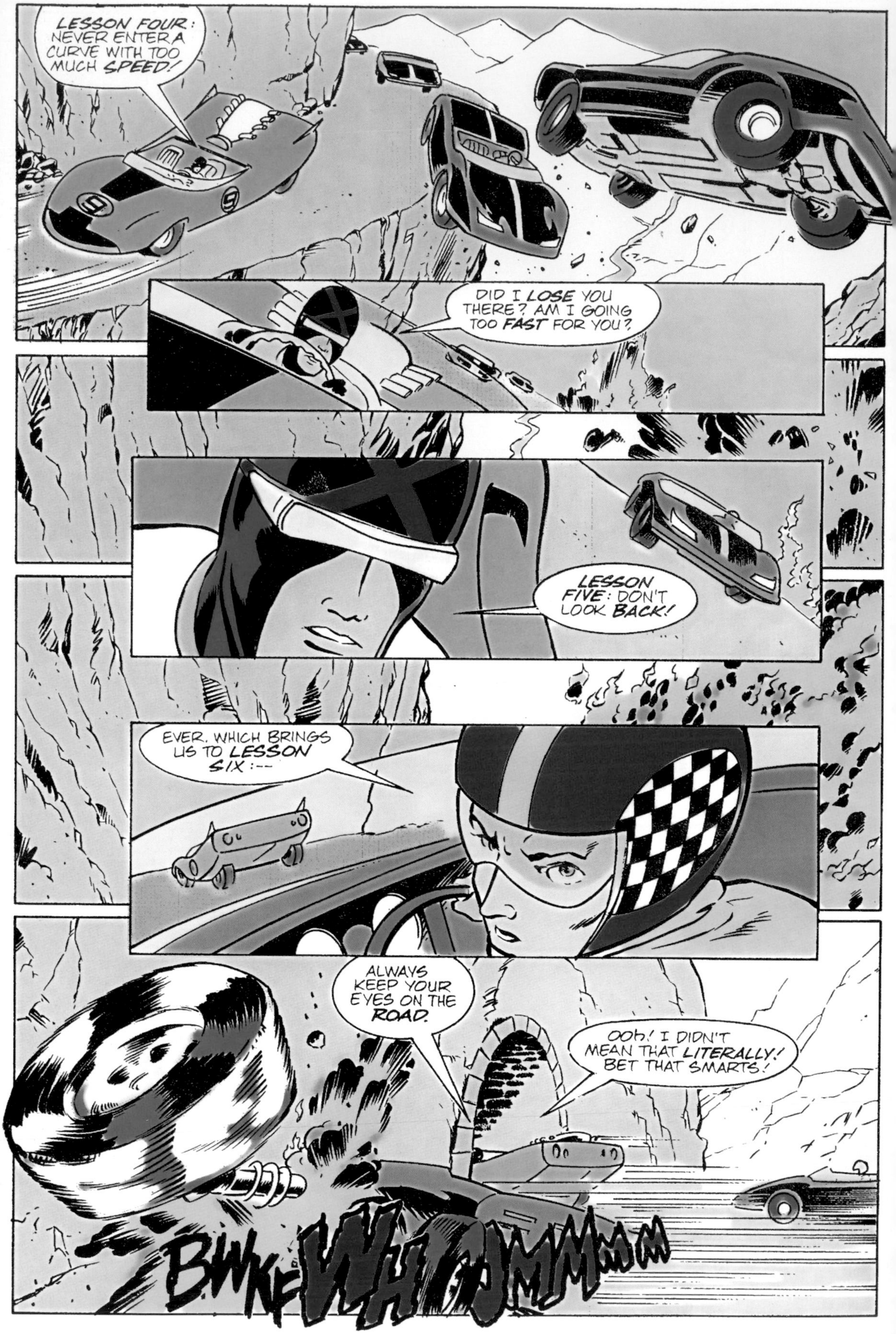
LESSON FOUR: NEVER ENTER A CURVE WITH TOO MUCH SPEED!
DID I LOSE YOU THERE? AM I GOING TOO FAST FOR YOU?
LESSON FIVE: DON'T LOOK BACK!
EVER. WHICH BRINGS US TO LESSON SIX:--
ALWAYS KEEP YOUR EYES ON THE ROAD.
OOH! I DIDN'T MEAN THAT LITERALLY! BET THAT SMARTS!
BWKFWHOMMMMM

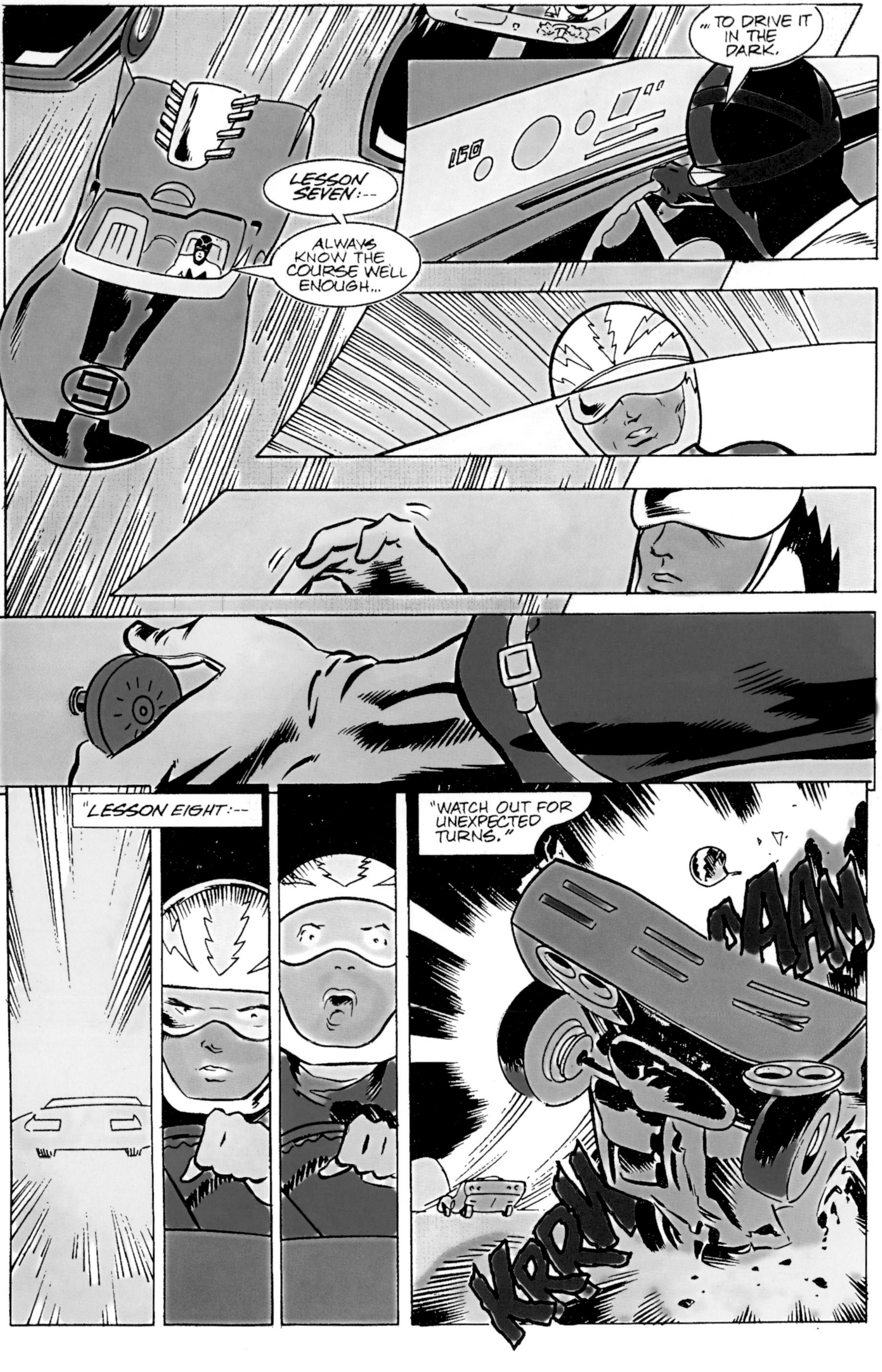
LESSON SEVEN:--
ALWAYS KNOW THE COURSE WELL ENOUGH...
...TO DRIVE IT IN THE DARK.
"LESSON EIGHT:--
"WATCH OUT FOR UNEXPECTED TURNS."
KRRW
AAM

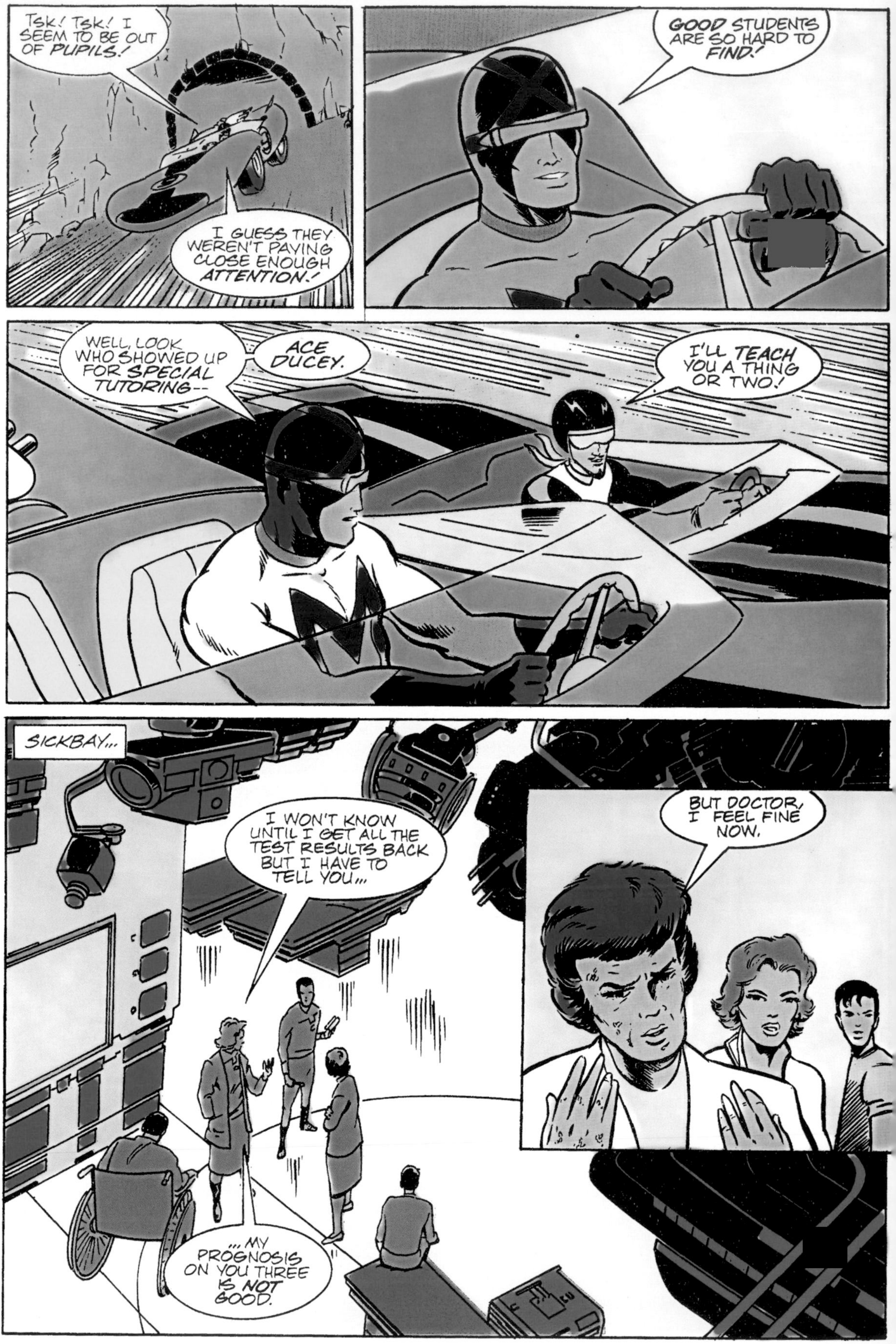
TSK! TSK! I SEEM TO BE OUT OF PUPILS!
I GUESS THEY WEREN'T PAYING CLOSE ENOUGH ATTENTION!
GOOD STUDENTS ARE SO HARD TO FIND!
WELL, LOOK WHO SHOWED UP FOR SPECIAL TUTORING--
ACE DUCEY.
I'LL TEACH YOU A THING OR TWO!
SICKBAY...
I WON'T KNOW UNTIL I GET ALL THE TEST RESULTS BACK BUT I HAVE TO TELL YOU...
...MY PROGNOSIS ON YOU THREE IS NOT GOOD.
BUT DOCTOR, I FEEL FINE NOW.

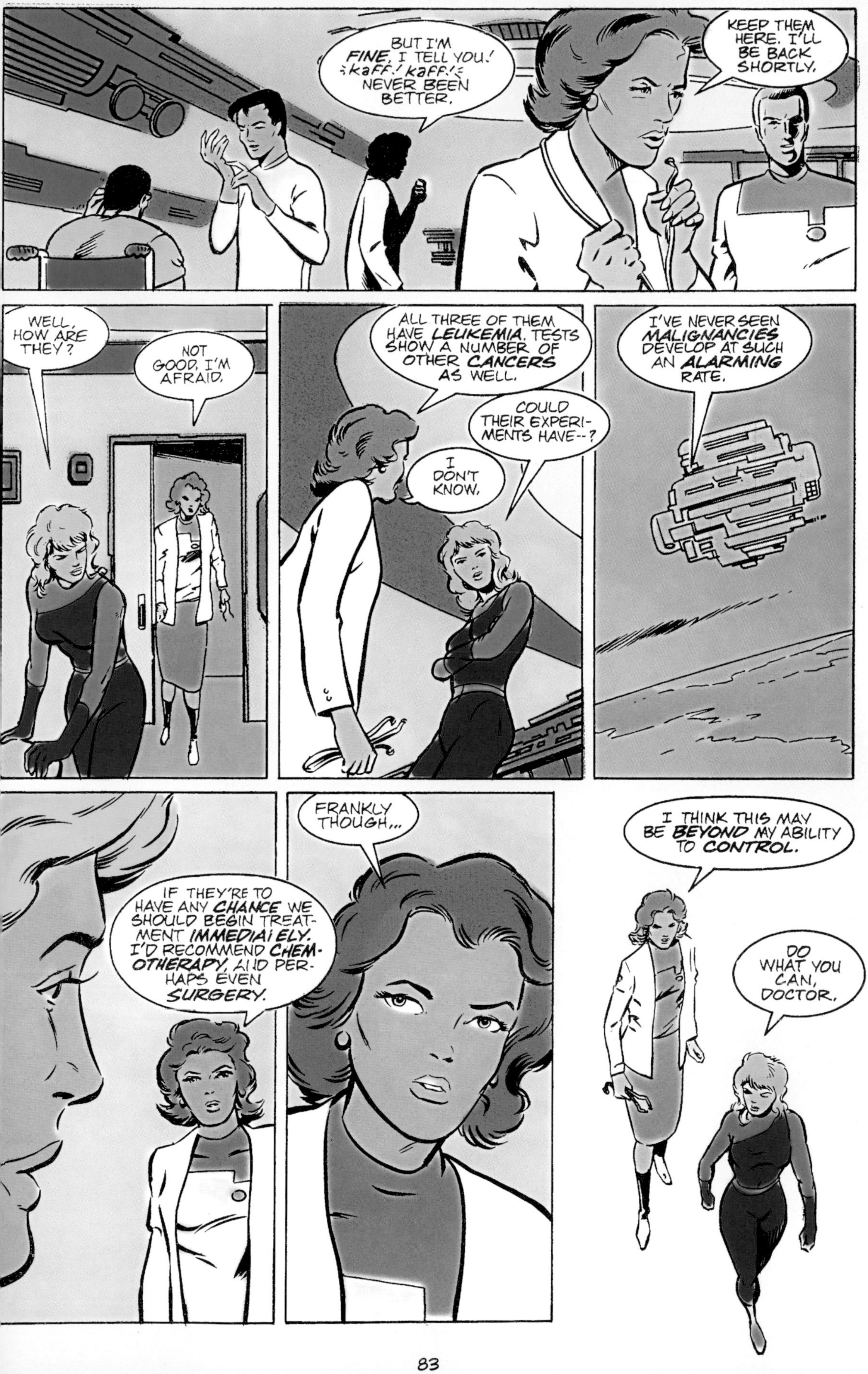
BUT I'M FINE, I TELL YOU! ¡kaff! kaff! NEVER BEEN BETTER.
KEEP THEM HERE. I'LL BE BACK SHORTLY.
WELL, HOW ARE THEY?
NOT GOOD, I'M AFRAID.
ALL THREE OF THEM HAVE LEUKEMIA. TESTS SHOW A NUMBER OF OTHER CANCERS AS WELL.
COULD THEIR EXPERI-MENTS HAVE--?
I DON'T KNOW.
I'VE NEVER SEEN MALIGNANCIES DEVELOP AT SUCH AN ALARMING RATE.
IF THEY'RE TO HAVE ANY CHANCE WE SHOULD BEGIN TREAT-MENT IMMEDIATELY. I'D RECOMMEND CHEM-OTHERAPY, AND PER-HAPS EVEN SURGERY.
FRANKLY THOUGH...
I THINK THIS MAY BE BEYOND MY ABILITY TO CONTROL.
DO WHAT YOU CAN, DOCTOR.

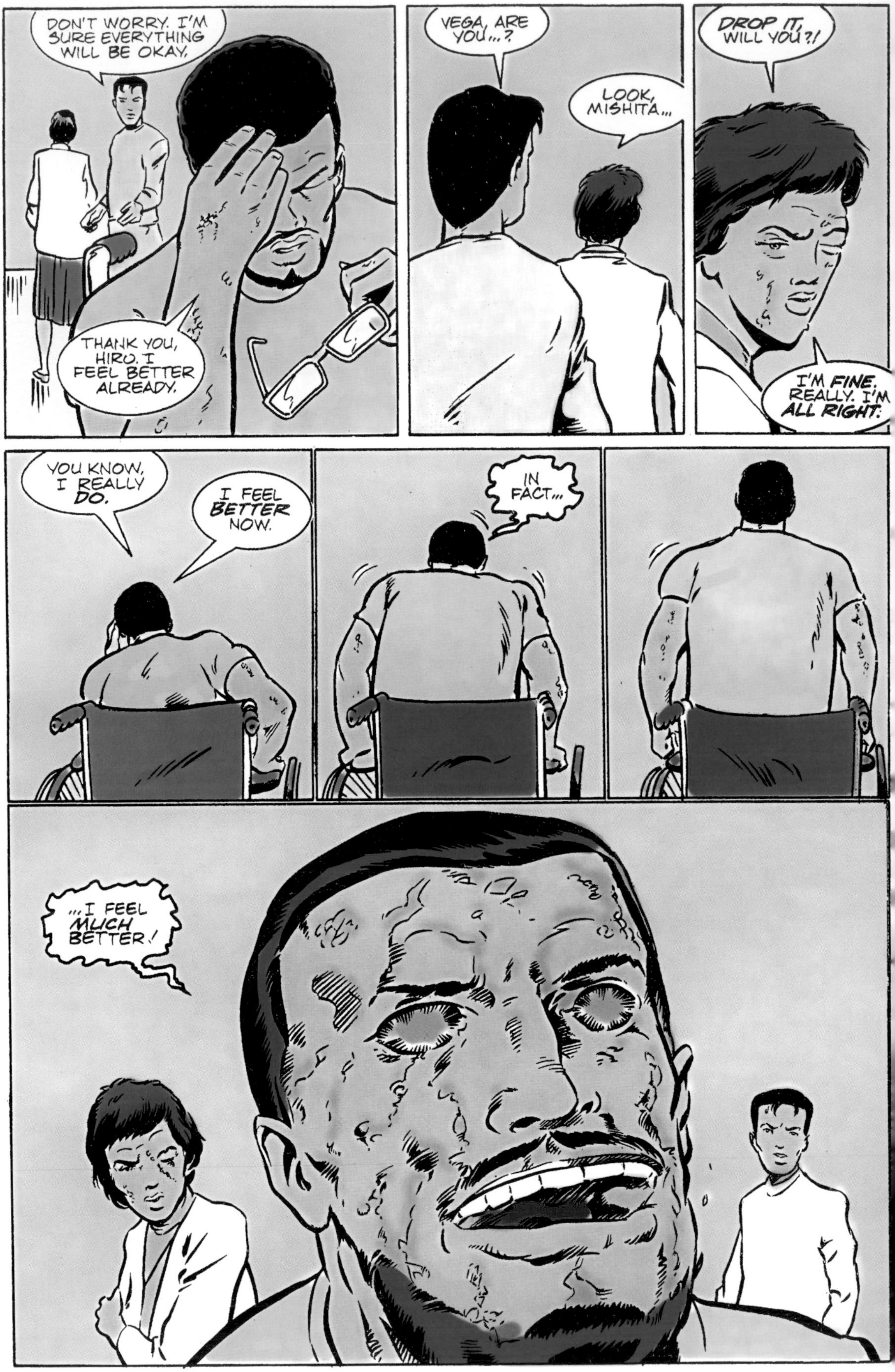
DON'T WORRY. I'M SURE EVERYTHING WILL BE OKAY.
THANK YOU, HIRO. I FEEL BETTER ALREADY.
VEGA, ARE YOU...?
LOOK, MISHITA...
DROP IT, WILL YOU?!
I'M FINE. REALLY. I'M ALL RIGHT.
YOU KNOW, I REALLY DO.
I FEEL BETTER NOW.
IN FACT...
...I FEEL MUCH BETTER!

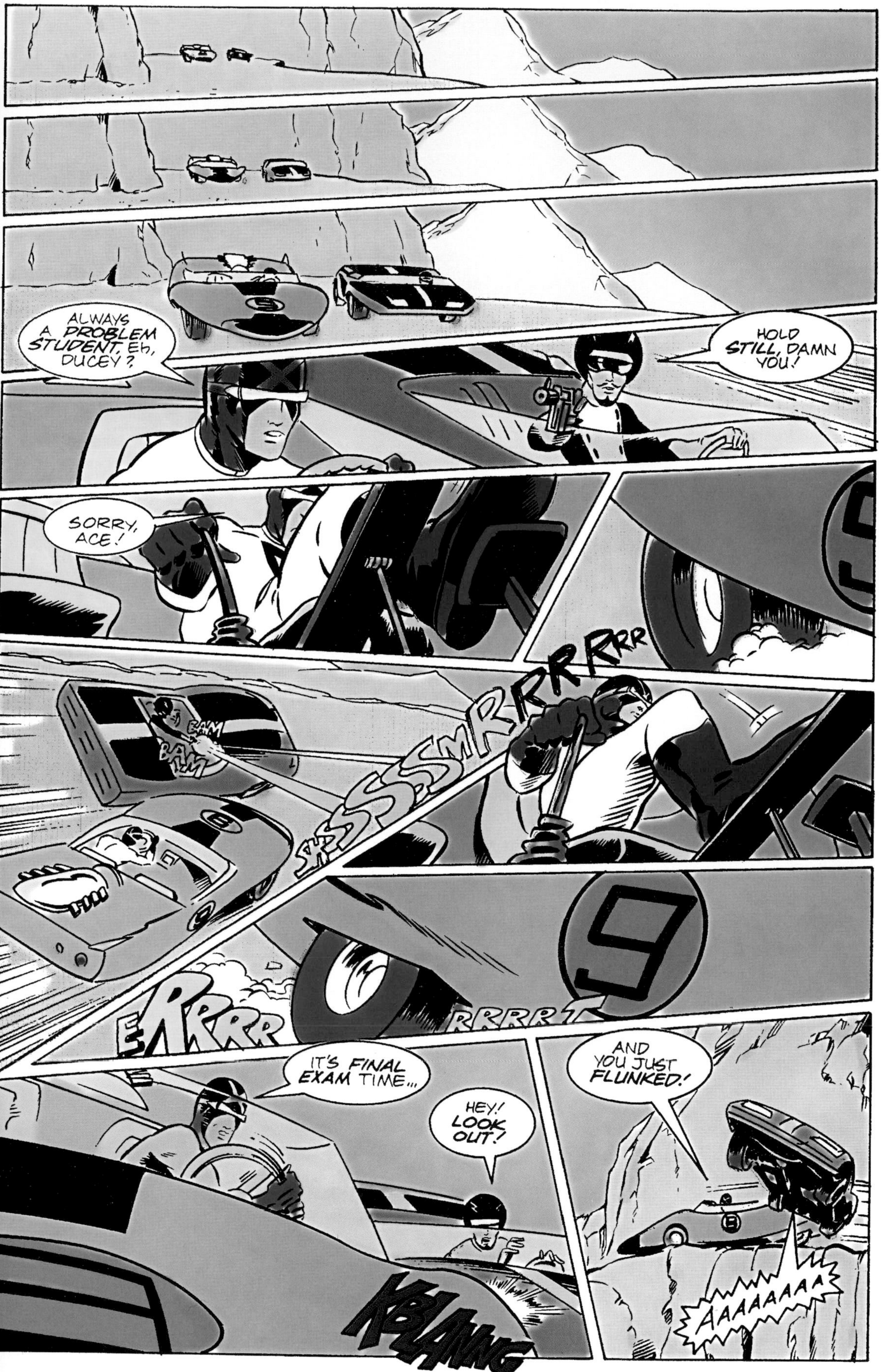

ALWAYS A PROBLEM STUDENT, Eh, DUCEY?
HOLD STILL, DAMN YOU!
SORRY, ACE!
RRRRRR
SSSSMRRR
BAM BAM
ERRRR
RRRRRT
IT'S FINAL EXAM TIME...
HEY! LOOK OUT!
AND YOU JUST FLUNKED!
AAAAAAA
KBLANNG

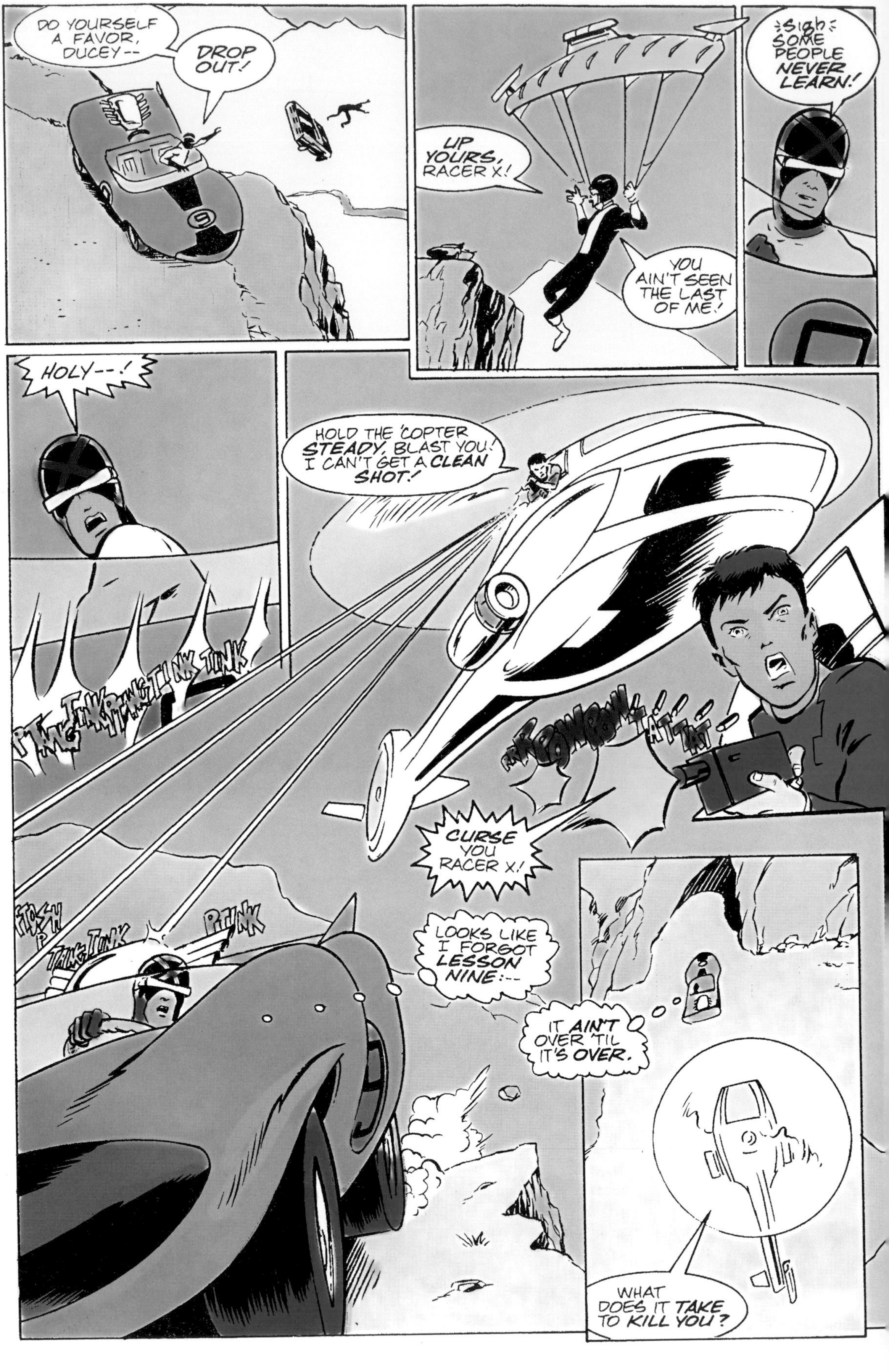
DO YOURSELF A FAVOR, DUCEY--
DROP OUT!
UP YOURS, RACER X!
YOU AIN'T SEEN THE LAST OF ME!
SIGH SOME PEOPLE NEVER LEARN!
HOLY--!
HOLD THE 'COPTER STEADY, BLAST YOU! I CAN'T GET A CLEAN SHOT!
TINK TINK
CURSE YOU RACER X!
PTINK
LOOKS LIKE I FORGOT LESSON NINE:--
IT AIN'T OVER 'TIL IT'S OVER.
WHAT DOES IT TAKE TO KILL YOU?

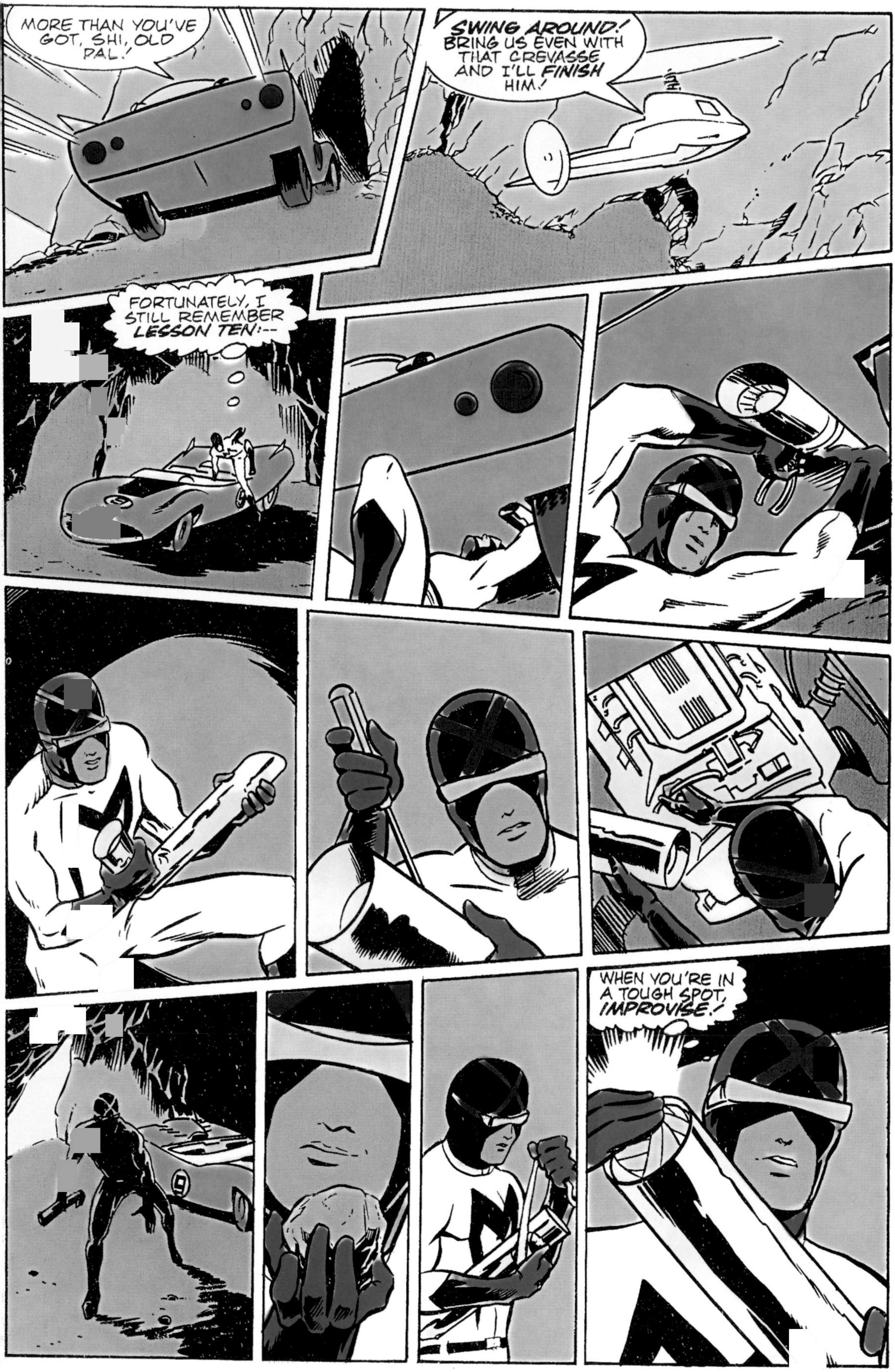
MORE THAN YOU'VE GOT, SHI, OLD PAL!
SWING AROUND! BRING US EVEN WITH THAT CREVASSE AND I'LL FINISH HIM!
FORTUNATELY, I STILL REMEMBER LESSON TEN:--
WHEN YOU'RE IN A TOUGH SPOT, IMPROVISE!

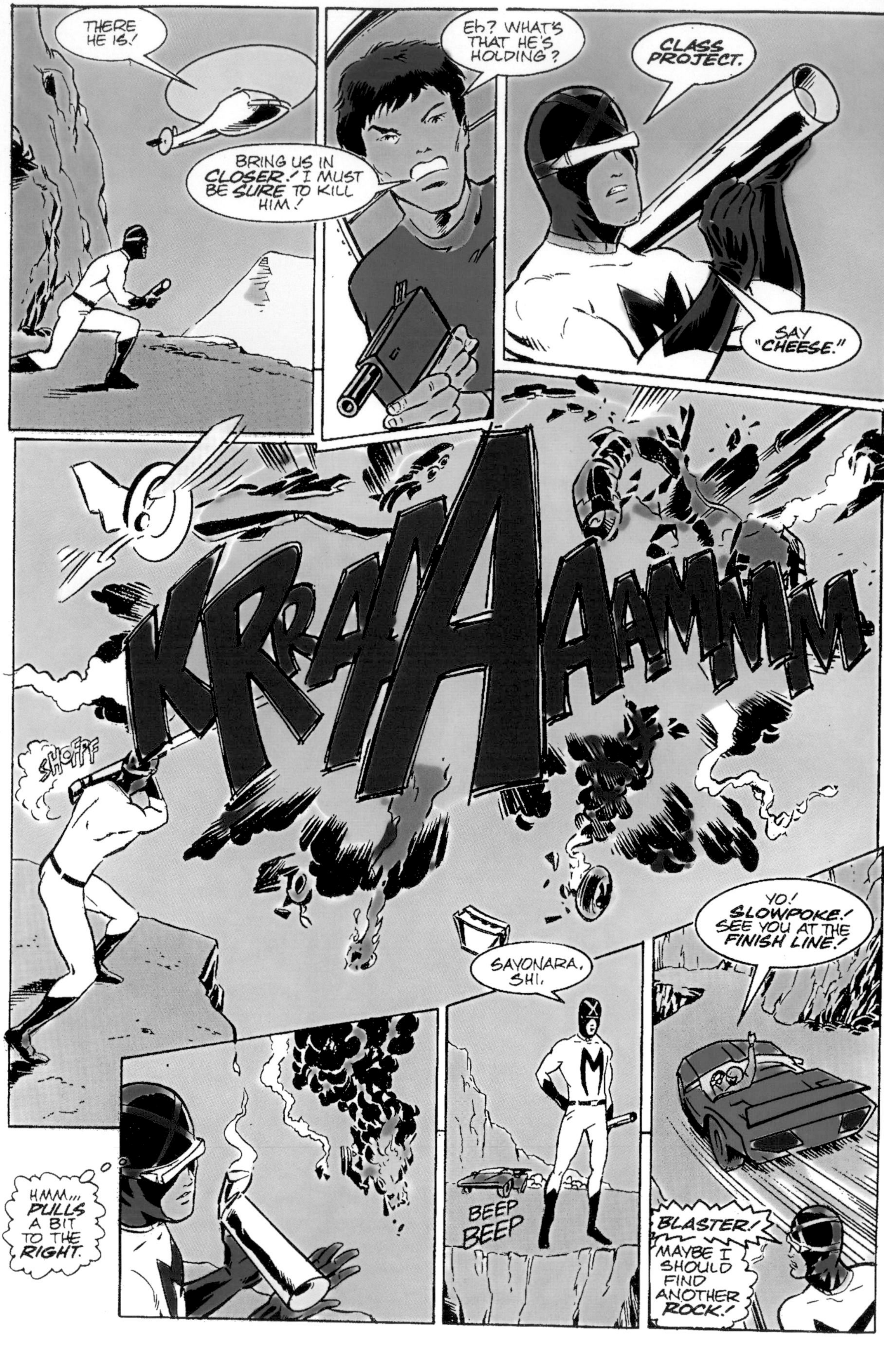
THERE HE IS!
Eh? WHAT'S THAT HE'S HOLDING?
BRING US IN CLOSER! I MUST BE SURE TO KILL HIM!
CLASS PROJECT.
SAY "CHEESE."
KRRAAAAAMMM
SHOFFF
SAYONARA, SHI.
YO! SLOWPOKE! SEE YOU AT THE FINISH LINE!
HMM... PULLS A BIT TO THE RIGHT.
BEEP BEEP
BLASTER!
MAYBE I SHOULD FIND ANOTHER ROCK!

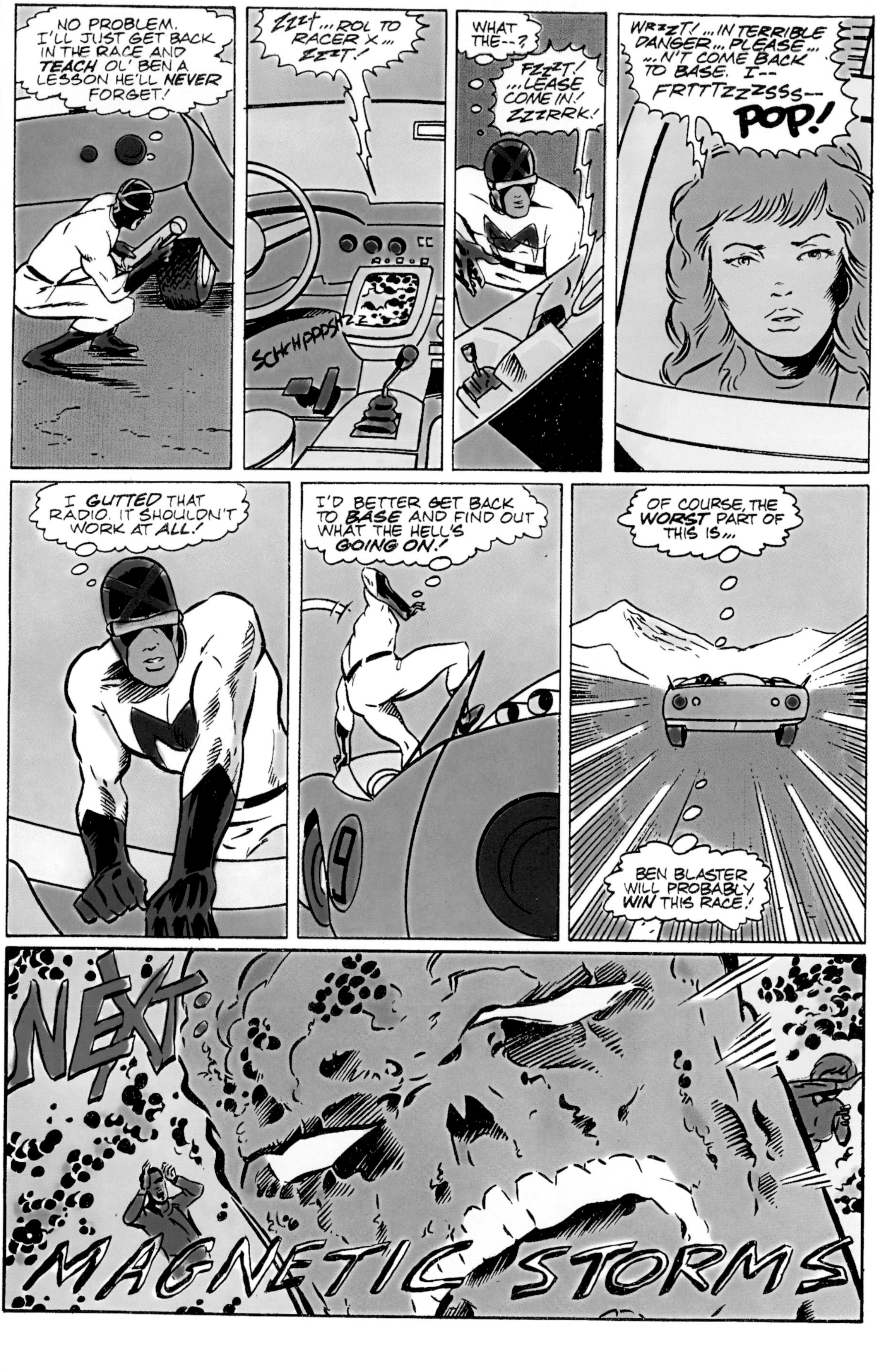
NO PROBLEM. I'LL JUST GET BACK IN THE RACE AND TEACH OL' BEN A LESSON HE'LL NEVER FORGET!
ZZZT... ROL TO RACER X... ZZZT!
SCHHPPPSHZZ
WHAT THE--?
FZZZT! ...LEASE COME IN! ZZZRRK!
WRZZT! ...IN TERRIBLE DANGER... PLEASE... ...N'T COME BACK TO BASE. I--
FRTTTZZZSSS--
POP!
I GUTTED THAT RADIO. IT SHOULDN'T WORK AT ALL!
I'D BETTER GET BACK TO BASE AND FIND OUT WHAT THE HELL'S GOING ON!
OF COURSE, THE WORST PART OF THIS IS...
BEN BLASTER WILL PROBABLY WIN THIS RACE!
NEXT
MAGNETIC STORMS

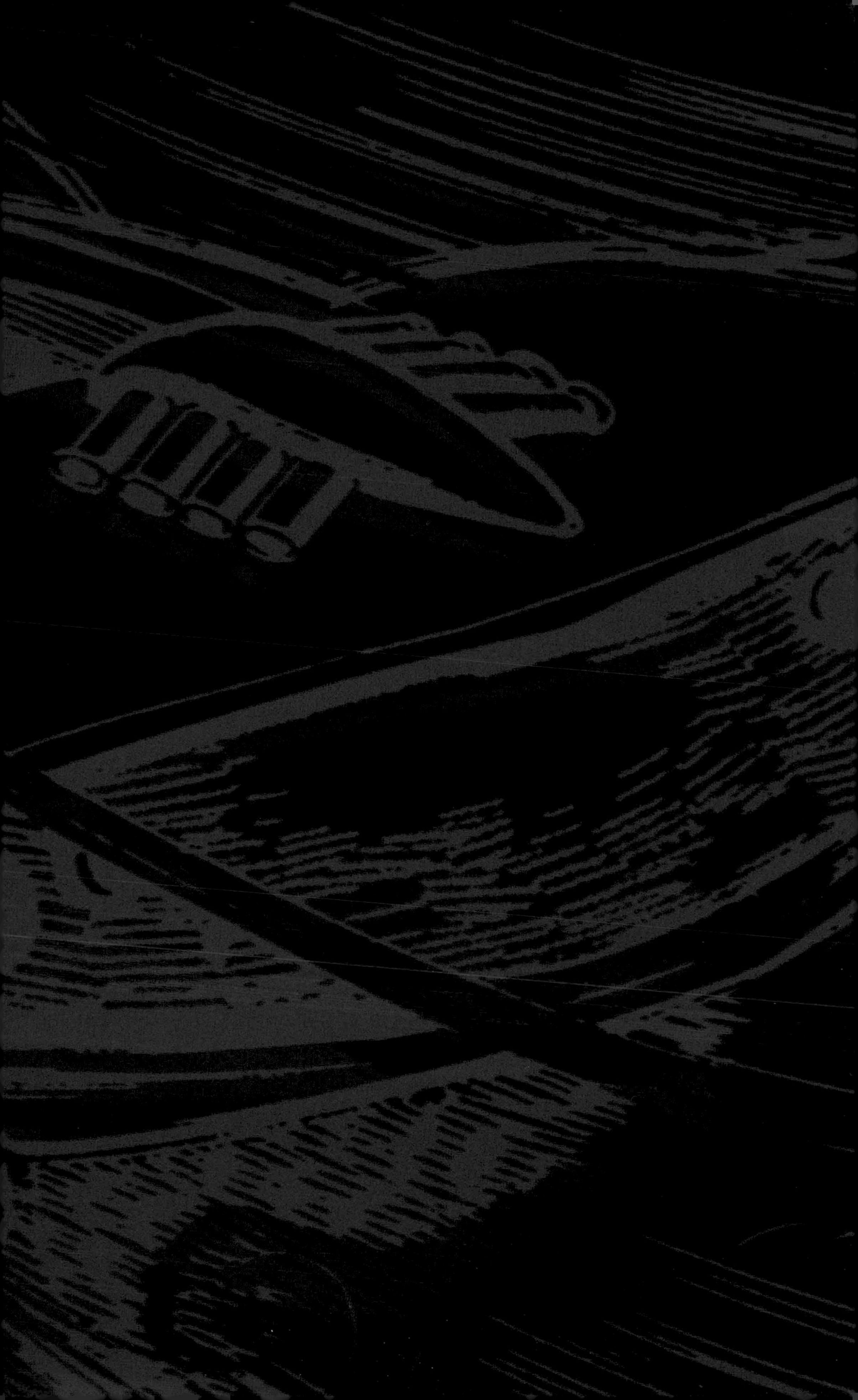

Racer X #4

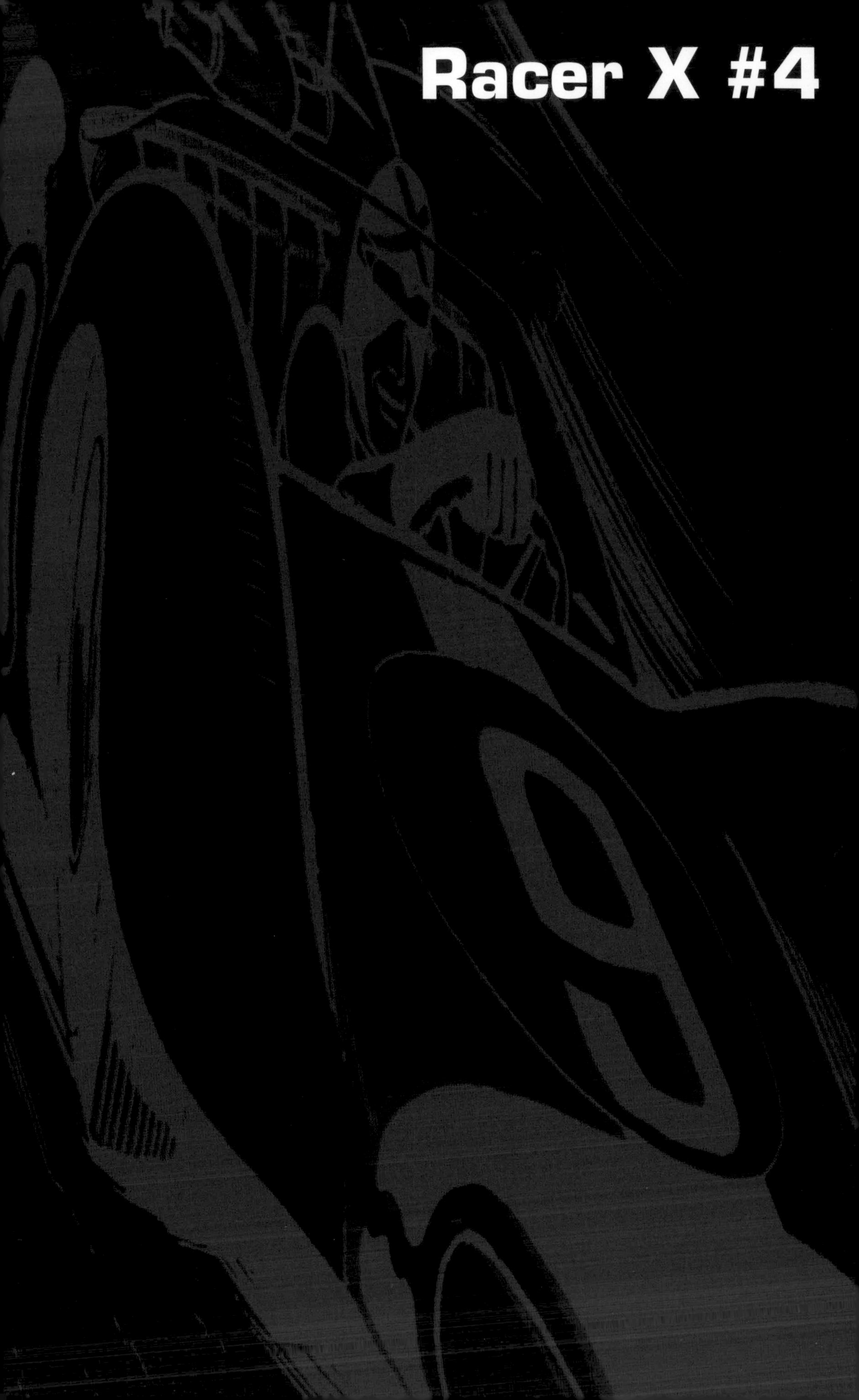

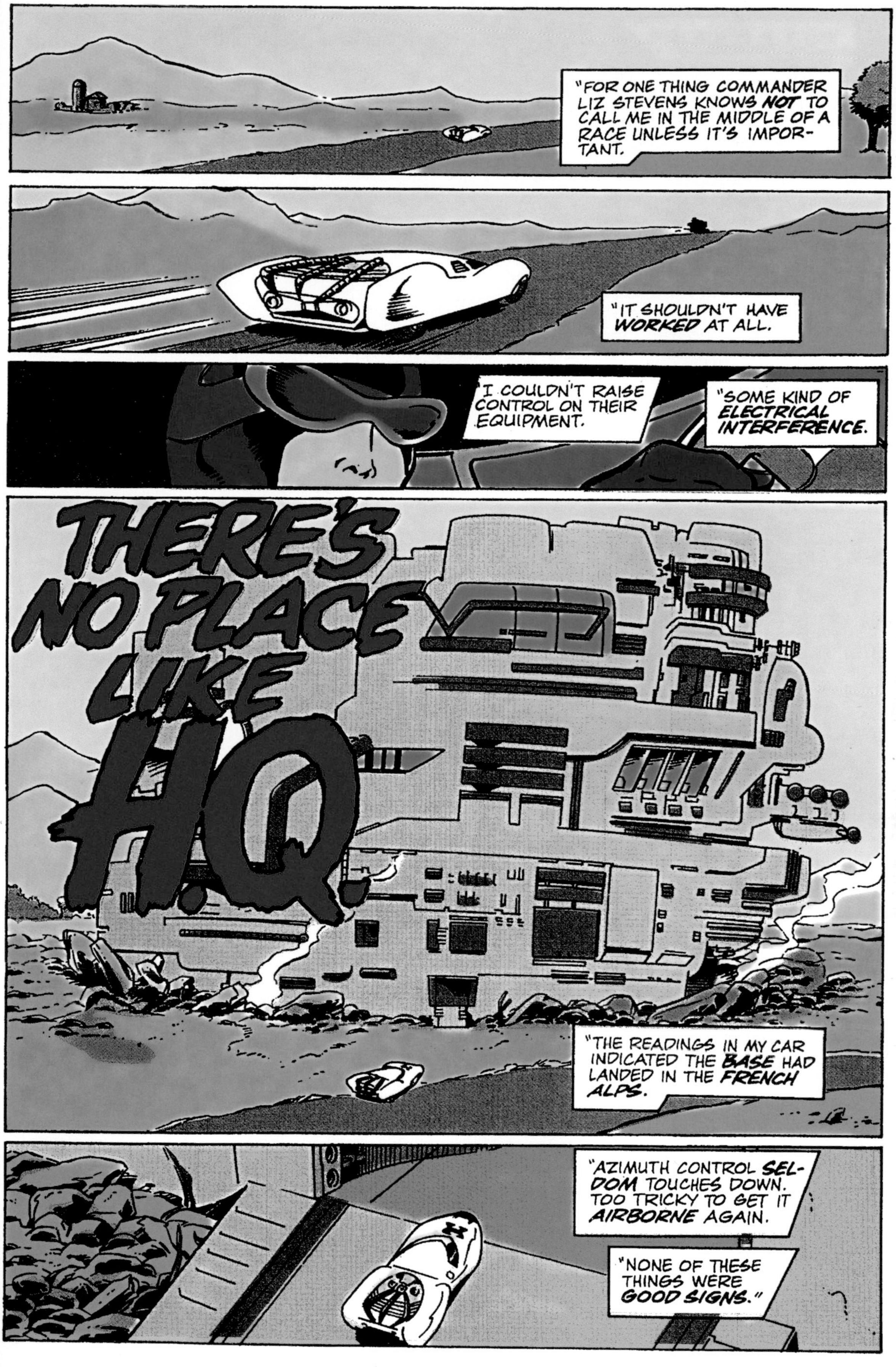
"FOR ONE THING COMMANDER LIZ STEVENS KNOWS NOT TO CALL ME IN THE MIDDLE OF A RACE UNLESS IT'S IMPORTANT.
"IT SHOULDN'T HAVE WORKED AT ALL.
"I COULDN'T RAISE CONTROL ON THEIR EQUIPMENT.
"SOME KIND OF ELECTRICAL INTERFERENCE.
THERE'S NO PLACE LIKE H.Q.
"THE READINGS IN MY CAR INDICATED THE BASE HAD LANDED IN THE FRENCH ALPS.
"AZIMUTH CONTROL SELDOM TOUCHES DOWN. TOO TRICKY TO GET IT AIRBORNE AGAIN.
"NONE OF THESE THINGS WERE GOOD SIGNS."

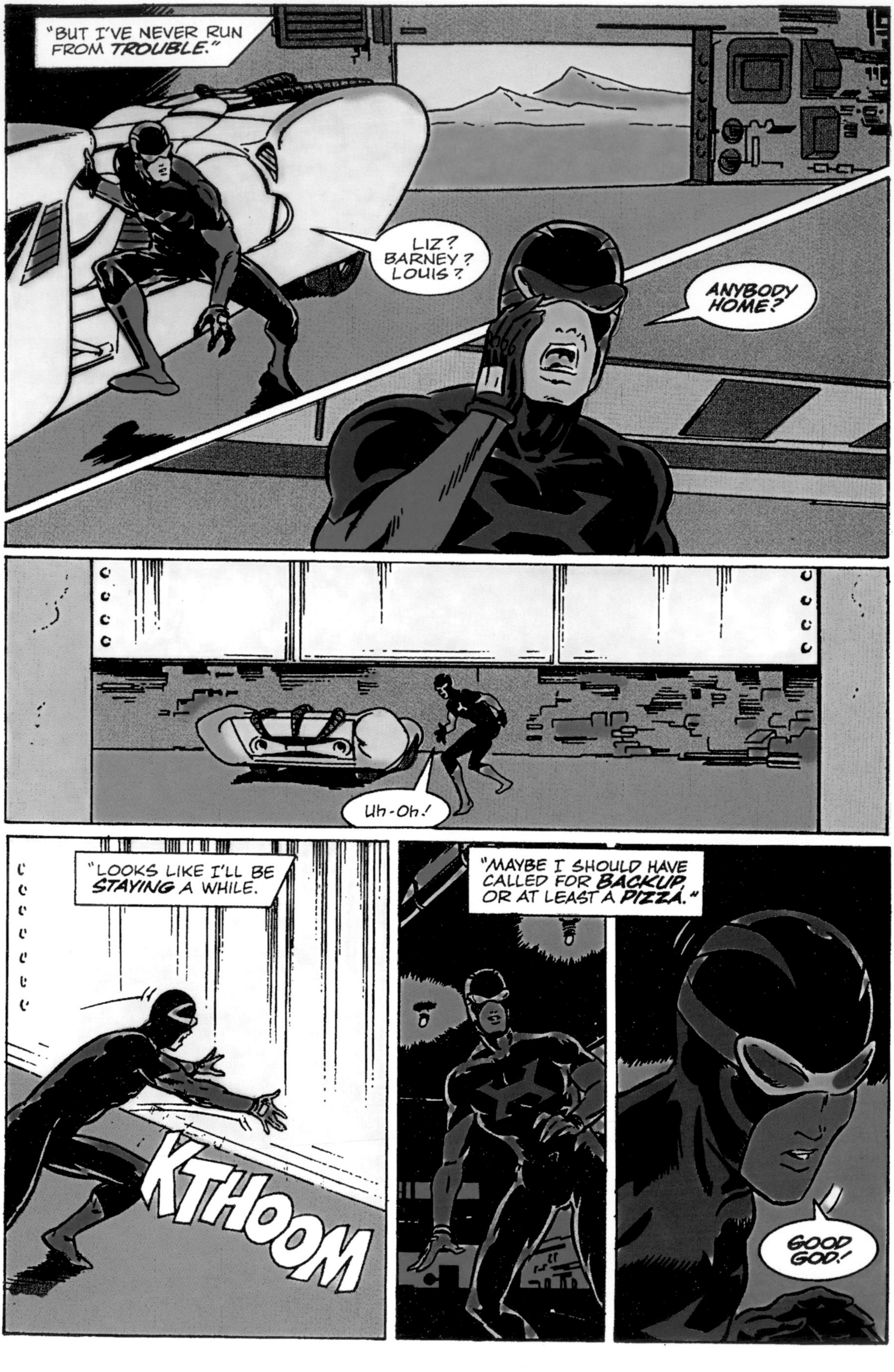
"BUT I'VE NEVER RUN FROM TROUBLE."
LIZ? BARNEY? LOUIS?
ANYBODY HOME?
Uh-Oh!
"LOOKS LIKE I'LL BE STAYING A WHILE.
KTHOOM
"MAYBE I SHOULD HAVE CALLED FOR BACKUP, OR AT LEAST A PIZZA."
GOOD GOD!

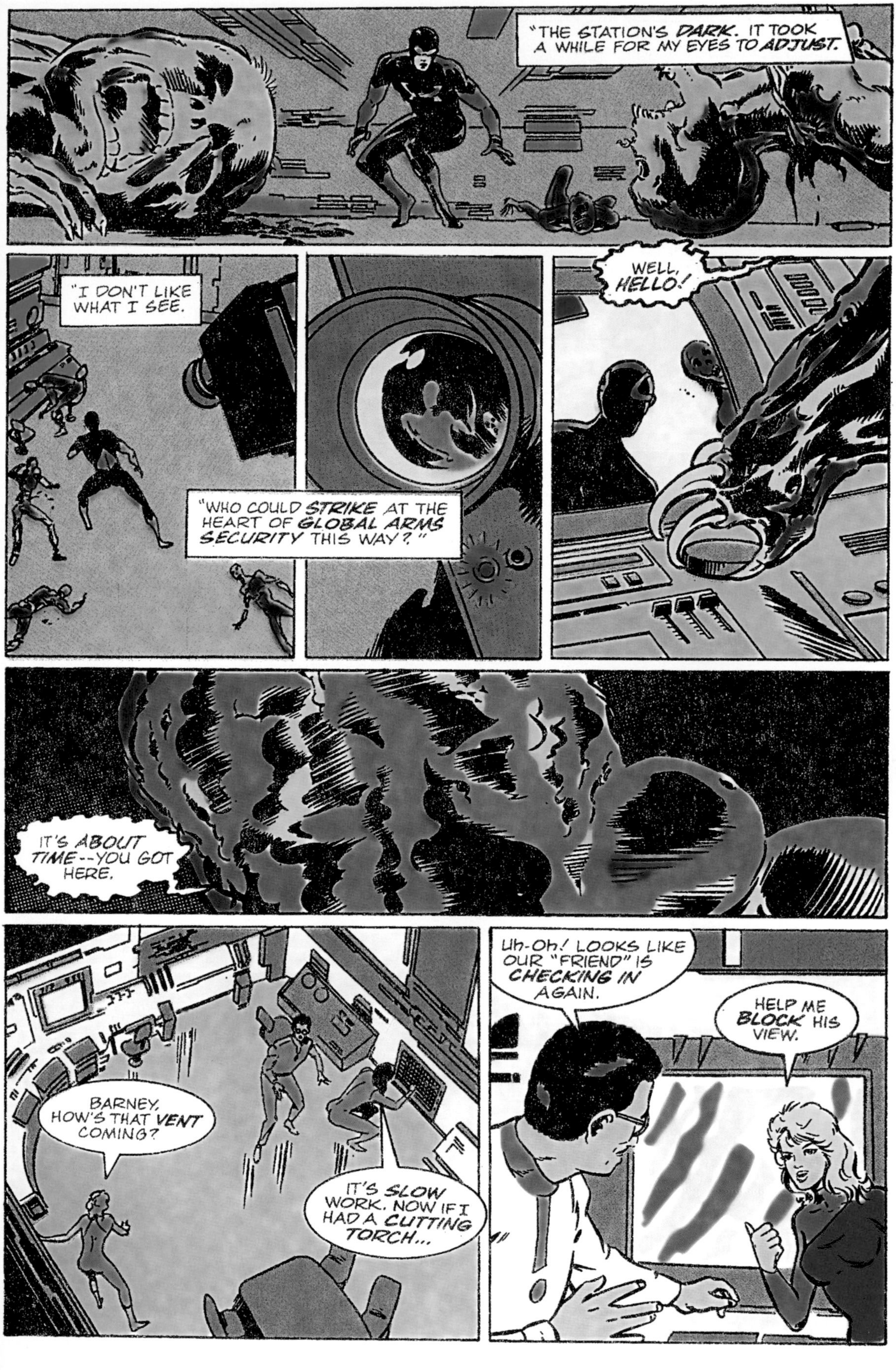
"THE STATION'S DARK. IT TOOK A WHILE FOR MY EYES TO ADJUST.
"I DON'T LIKE WHAT I SEE.
"WHO COULD STRIKE AT THE HEART OF GLOBAL ARMS SECURITY THIS WAY?"
WELL, HELLO!
IT'S ABOUT TIME--YOU GOT HERE.
BARNEY, HOW'S THAT VENT COMING?
IT'S SLOW WORK. NOW IF I HAD A CUTTING TORCH...
Uh-Oh! LOOKS LIKE OUR "FRIEND" IS CHECKING IN AGAIN.
HELP ME BLOCK HIS VIEW.

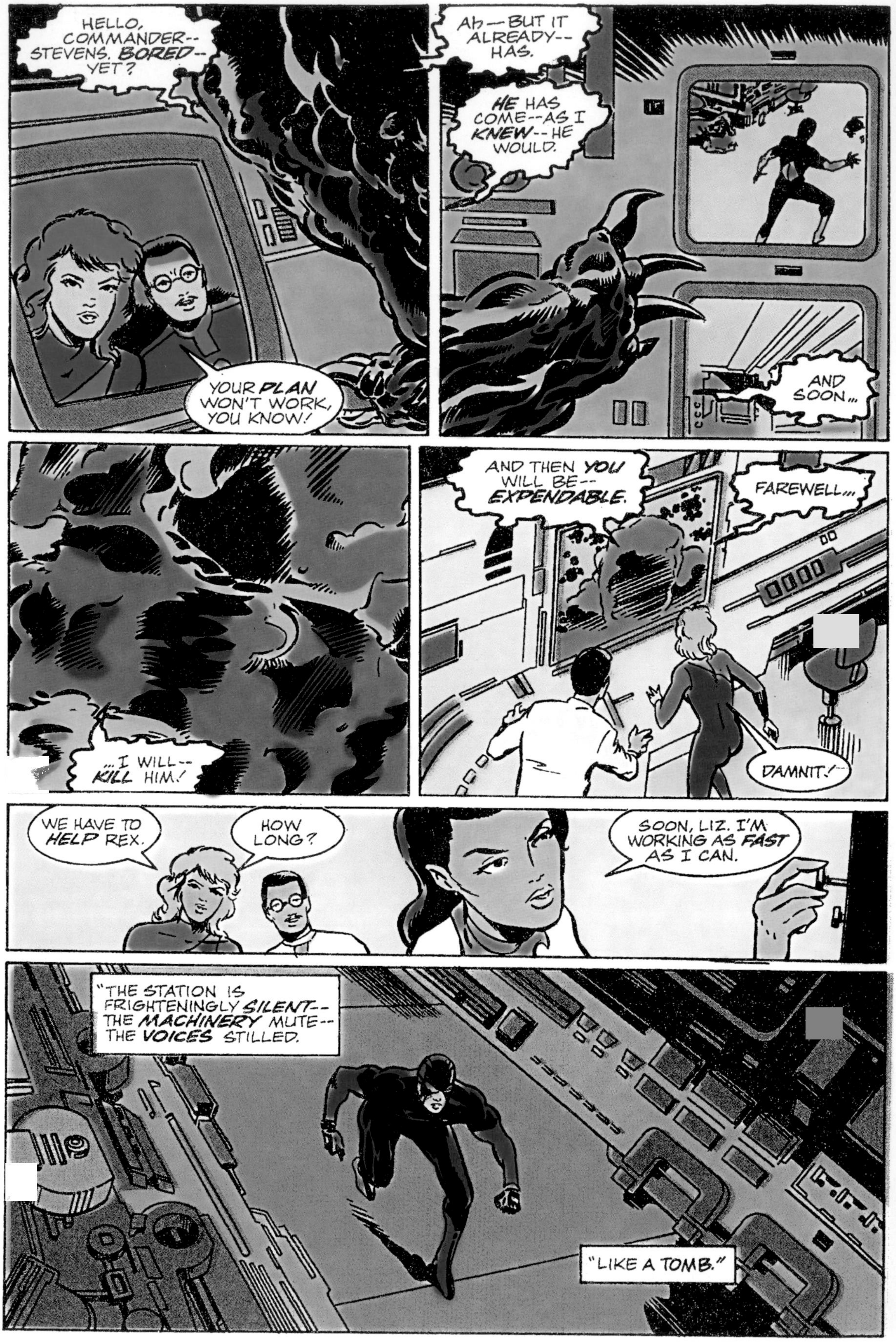
HELLO, COMMANDER-- STEVENS. BORED-- YET?
YOUR PLAN WON'T WORK, YOU KNOW!
Ah--BUT IT ALREADY-- HAS.
HE HAS COME--AS I KNEW--HE WOULD.
AND SOON...
...I WILL-- KILL HIM!
AND THEN YOU WILL BE-- EXPENDABLE.
FAREWELL...
DAMNIT!
WE HAVE TO HELP REX.
HOW LONG?
SOON, LIZ. I'M WORKING AS FAST AS I CAN.
"THE STATION IS FRIGHTENINGLY SILENT-- THE MACHINERY MUTE-- THE VOICES STILLED.
"LIKE A TOMB."

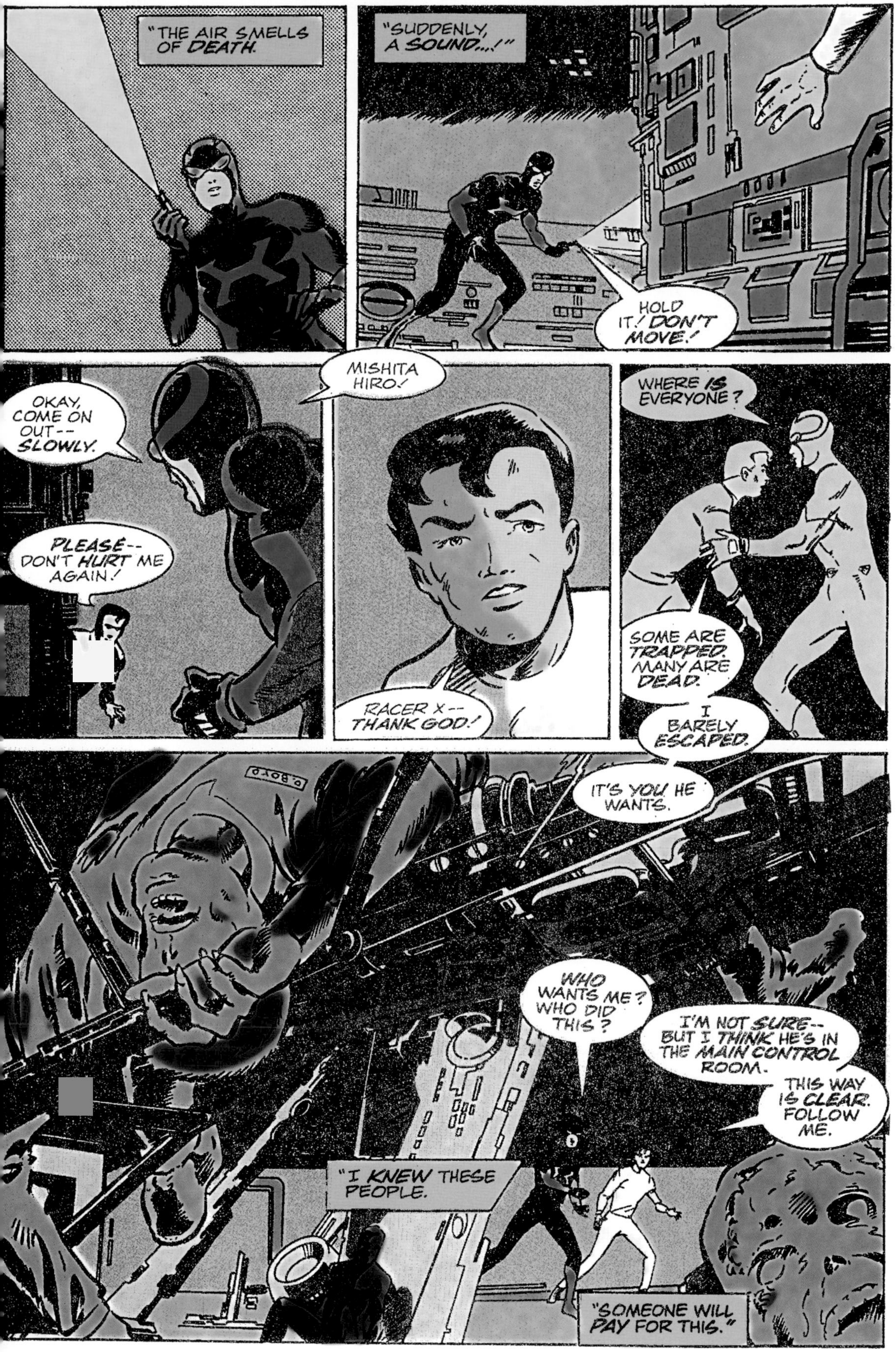
"THE AIR SMELLS OF DEATH.
"SUDDENLY, A SOUND...!"
HOLD IT! DON'T MOVE!
OKAY, COME ON OUT-- SLOWLY.
PLEASE-- DON'T HURT ME AGAIN!
MISHITA HIRO!
RACER X-- THANK GOD!
WHERE IS EVERYONE?
SOME ARE TRAPPED. MANY ARE DEAD.
I BARELY ESCAPED.
IT'S YOU HE WANTS.
WHO WANTS ME? WHO DID THIS?
I'M NOT SURE-- BUT I THINK HE'S IN THE MAIN CONTROL ROOM.
THIS WAY IS CLEAR. FOLLOW ME.
"I KNEW THESE PEOPLE.
"SOMEONE WILL PAY FOR THIS."

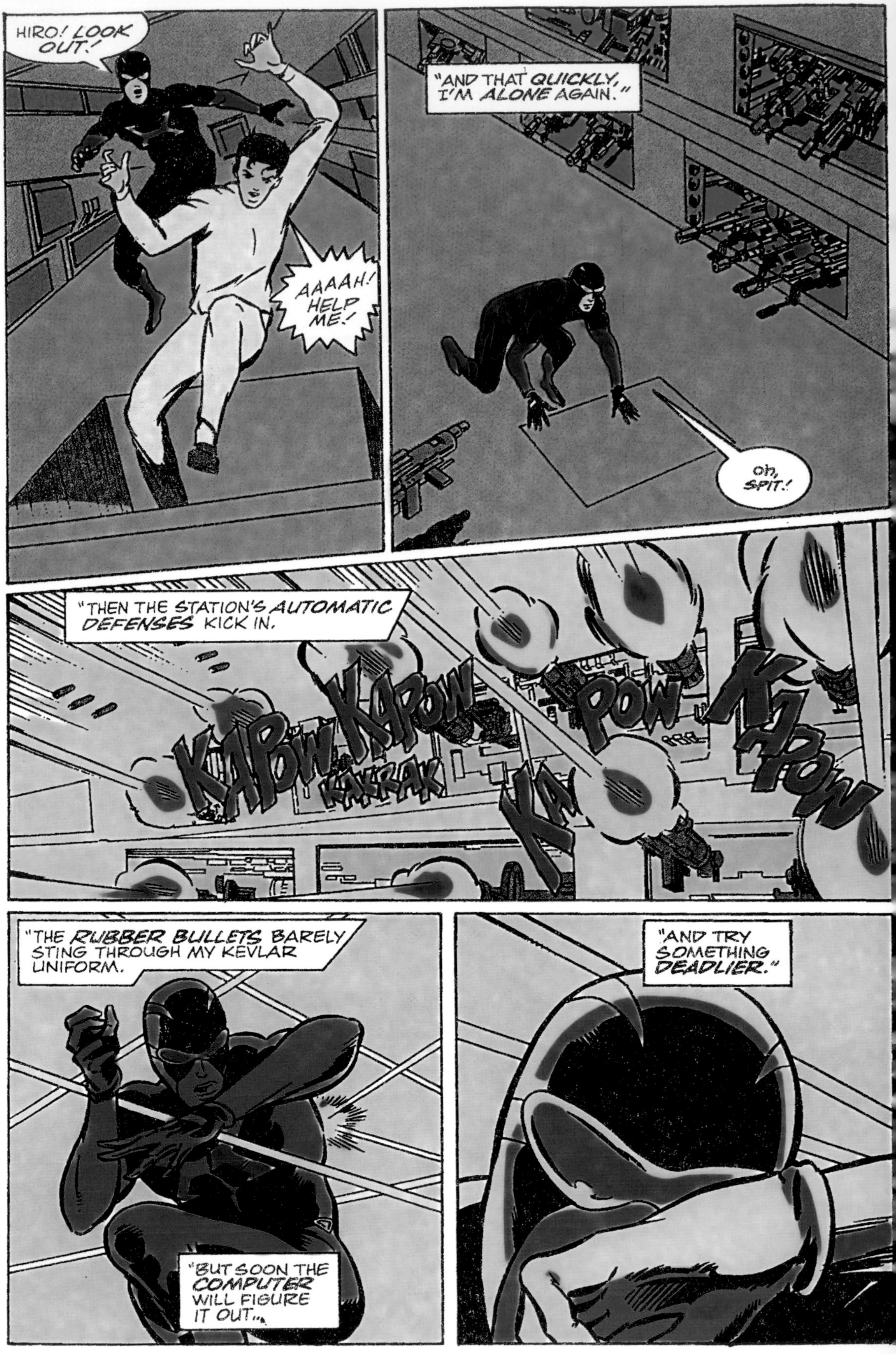
HIRO! LOOK OUT!
AAAAH! HELP ME!
"AND THAT QUICKLY, I'M ALONE AGAIN."
oh, SPIT!
"THEN THE STATION'S AUTOMATIC DEFENSES KICK IN.
KAPOW KAPOW
KAKRAK
KAPOW
KAPOW
"THE RUBBER BULLETS BARELY STING THROUGH MY KEVLAR UNIFORM.
"BUT SOON THE COMPUTER WILL FIGURE IT OUT...
"AND TRY SOMETHING DEADLIER."

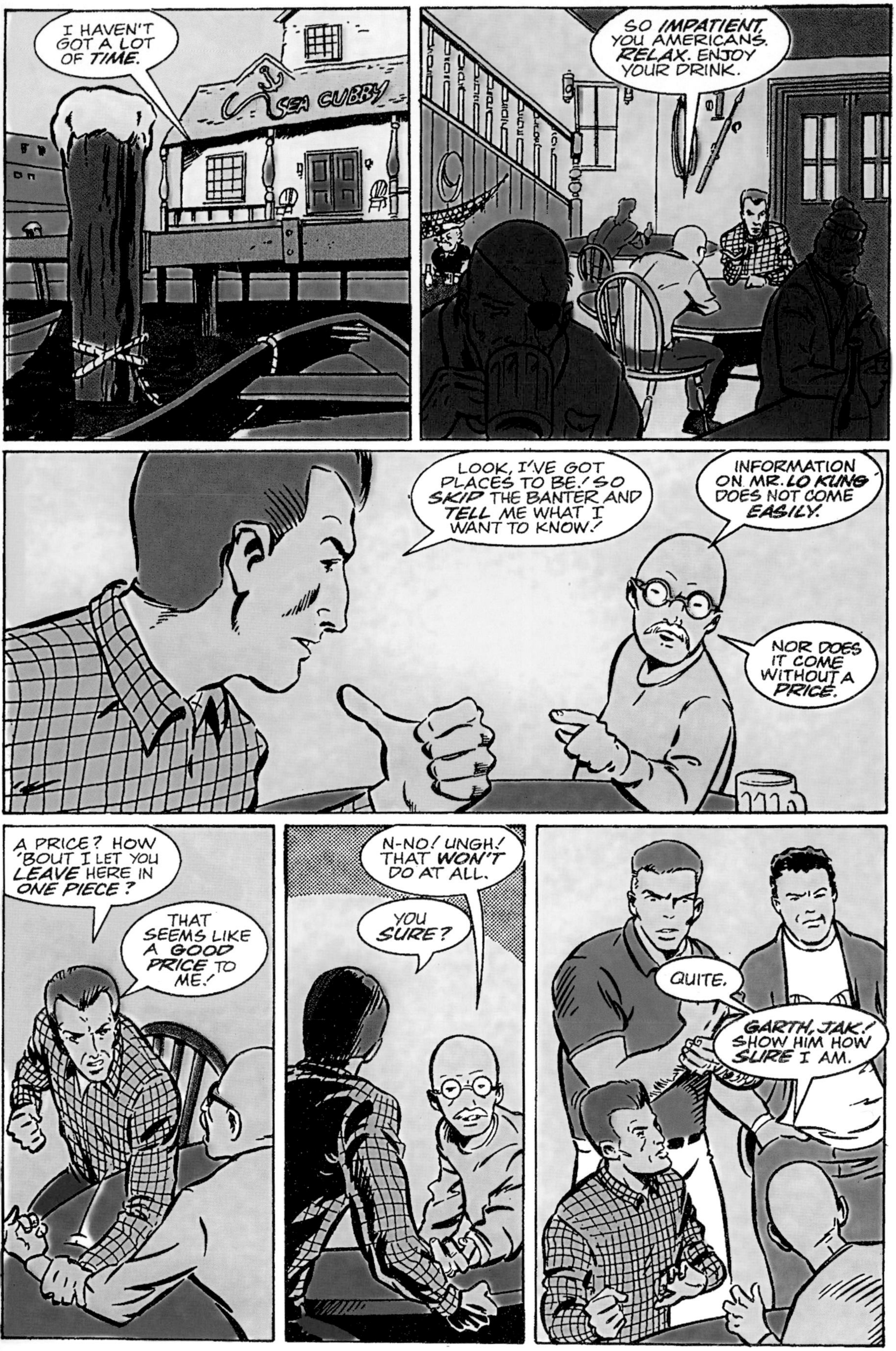
I HAVEN'T GOT A LOT OF TIME.
SEA CUBBY
SO IMPATIENT, YOU AMERICANS. RELAX. ENJOY YOUR DRINK.
LOOK, I'VE GOT PLACES TO BE.! SO SKIP THE BANTER AND TELL ME WHAT I WANT TO KNOW.!
INFORMATION ON MR. LO KUNG DOES NOT COME EASILY.
NOR DOES IT COME WITHOUT A PRICE.
A PRICE? HOW 'BOUT I LET YOU LEAVE HERE IN ONE PIECE?
THAT SEEMS LIKE A GOOD PRICE TO ME.!
N-NO! UNGH! THAT WON'T DO AT ALL.
YOU SURE?
QUITE.
GARTH, JAK! SHOW HIM HOW SURE I AM.

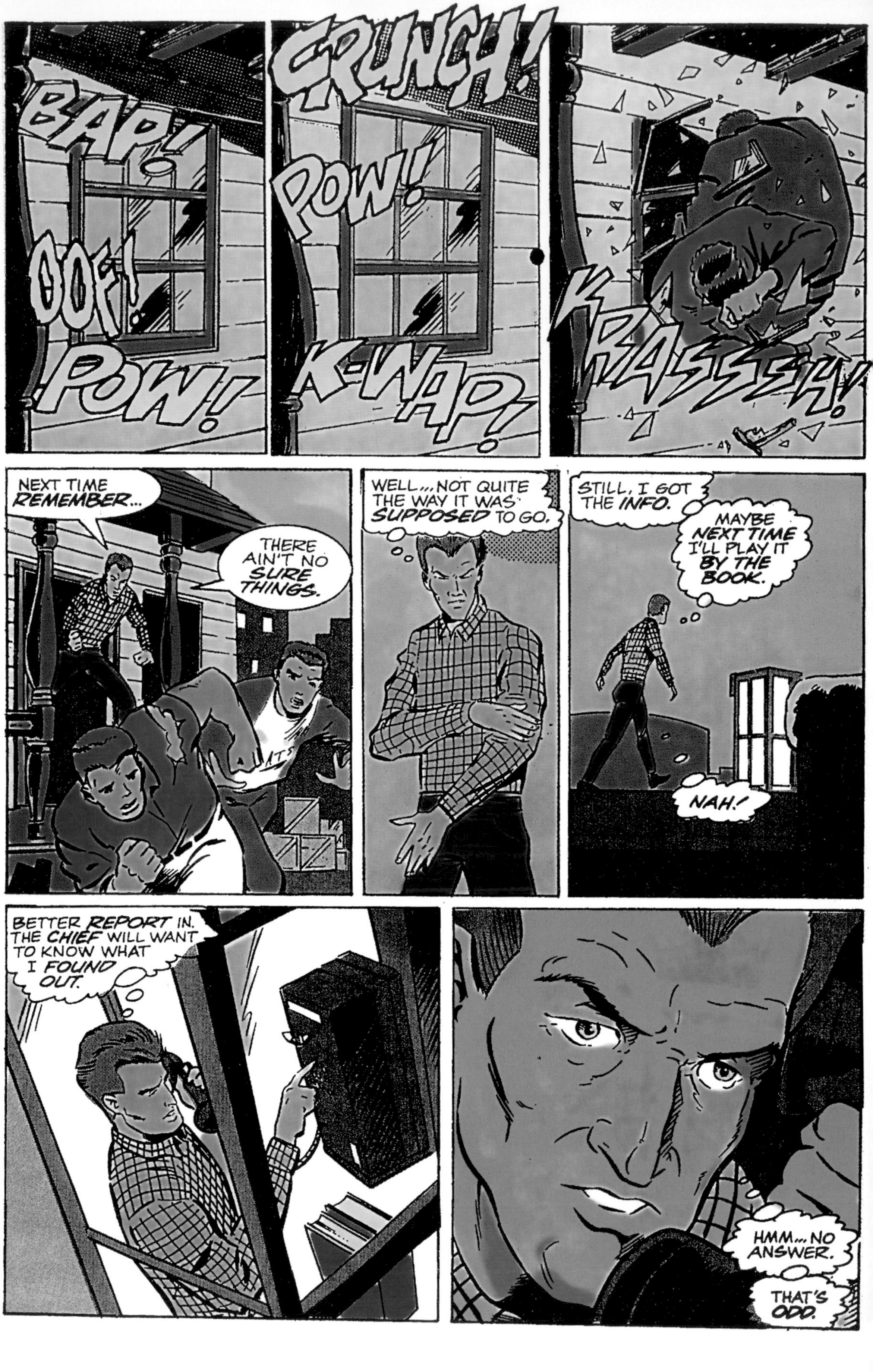
BAP!
OOF!
POW!
CRUNCH!
POW!
K-WAP!
KRASSSH!
NEXT TIME REMEMBER...
THERE AIN'T NO SURE THINGS.
WELL... NOT QUITE THE WAY IT WAS SUPPOSED TO GO.
STILL, I GOT THE INFO.
MAYBE NEXT TIME I'LL PLAY IT BY THE BOOK.
NAH!
BETTER REPORT IN. THE CHIEF WILL WANT TO KNOW WHAT I FOUND OUT.
HMM... NO ANSWER.
THAT'S ODD.

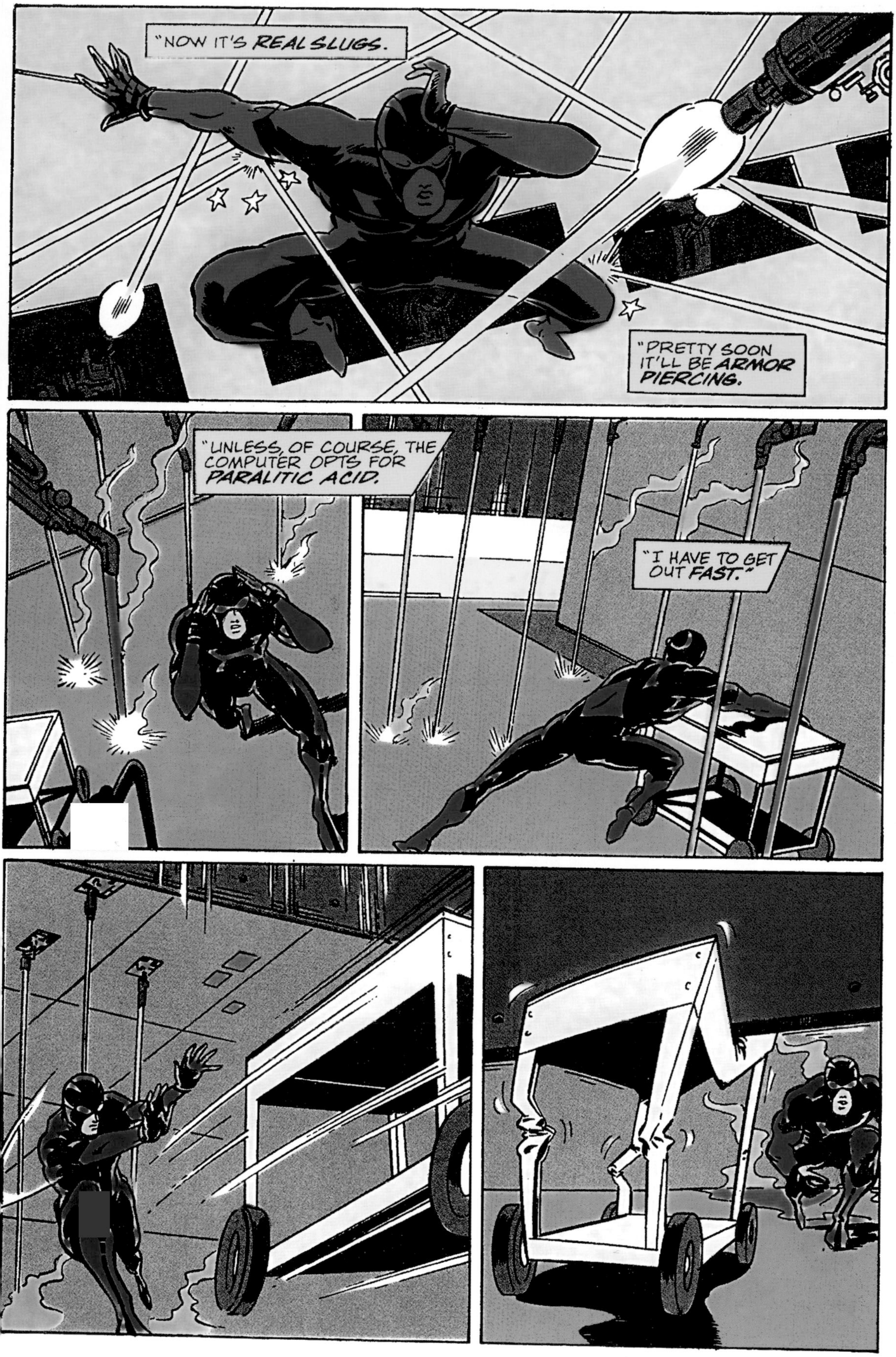
"NOW IT'S REAL SLUGS.
"PRETTY SOON IT'LL BE ARMOR PIERCING.
"UNLESS, OF COURSE, THE COMPUTER OPTS FOR PARALITIC ACID.
"I HAVE TO GET OUT FAST."

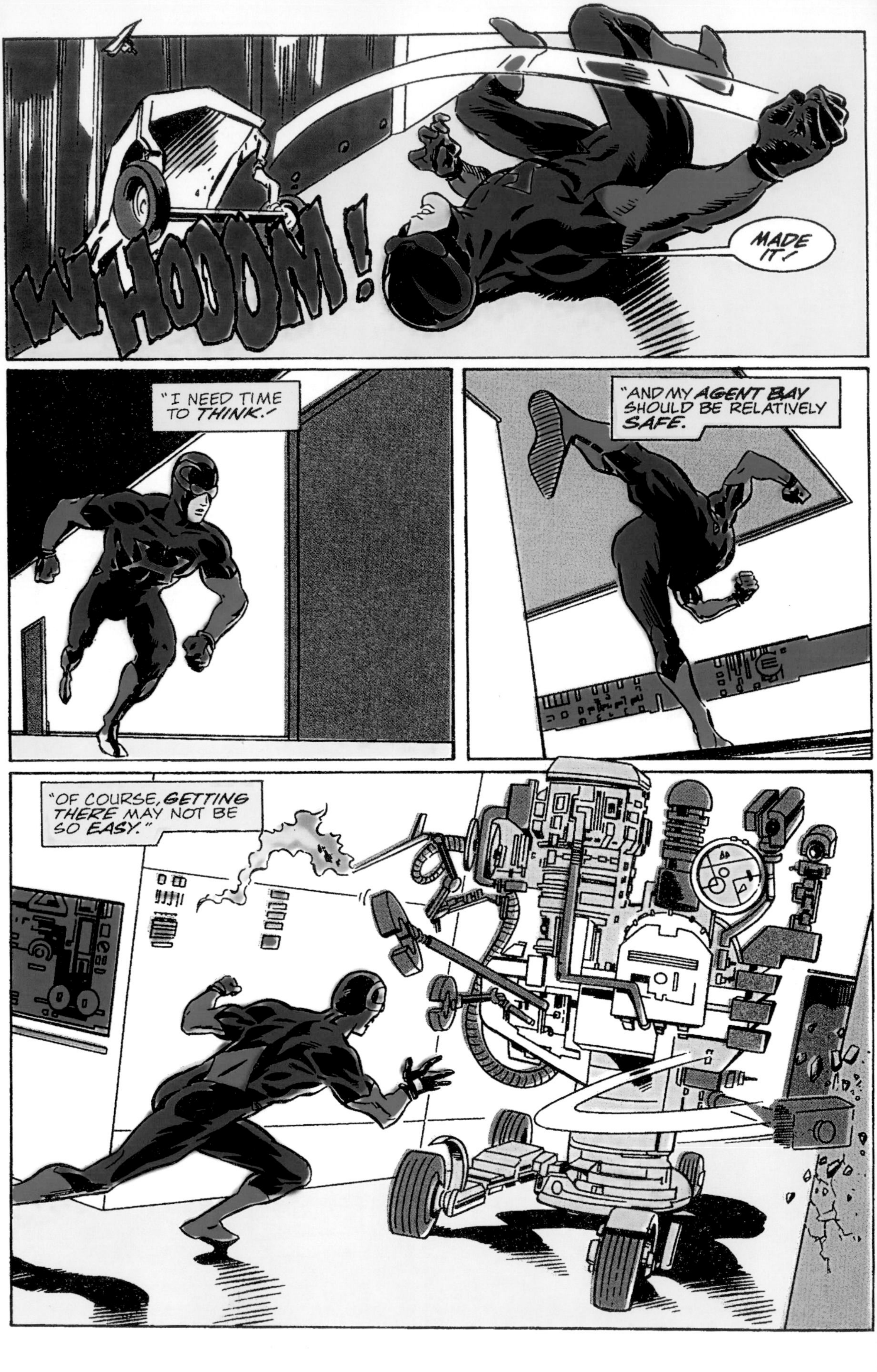
WHOOOM!
MADE IT!
"I NEED TIME TO THINK.
"AND MY AGENT BAY SHOULD BE RELATIVELY SAFE.
"OF COURSE, GETTING THERE MAY NOT BE SO EASY."

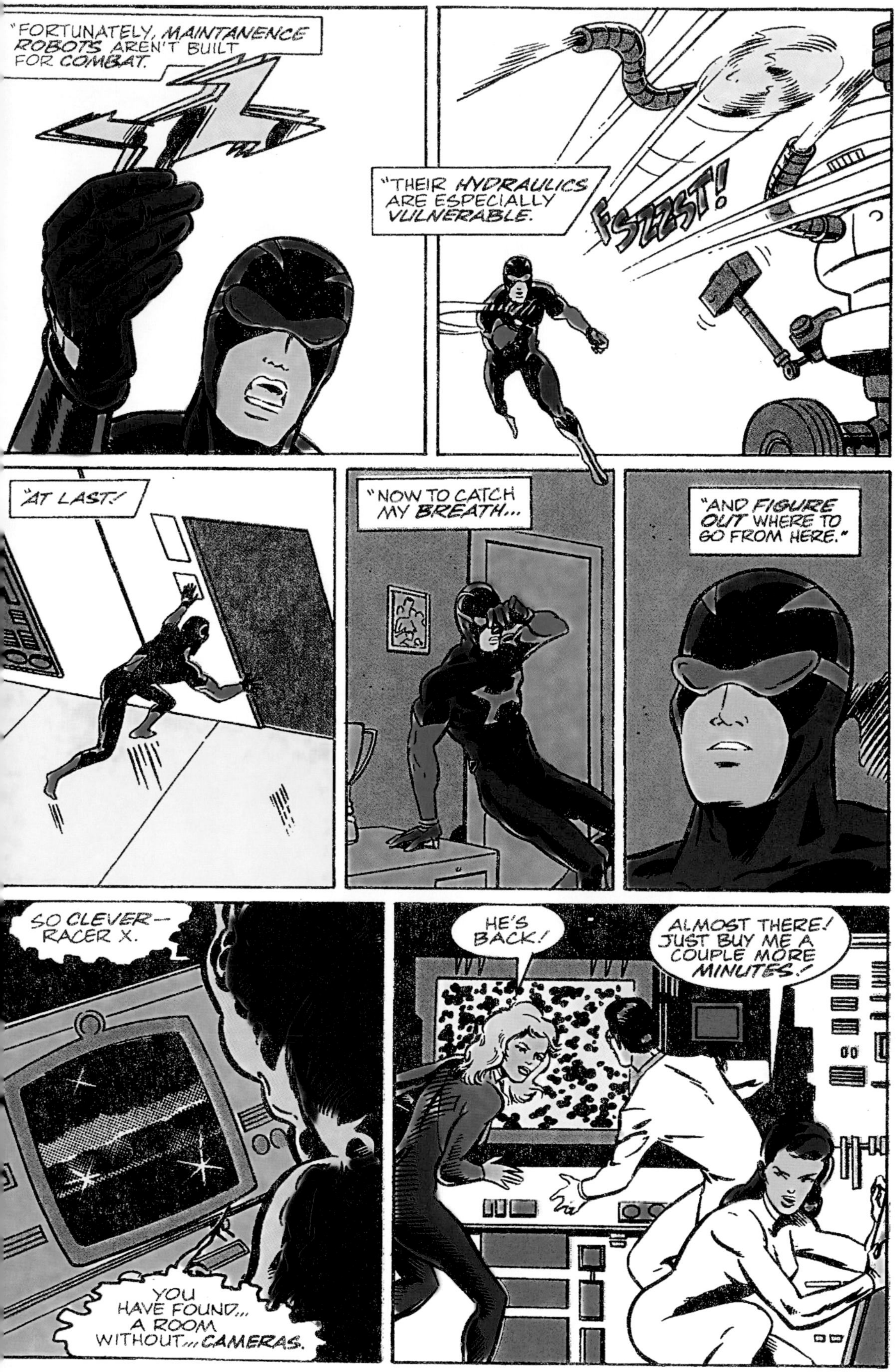

"FORTUNATELY, MAINTANENCE ROBOTS AREN'T BUILT FOR COMBAT.
"THEIR HYDRAULICS ARE ESPECIALLY VULNERABLE.
FSZZST!
"AT LAST!
"NOW TO CATCH MY BREATH...
"AND FIGURE OUT WHERE TO GO FROM HERE."
SO CLEVER— RACER X.
YOU HAVE FOUND... A ROOM WITHOUT... CAMERAS.
HE'S BACK!
ALMOST THERE! JUST BUY ME A COUPLE MORE MINUTES!

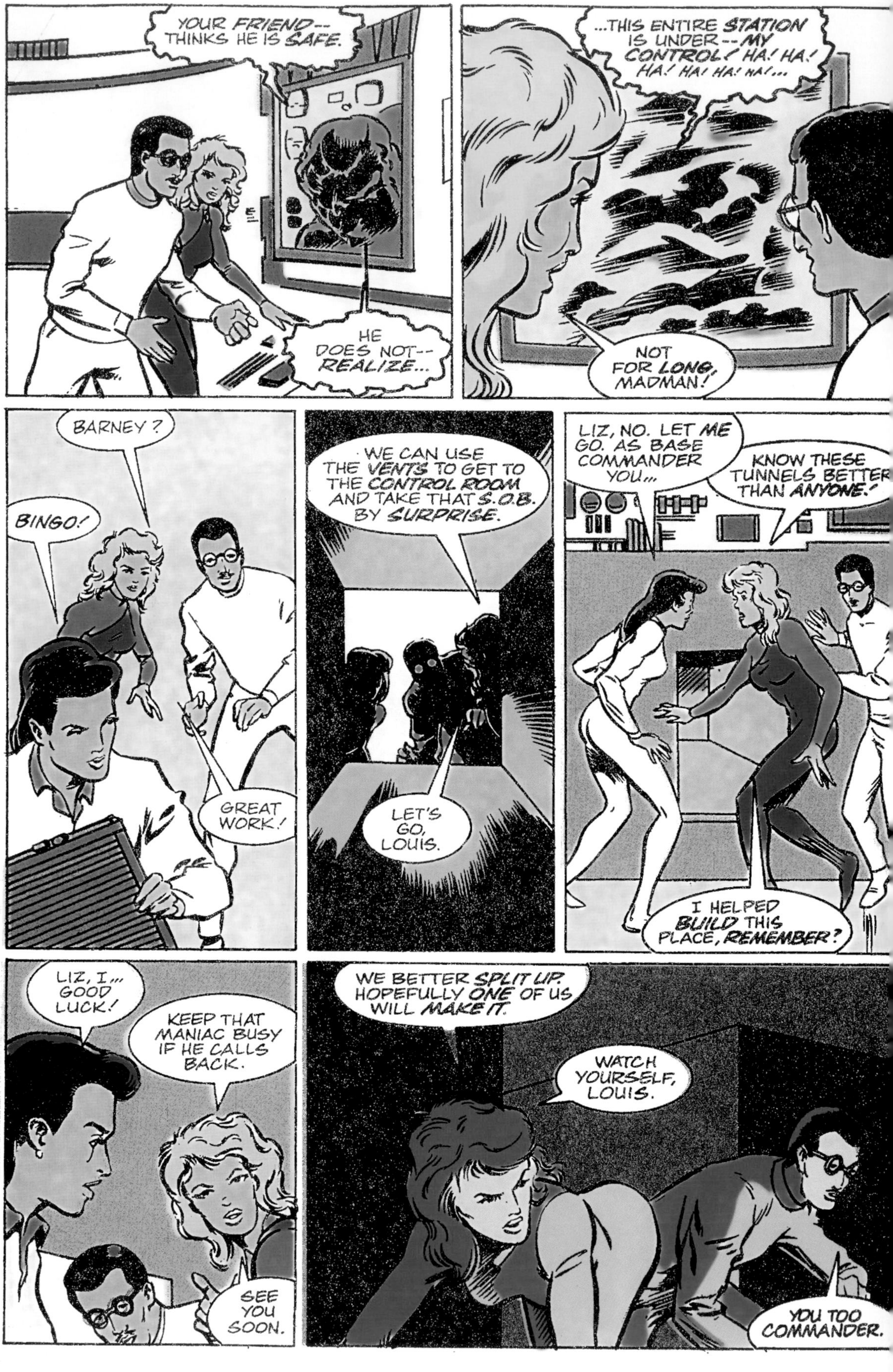
YOUR FRIEND-- THINKS HE IS SAFE.
HE DOES NOT-- REALIZE...
...THIS ENTIRE STATION IS UNDER--MY CONTROL! HA! HA! HA! HA! HA! HA!...
NOT FOR LONG, MADMAN!
BARNEY?
BINGO!
GREAT WORK!
WE CAN USE THE VENTS TO GET TO THE CONTROL ROOM AND TAKE THAT S.O.B. BY SURPRISE.
LET'S GO, LOUIS.
LIZ, NO. LET ME GO. AS BASE COMMANDER YOU...
KNOW THESE TUNNELS BETTER THAN ANYONE!
I HELPED BUILD THIS PLACE, REMEMBER?
LIZ, I... GOOD LUCK!
KEEP THAT MANIAC BUSY IF HE CALLS BACK.
SEE YOU SOON.
WE BETTER SPLIT UP. HOPEFULLY ONE OF US WILL MAKE IT.
WATCH YOURSELF, LOUIS.
YOU TOO COMMANDER.

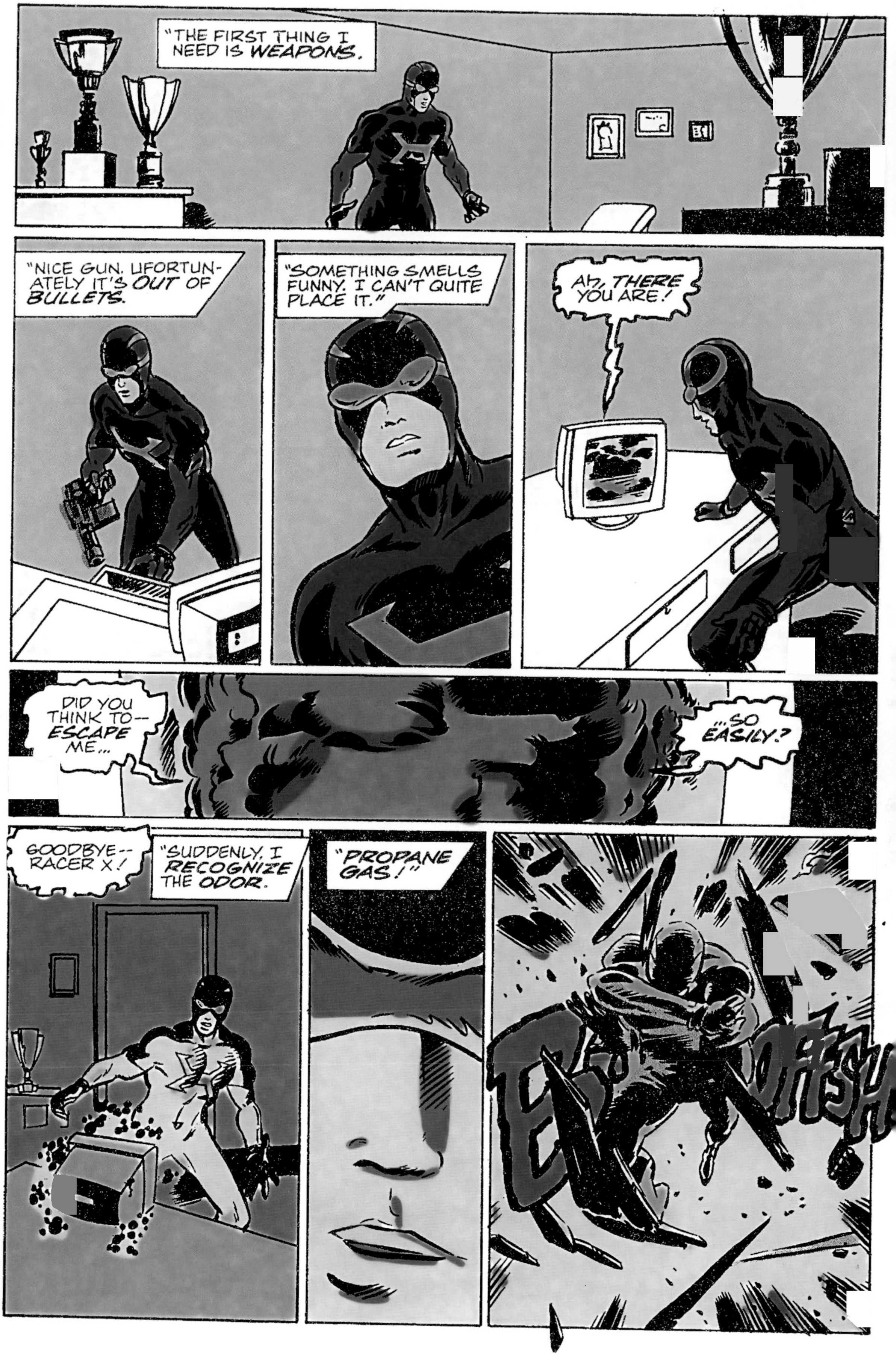
"THE FIRST THING I NEED IS WEAPONS.
"NICE GUN. UFORTUNATELY IT'S OUT OF BULLETS.
"SOMETHING SMELLS FUNNY. I CAN'T QUITE PLACE IT."
AH, THERE YOU ARE!
DID YOU THINK TO-- ESCAPE ME...
...SO EASILY?
GOODBYE-- RACER X!
"SUDDENLY, I RECOGNIZE THE ODOR.
"PROPANE GAS!"

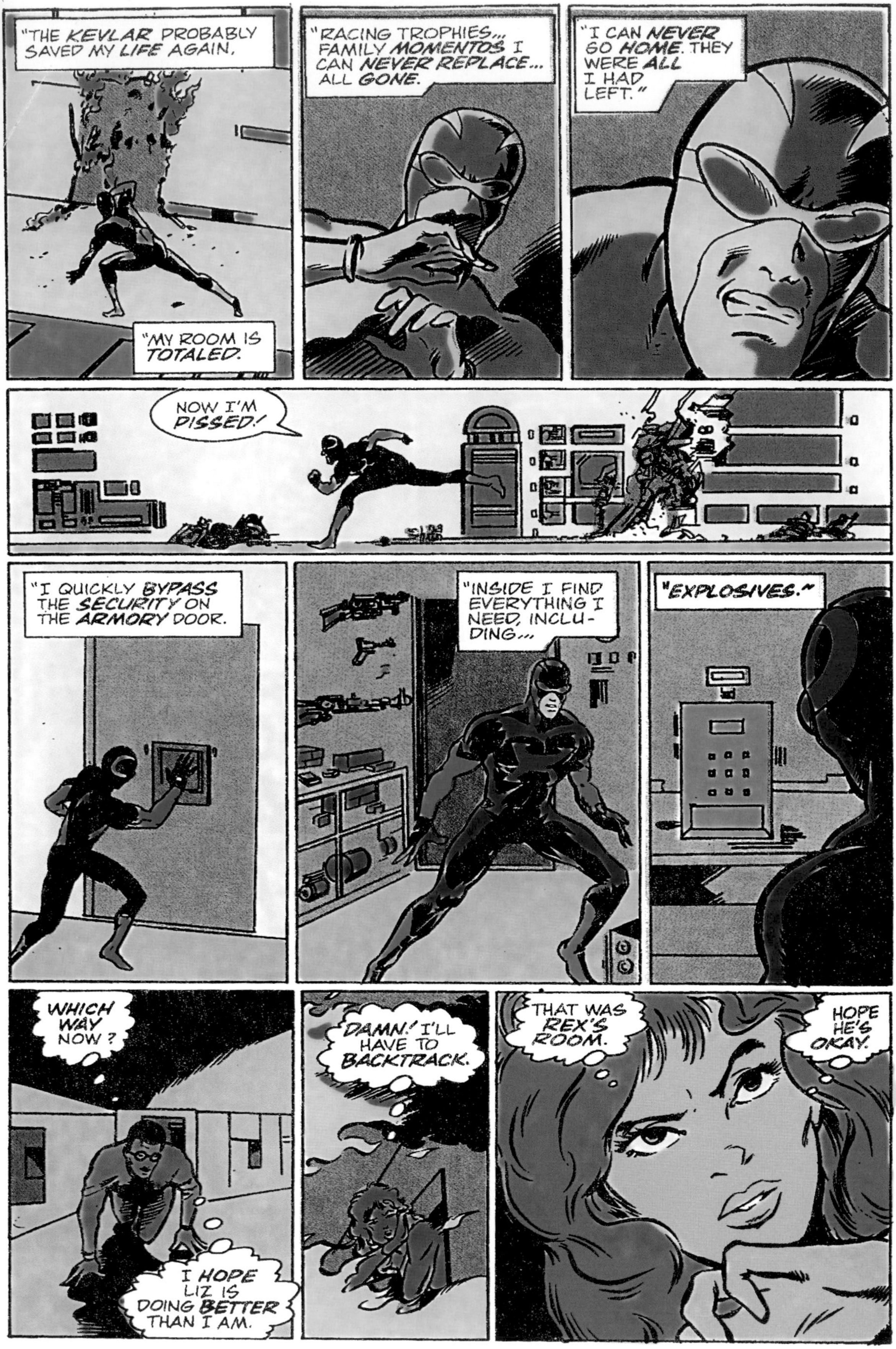
"THE KEVLAR PROBABLY SAVED MY LIFE AGAIN.
"MY ROOM IS TOTALED.
"RACING TROPHIES... FAMILY MOMENTOS I CAN NEVER REPLACE... ALL GONE.
"I CAN NEVER GO HOME. THEY WERE ALL I HAD LEFT."
NOW I'M PISSED!
"I QUICKLY BYPASS THE SECURITY ON THE ARMORY DOOR.
"INSIDE I FIND EVERYTHING I NEED, INCLU-DING...
"EXPLOSIVES."
WHICH WAY NOW?
I HOPE LIZ IS DOING BETTER THAN I AM.
DAMN! I'LL HAVE TO BACKTRACK.
THAT WAS REX'S ROOM.
HOPE HE'S OKAY.

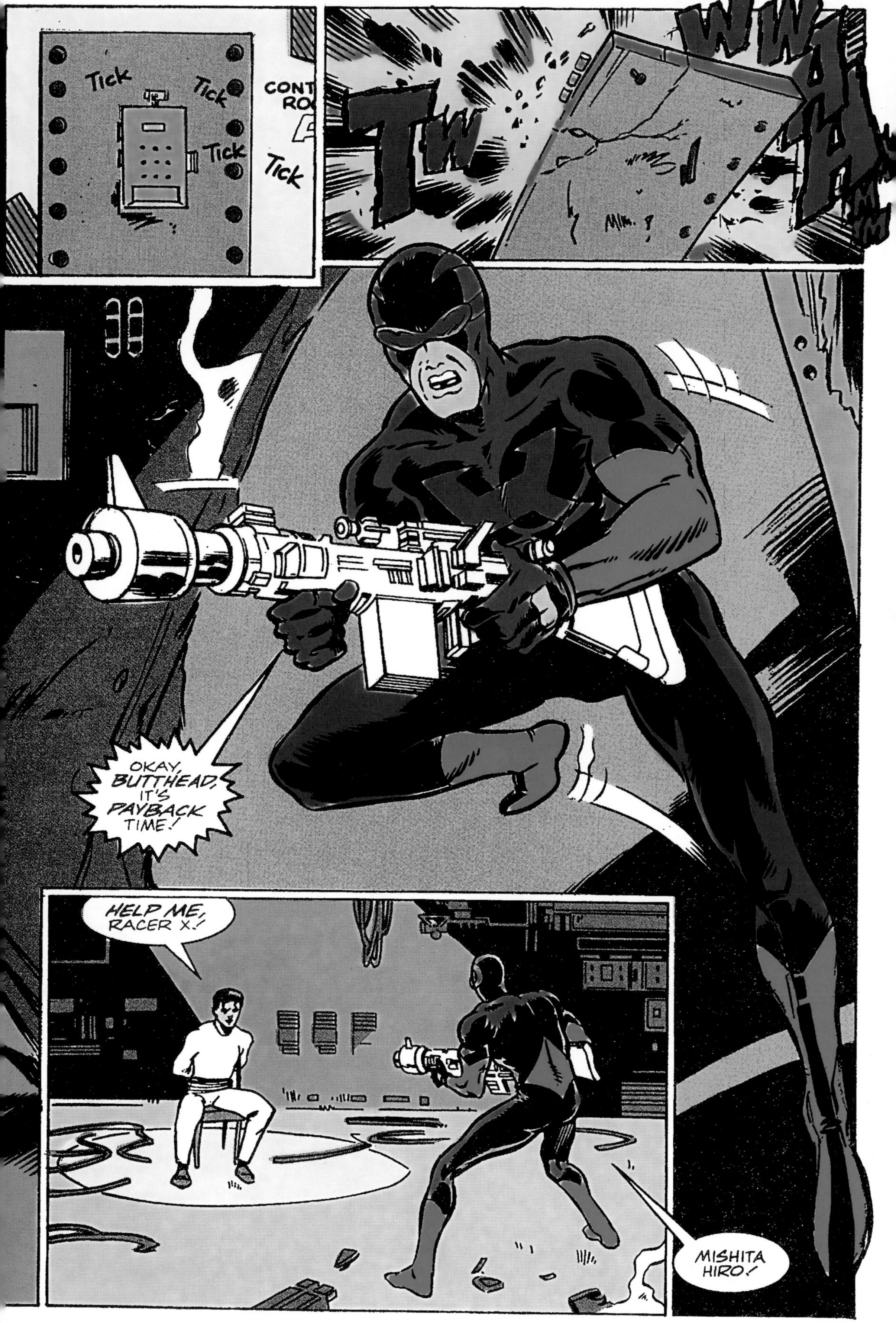
Tick
Tick
Tick
Tick
OKAY, BUTTHEAD, IT'S PAYBACK TIME!
HELP ME, RACER X!
MISHITA HIRO!

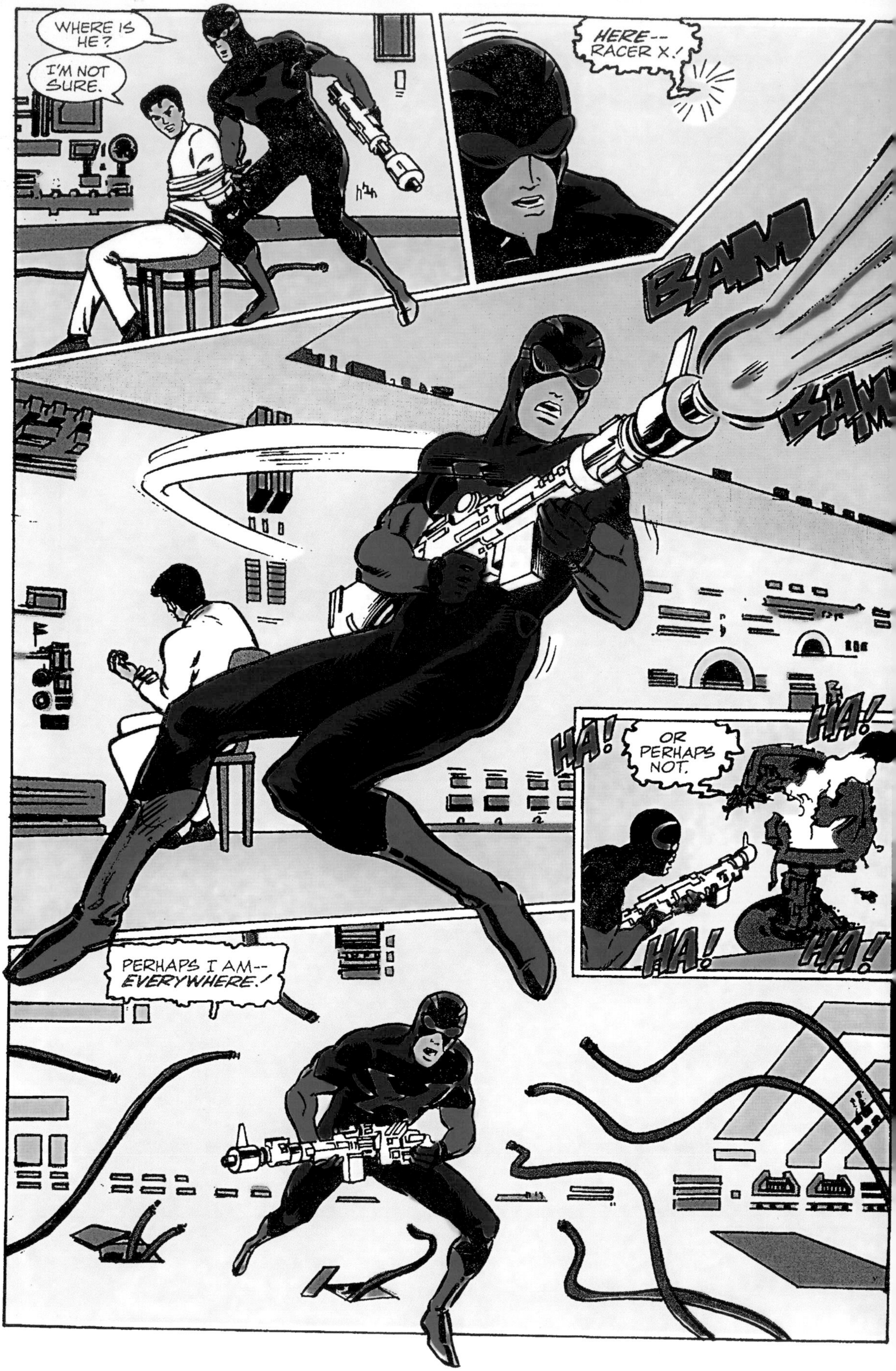
WHERE IS HE?
I'M NOT SURE.
HERE-- RACER X.!
BAM
BAM
HA!
OR PERHAPS NOT.
HA!
HA!
HA!
PERHAPS I AM-- EVERYWHERE!

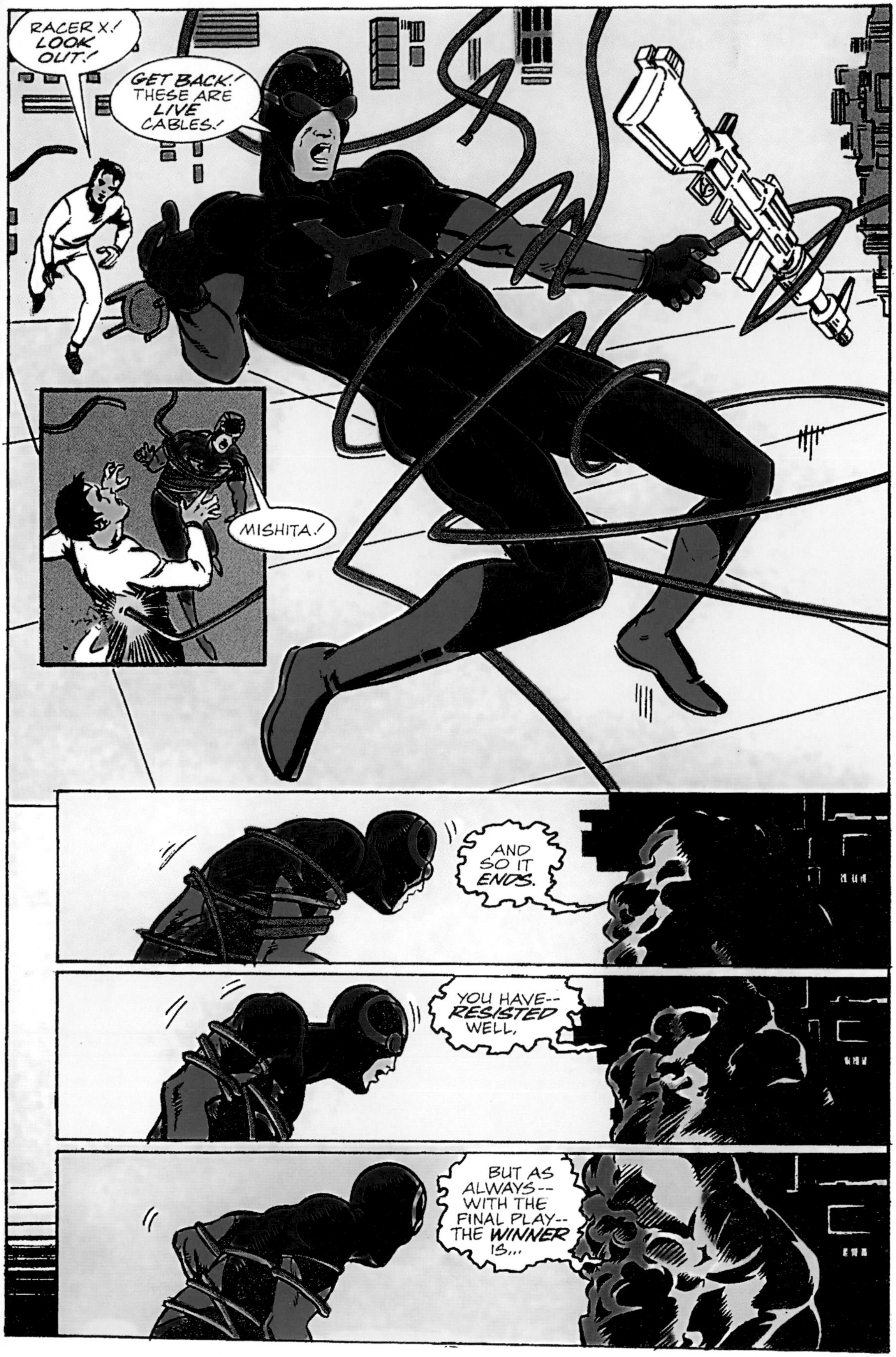
RACER X! LOOK OUT!
GET BACK! THESE ARE LIVE CABLES!
MISHITA!
AND SO IT ENDS.
YOU HAVE-- RESISTED WELL,
BUT AS ALWAYS-- WITH THE FINAL PLAY-- THE WINNER IS...

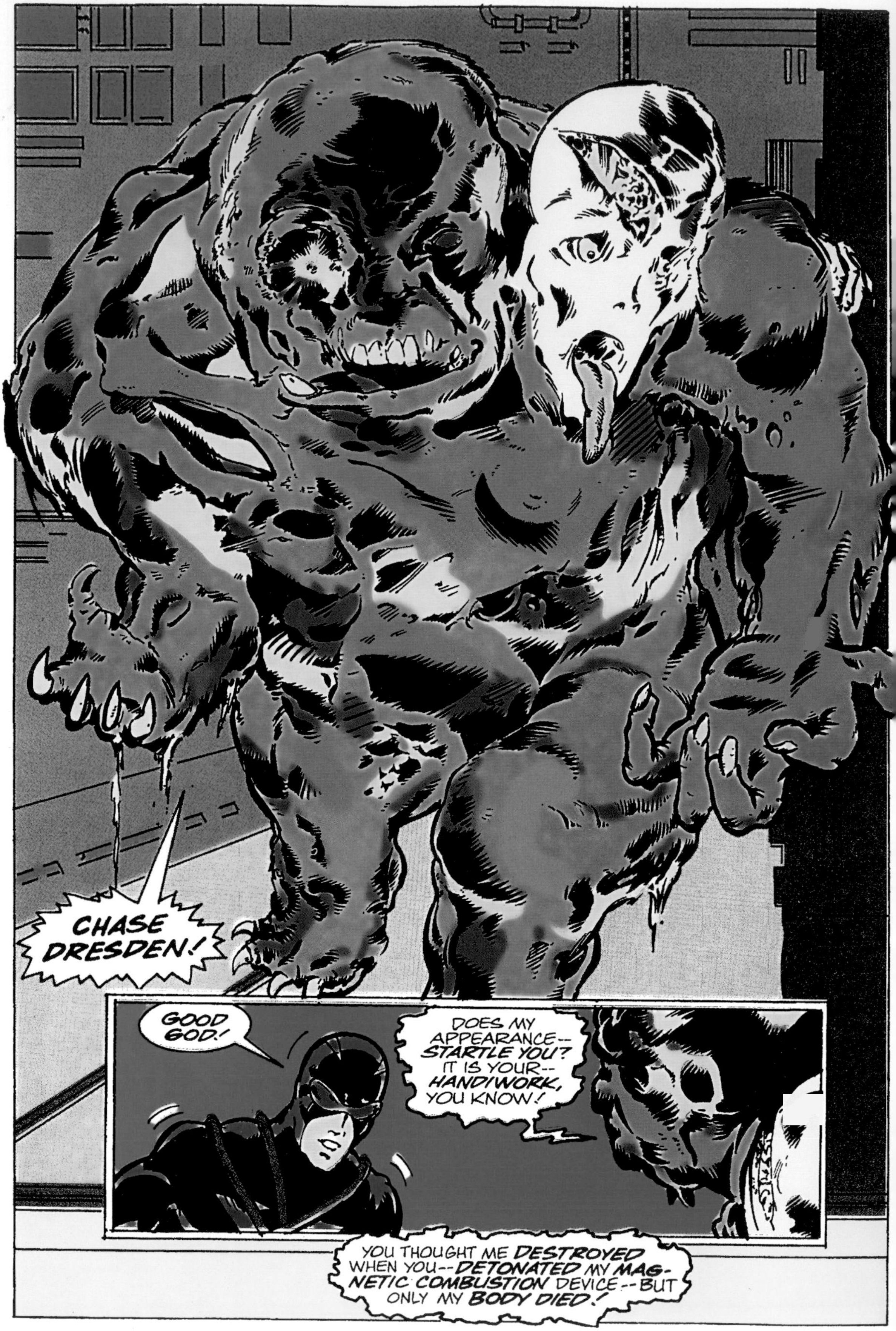
CHASE DRESDEN!
GOOD GOD!
DOES MY APPEARANCE-- STARTLE YOU? IT IS YOUR-- HANDIWORK, YOU KNOW!
YOU THOUGHT ME DESTROYED WHEN YOU--DETONATED MY MAG-NETIC COMBUSTION DEVICE--BUT ONLY MY BODY DIED!

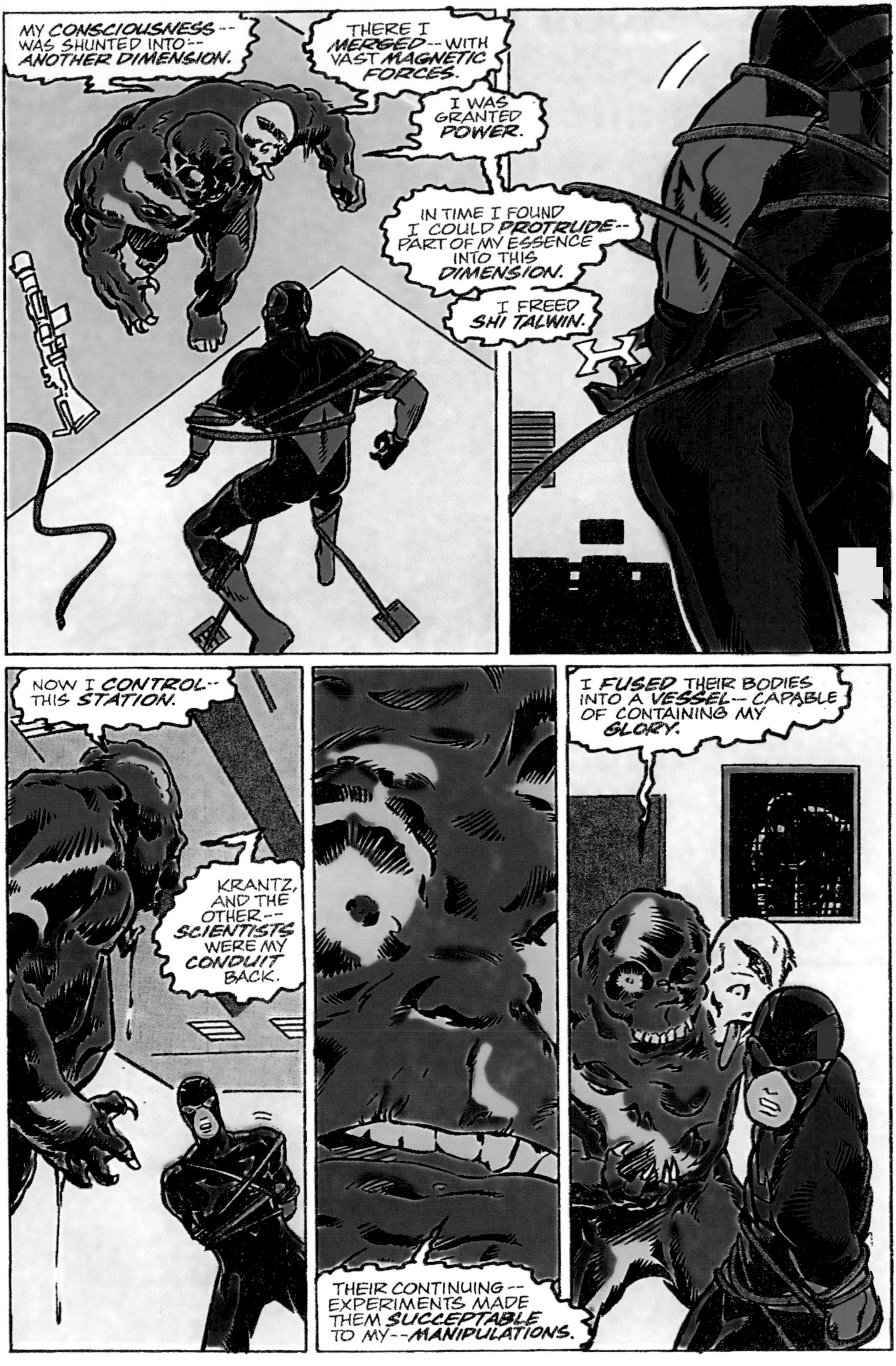
MY CONSCIOUSNESS-- WAS SHUNTED INTO-- ANOTHER DIMENSION.
THERE I MERGED--WITH VAST MAGNETIC FORCES.
I WAS GRANTED POWER.
IN TIME I FOUND I COULD PROTRUDE-- PART OF MY ESSENCE INTO THIS DIMENSION.
I FREED SHI TALWIN.
NOW I CONTROL-- THIS STATION.
KRANTZ, AND THE OTHER-- SCIENTISTS WERE MY CONDUIT BACK.
THEIR CONTINUING-- EXPERIMENTS MADE THEM SUCCEPTABLE TO MY--MANIPULATIONS.
I FUSED THEIR BODIES INTO A VESSEL--CAPABLE OF CONTAINING MY GLORY.

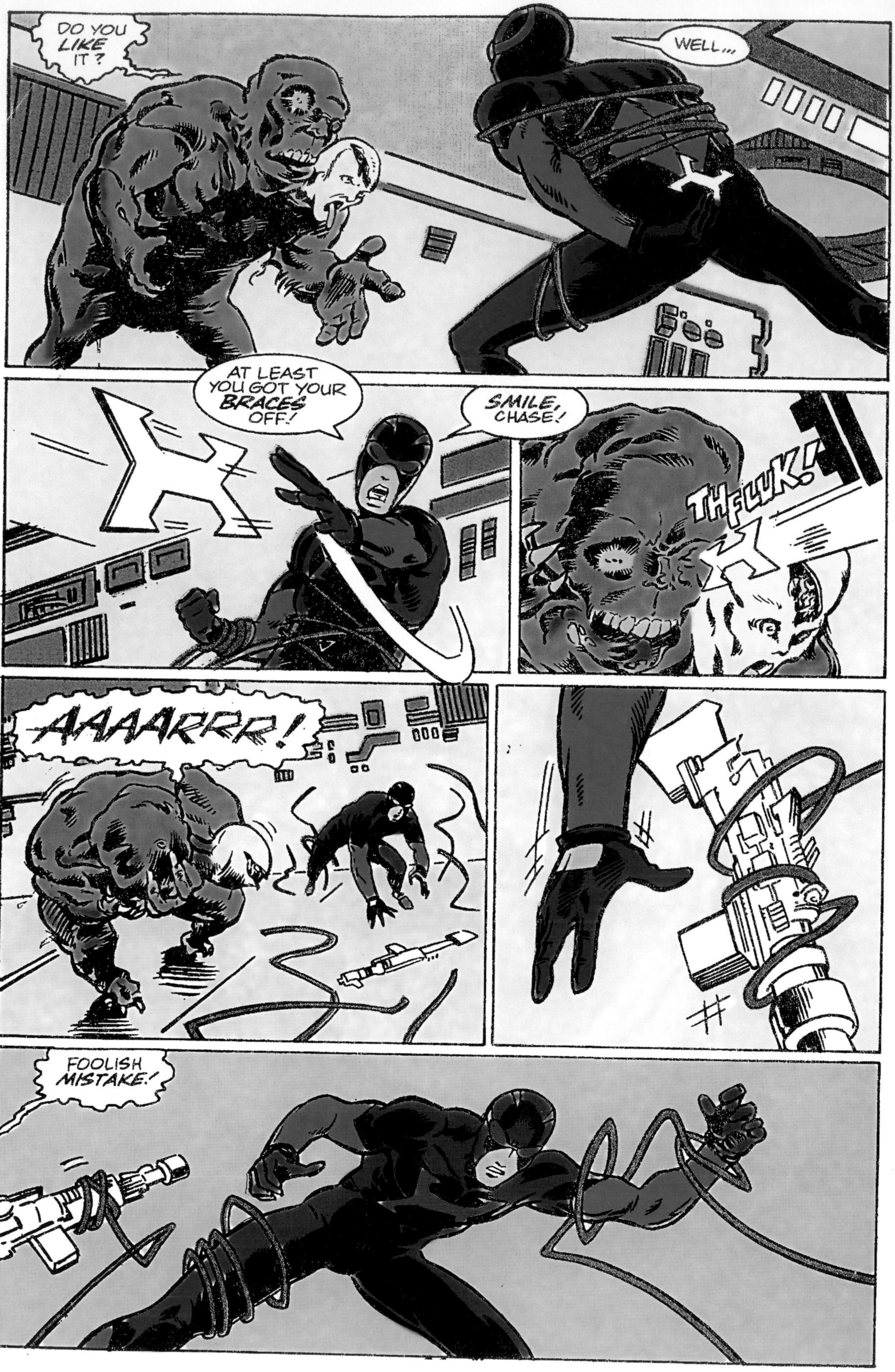
DO YOU LIKE IT?
WELL...
AT LEAST YOU GOT YOUR BRACES OFF!
SMILE, CHASE!
THFLUK!
AAAARRR!
FOOLISH MISTAKE!

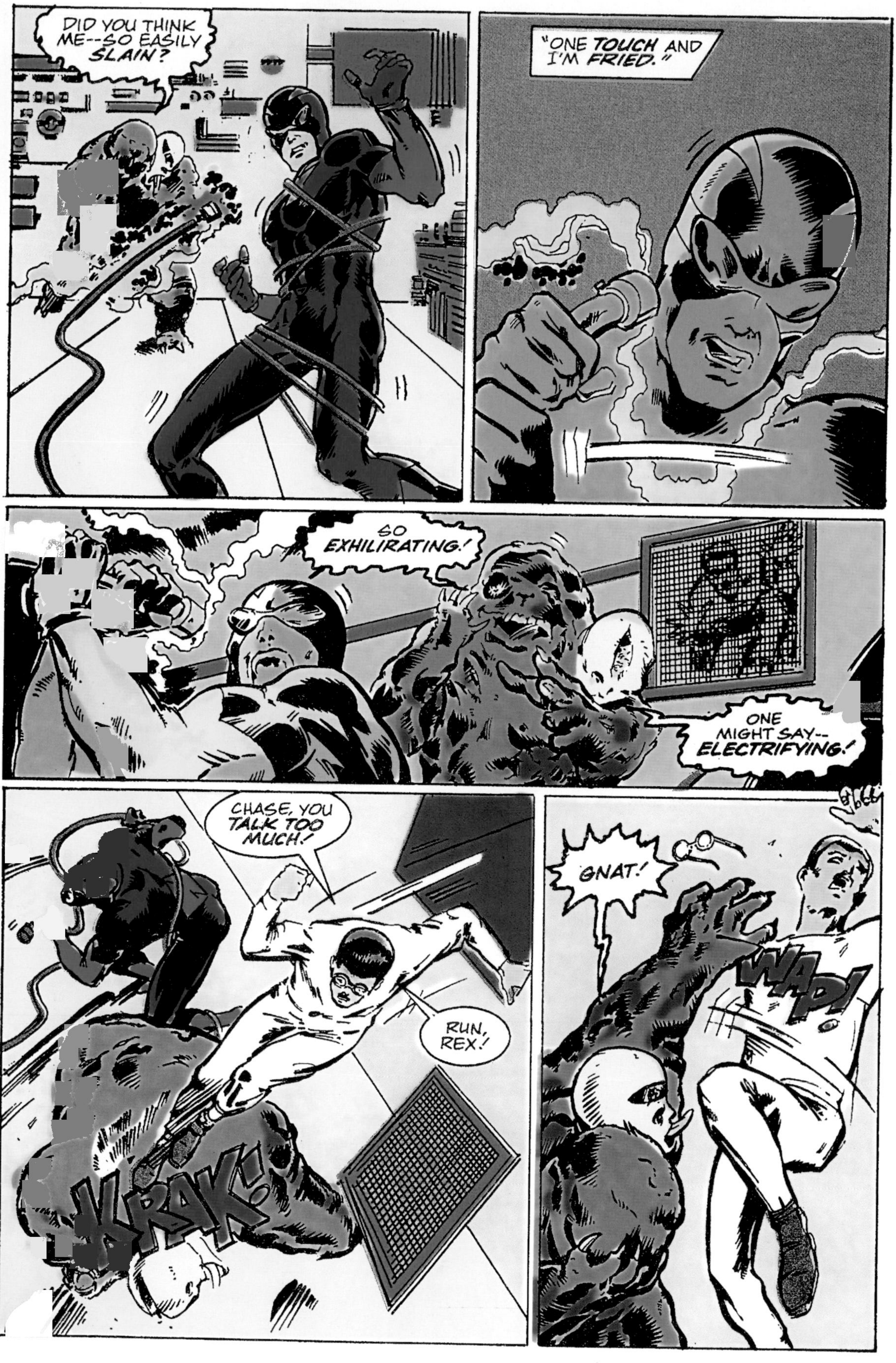
DID YOU THINK ME--SO EASILY SLAIN?
"ONE TOUCH AND I'M FRIED."
SO EXHILIRATING!
ONE MIGHT SAY-- ELECTRIFYING!
CHASE, YOU TALK TOO MUCH!
RUN, REX!
KRAK!
GNAT!
WAP!

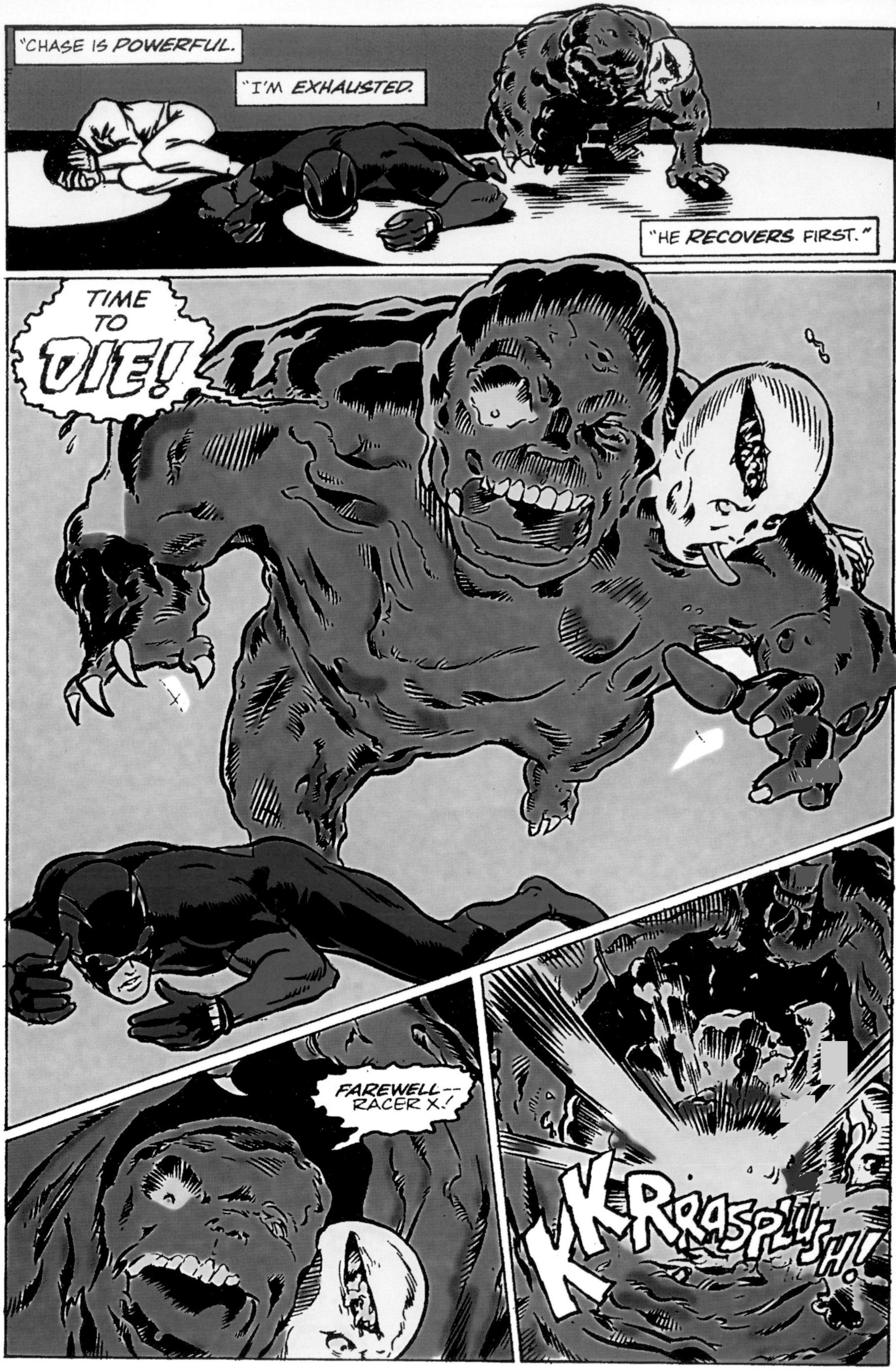
"CHASE IS POWERFUL.
"I'M EXHAUSTED.
"HE RECOVERS FIRST."
TIME TO DIE!
FAREWELL-- RACER X!
KKRRASPLUSH!

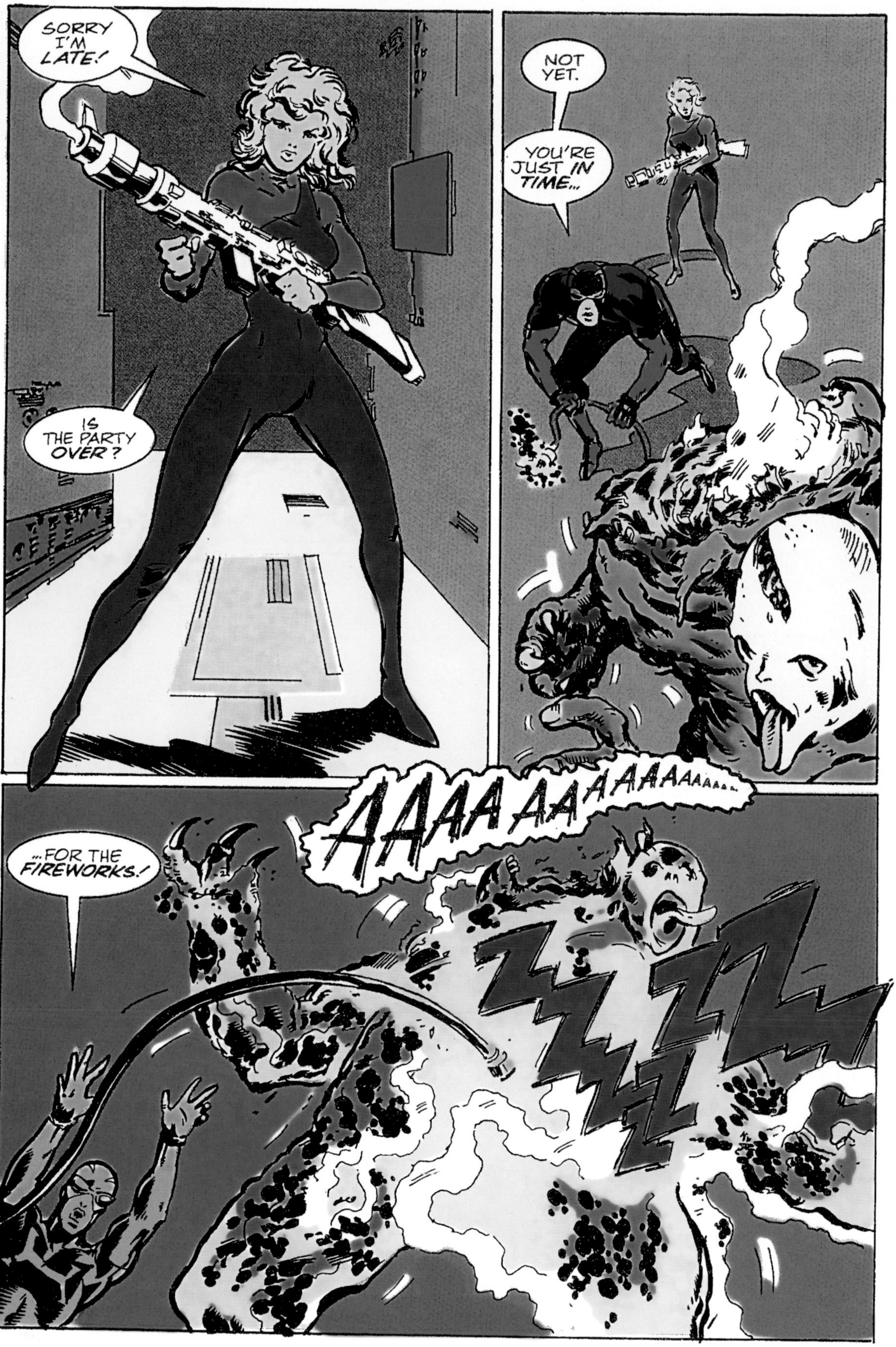
SORRY I'M *LATE!*
IS THE PARTY *OVER?*
NOT YET.
YOU'RE JUST *IN TIME...*
AAAAAAAAAAAAA...
...FOR THE *FIREWORKS!*

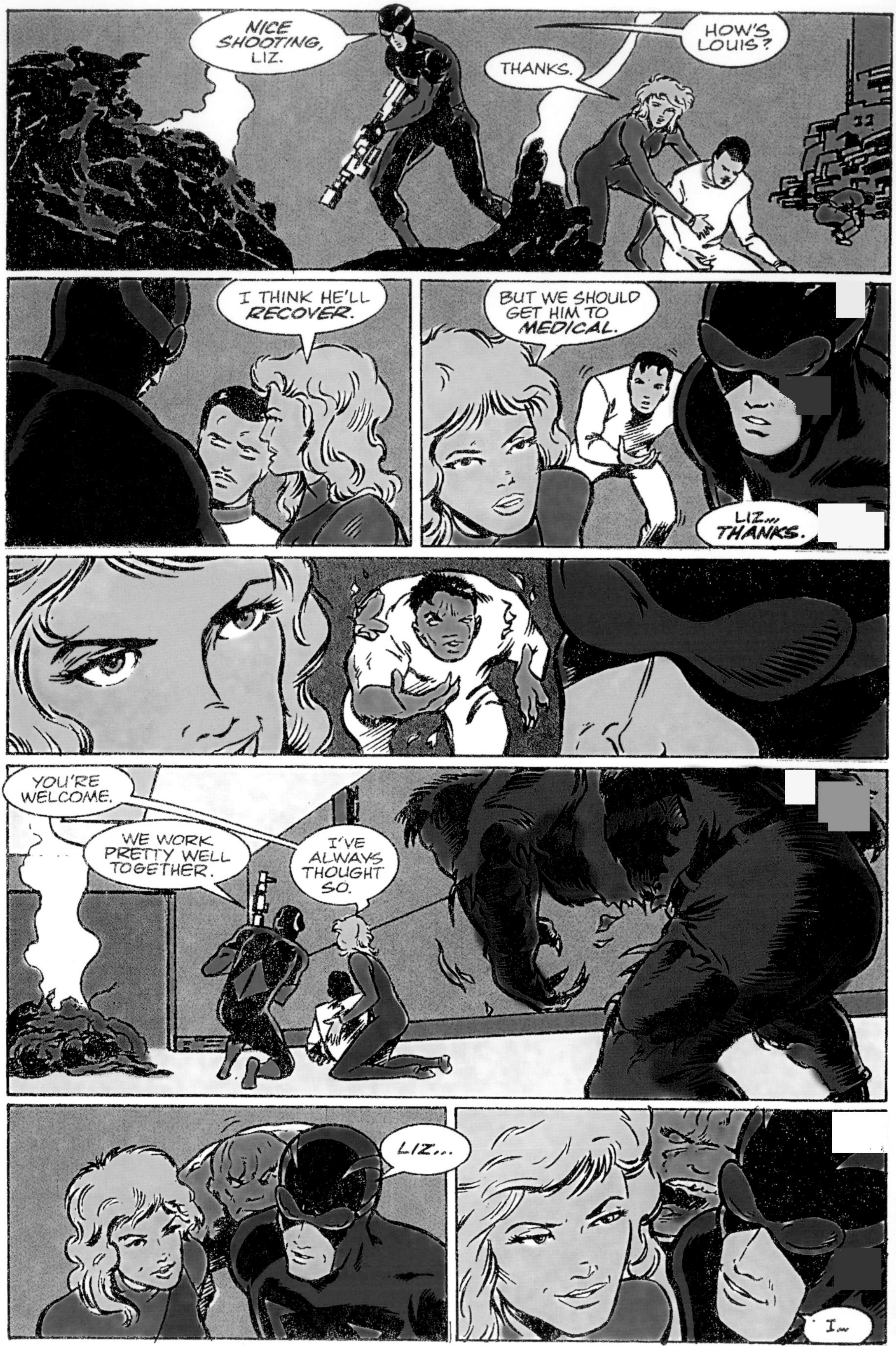
NICE SHOOTING, LIZ.
THANKS.
HOW'S LOUIS?
I THINK HE'LL RECOVER.
BUT WE SHOULD GET HIM TO MEDICAL.
LIZ... THANKS.
YOU'RE WELCOME.
WE WORK PRETTY WELL TOGETHER.
I'VE ALWAYS THOUGHT SO.
LIZ...
I...

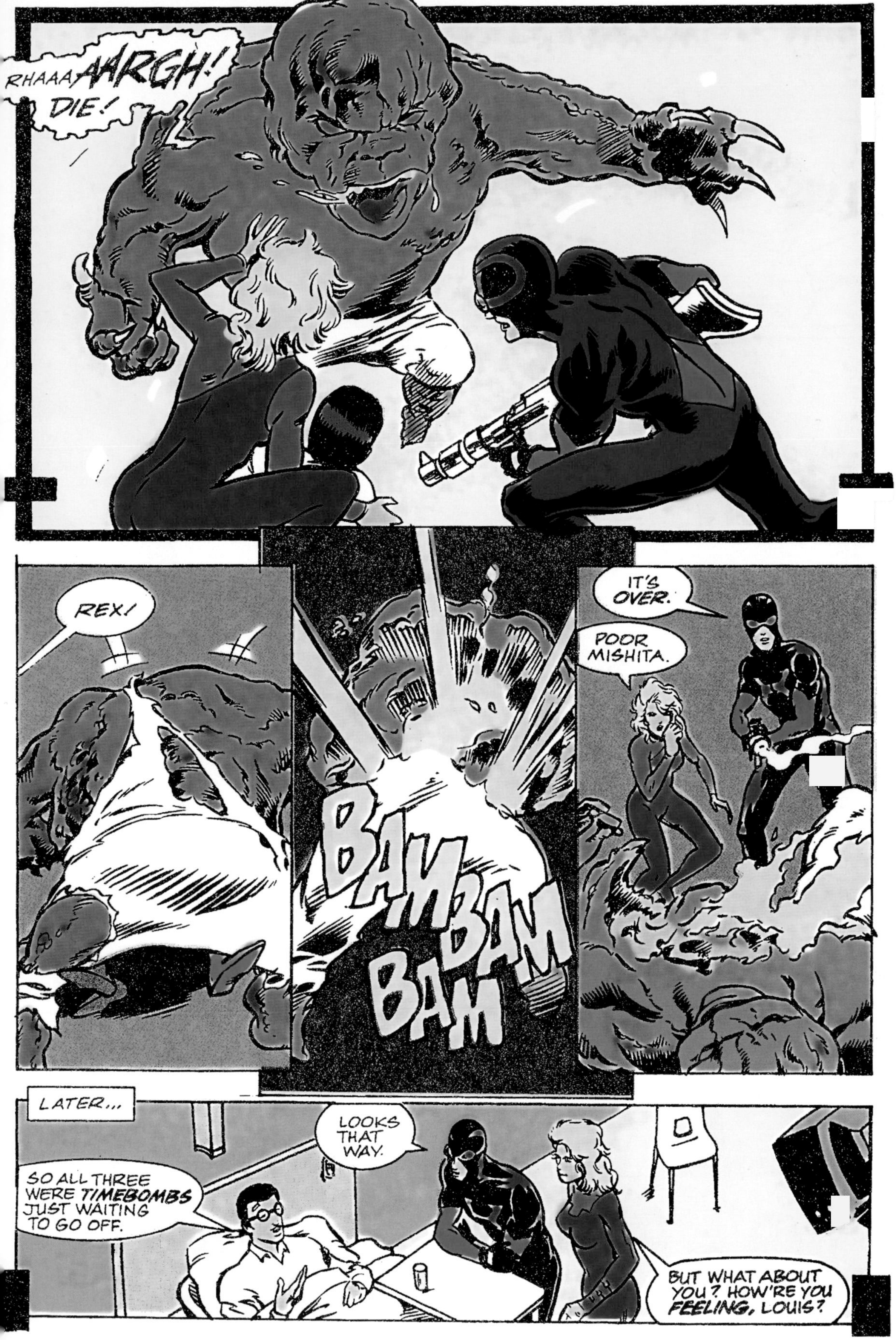
RHAAAAARGH! DIE!
REX!
BAM BAM BAM
IT'S OVER.
POOR MISHITA.
LATER...
SO ALL THREE WERE TIMEBOMBS JUST WAITING TO GO OFF.
LOOKS THAT WAY.
BUT WHAT ABOUT YOU? HOW'RE YOU FEELING, LOUIS?

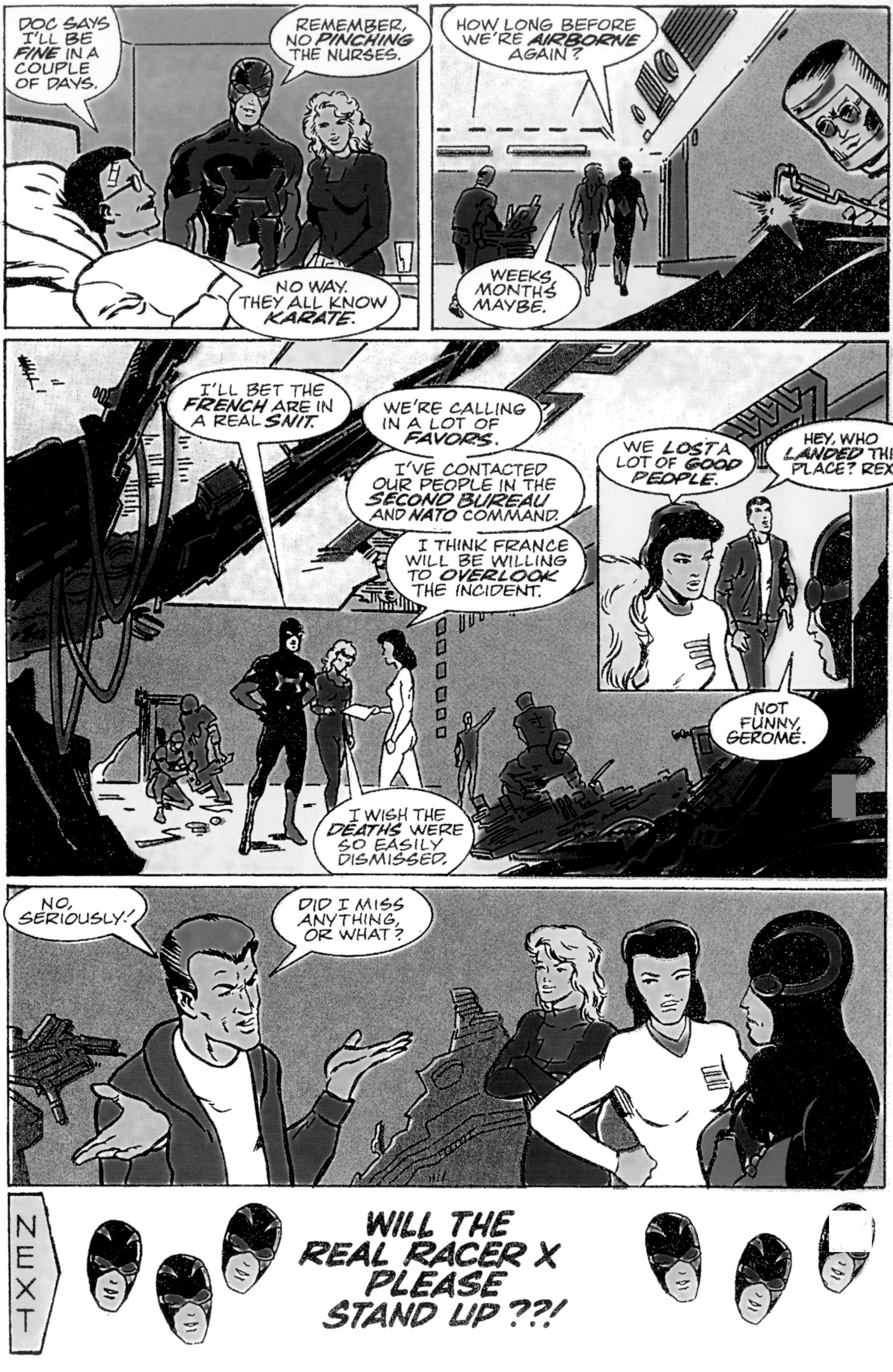
DOC SAYS I'LL BE FINE IN A COUPLE OF DAYS.
REMEMBER, NO PINCHING THE NURSES.
NO WAY. THEY ALL KNOW KARATE.
HOW LONG BEFORE WE'RE AIRBORNE AGAIN?
WEEKS, MONTHS MAYBE.
I'LL BET THE FRENCH ARE IN A REAL SNIT.
WE'RE CALLING IN A LOT OF FAVORS.
I'VE CONTACTED OUR PEOPLE IN THE SECOND BUREAU AND NATO COMMAND.
I THINK FRANCE WILL BE WILLING TO OVERLOOK THE INCIDENT.
I WISH THE DEATHS WERE SO EASILY DISMISSED.
WE LOST A LOT OF GOOD PEOPLE.
HEY, WHO LANDED THI PLACE? REX
NOT FUNNY, GEROME.
NO, SERIOUSLY!
DID I MISS ANYTHING, OR WHAT?
NEXT
WILL THE REAL RACER X PLEASE STAND UP ??!

Racer X #5

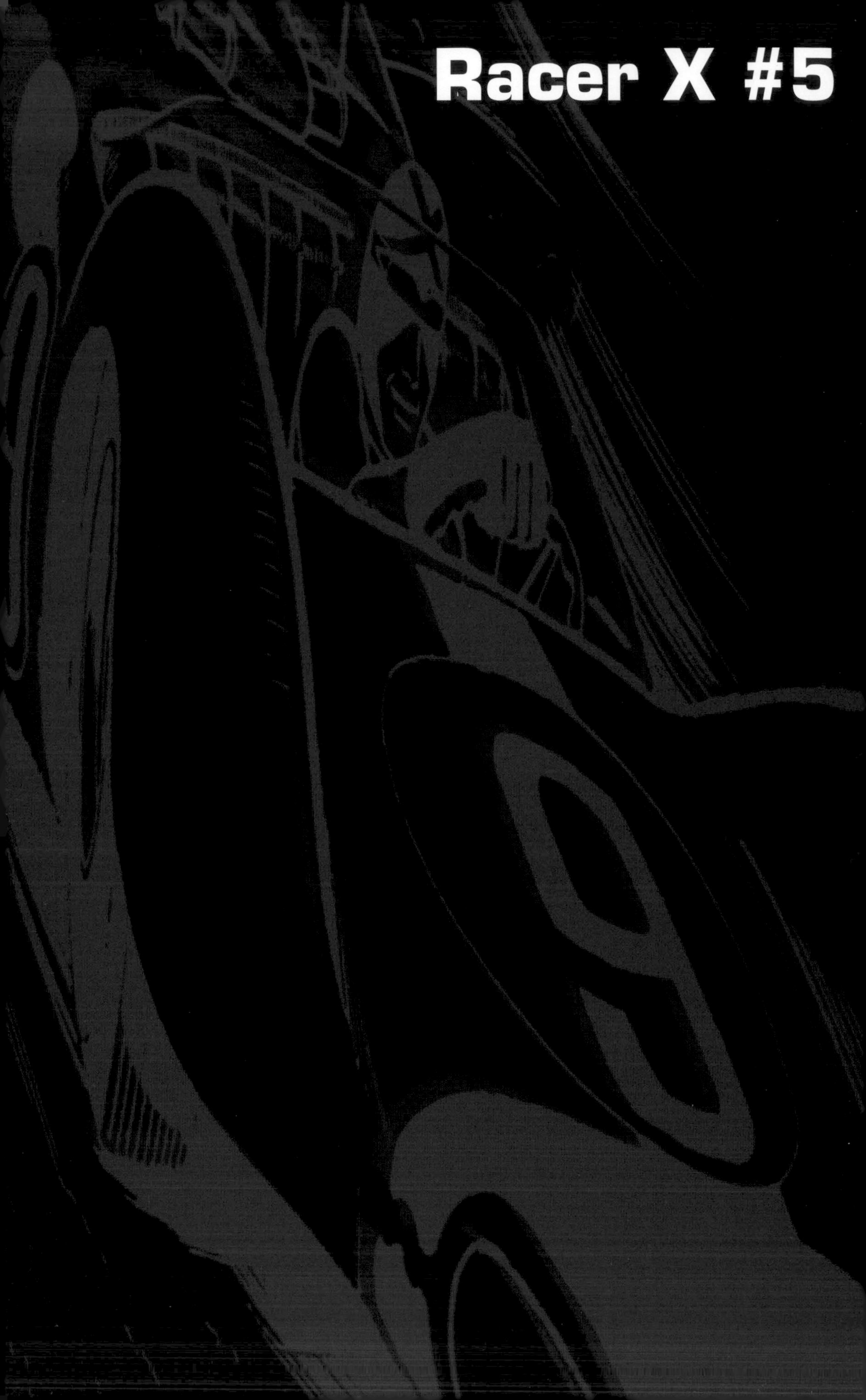

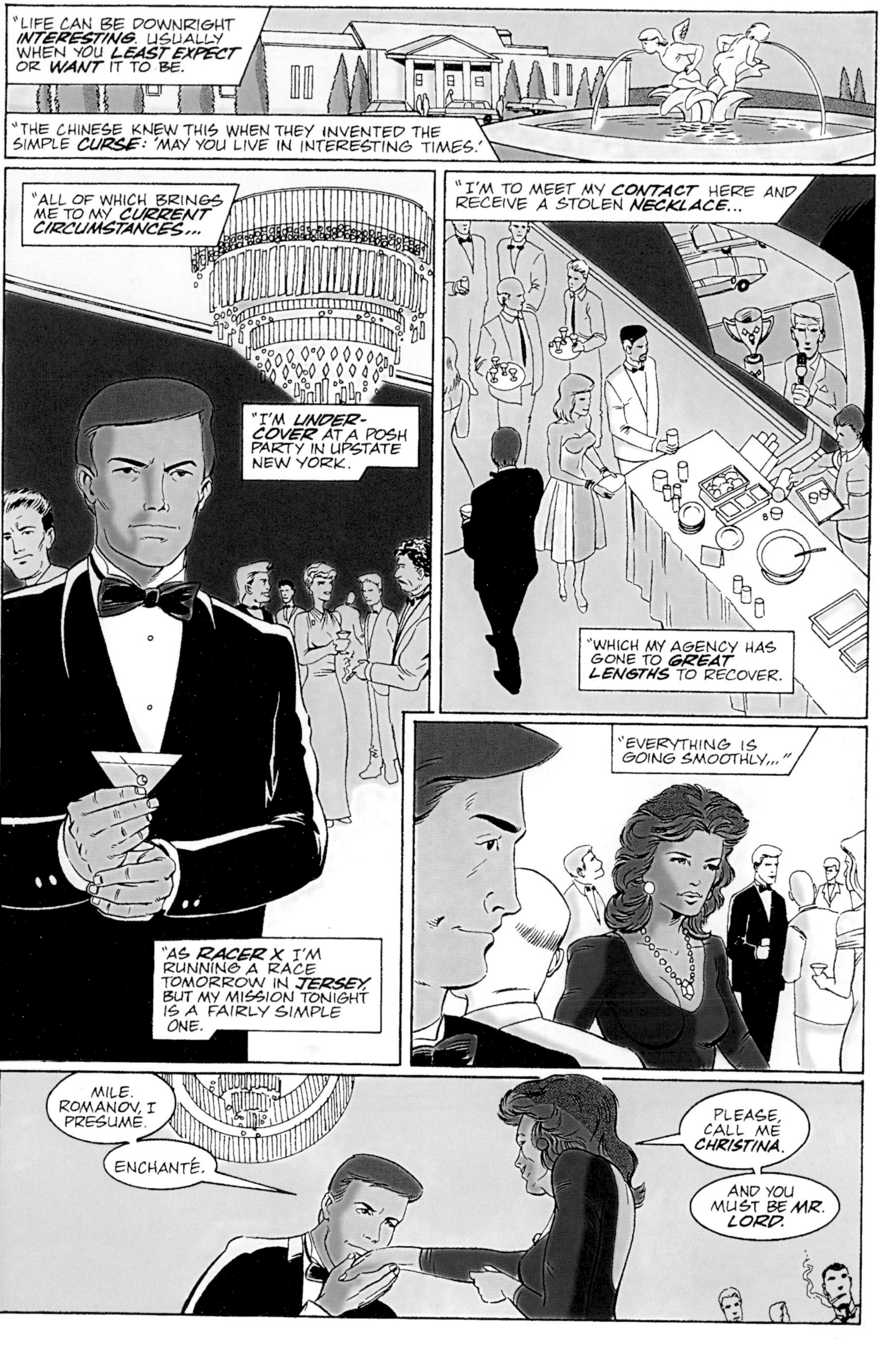
"LIFE CAN BE DOWNRIGHT INTERESTING. USUALLY WHEN YOU LEAST EXPECT OR WANT IT TO BE.
"THE CHINESE KNEW THIS WHEN THEY INVENTED THE SIMPLE CURSE: 'MAY YOU LIVE IN INTERESTING TIMES.'
"ALL OF WHICH BRINGS ME TO MY CURRENT CIRCUMSTANCES...
"I'M UNDER-COVER AT A POSH PARTY IN UPSTATE NEW YORK.
"AS RACER X I'M RUNNING A RACE TOMORROW IN JERSEY, BUT MY MISSION TONIGHT IS A FAIRLY SIMPLE ONE.
"I'M TO MEET MY CONTACT HERE AND RECEIVE A STOLEN NECKLACE...
"WHICH MY AGENCY HAS GONE TO GREAT LENGTHS TO RECOVER.
"EVERYTHING IS GOING SMOOTHLY..."
MLLE. ROMANOV, I PRESUME.
ENCHANTÉ.
PLEASE, CALL ME CHRISTINA.
AND YOU MUST BE MR. LORD.

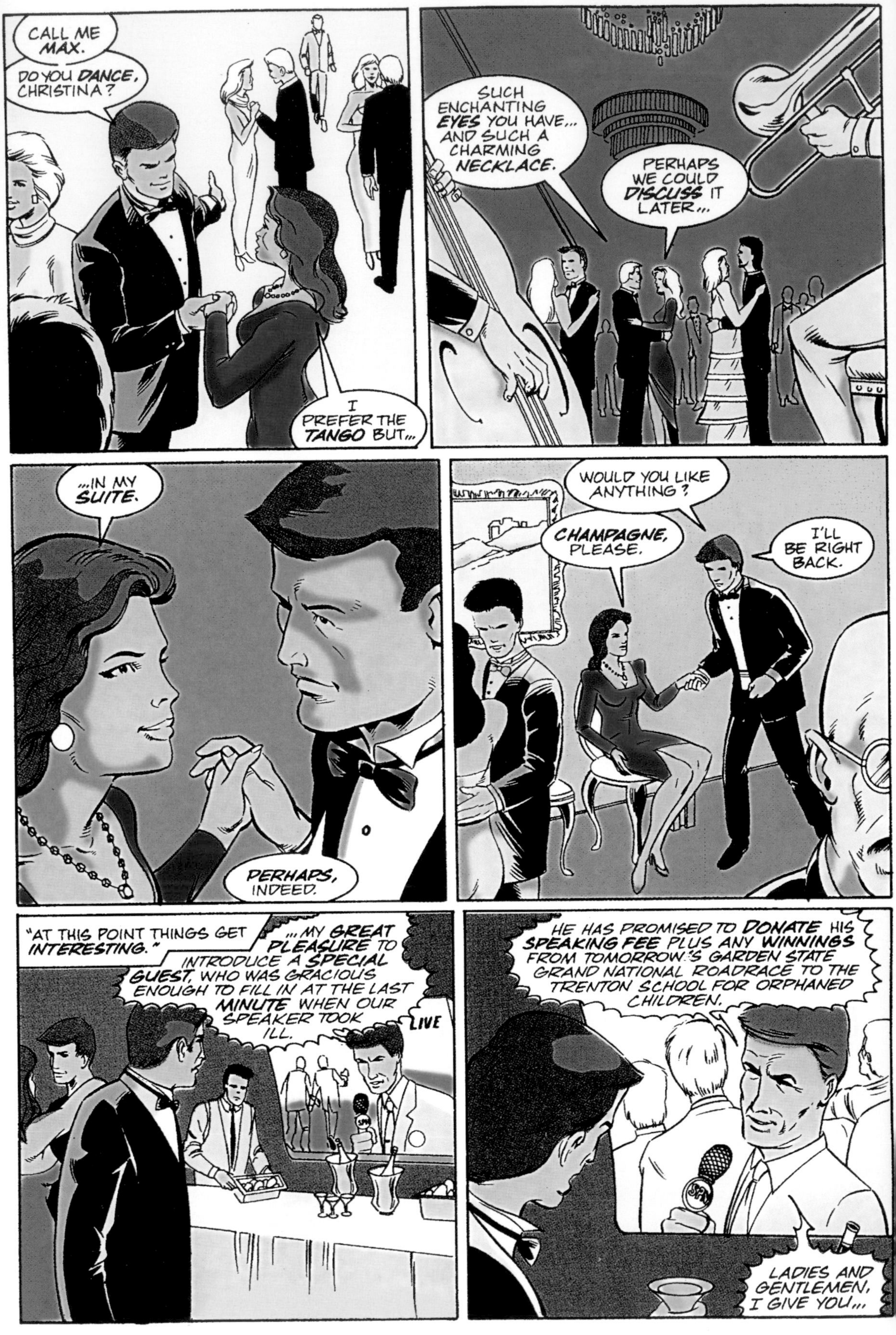
CALL ME MAX.
DO YOU DANCE, CHRISTINA?
I PREFER THE TANGO BUT...
SUCH ENCHANTING EYES YOU HAVE... AND SUCH A CHARMING NECKLACE.
PERHAPS WE COULD DISCUSS IT LATER...
...IN MY SUITE.
PERHAPS, INDEED.
WOULD YOU LIKE ANYTHING?
CHAMPAGNE, PLEASE.
I'LL BE RIGHT BACK.
"AT THIS POINT THINGS GET INTERESTING."
...MY GREAT PLEASURE TO INTRODUCE A SPECIAL GUEST, WHO WAS GRACIOUS ENOUGH TO FILL IN AT THE LAST MINUTE WHEN OUR SPEAKER TOOK ILL.
LIVE
HE HAS PROMISED TO DONATE HIS SPEAKING FEE PLUS ANY WINNINGS FROM TOMORROW'S GARDEN STATE GRAND NATIONAL ROADRACE TO THE TRENTON SCHOOL FOR ORPHANED CHILDREN.
LADIES AND GENTLEMEN, I GIVE YOU...

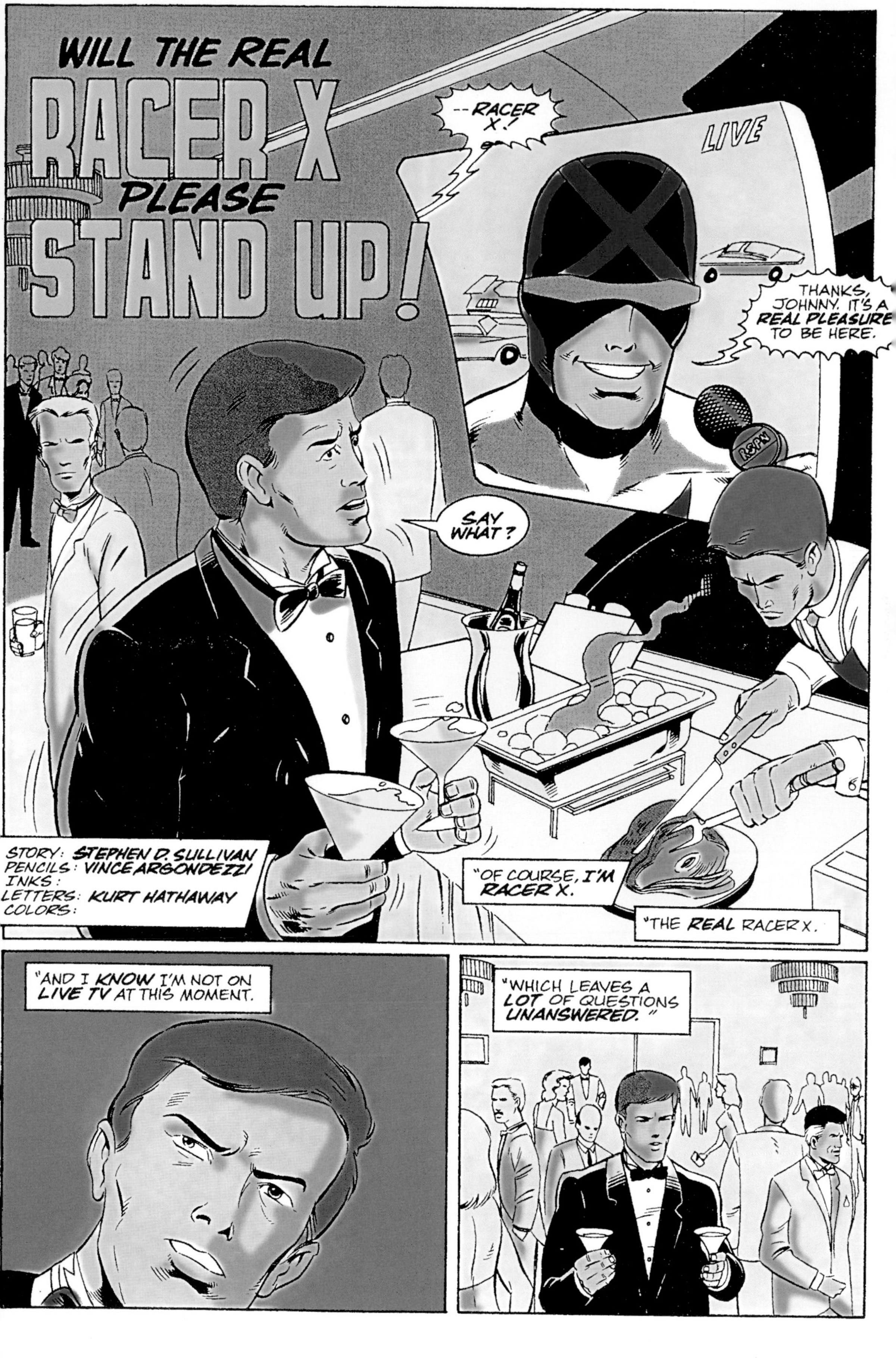
WILL THE REAL RACER X PLEASE STAND UP!
--RACER X!
LIVE
THANKS, JOHNNY. IT'S A REAL PLEASURE TO BE HERE.
SAY WHAT?
STORY: STEPHEN D. SULLIVAN
PENCILS: VINCE ARGONDEZZI
INKS:
LETTERS: KURT HATHAWAY
COLORS:
"OF COURSE, I'M RACER X.
"THE REAL RACER X.
"AND I KNOW I'M NOT ON LIVE TV AT THIS MOMENT.
"WHICH LEAVES A LOT OF QUESTIONS UNANSWERED."

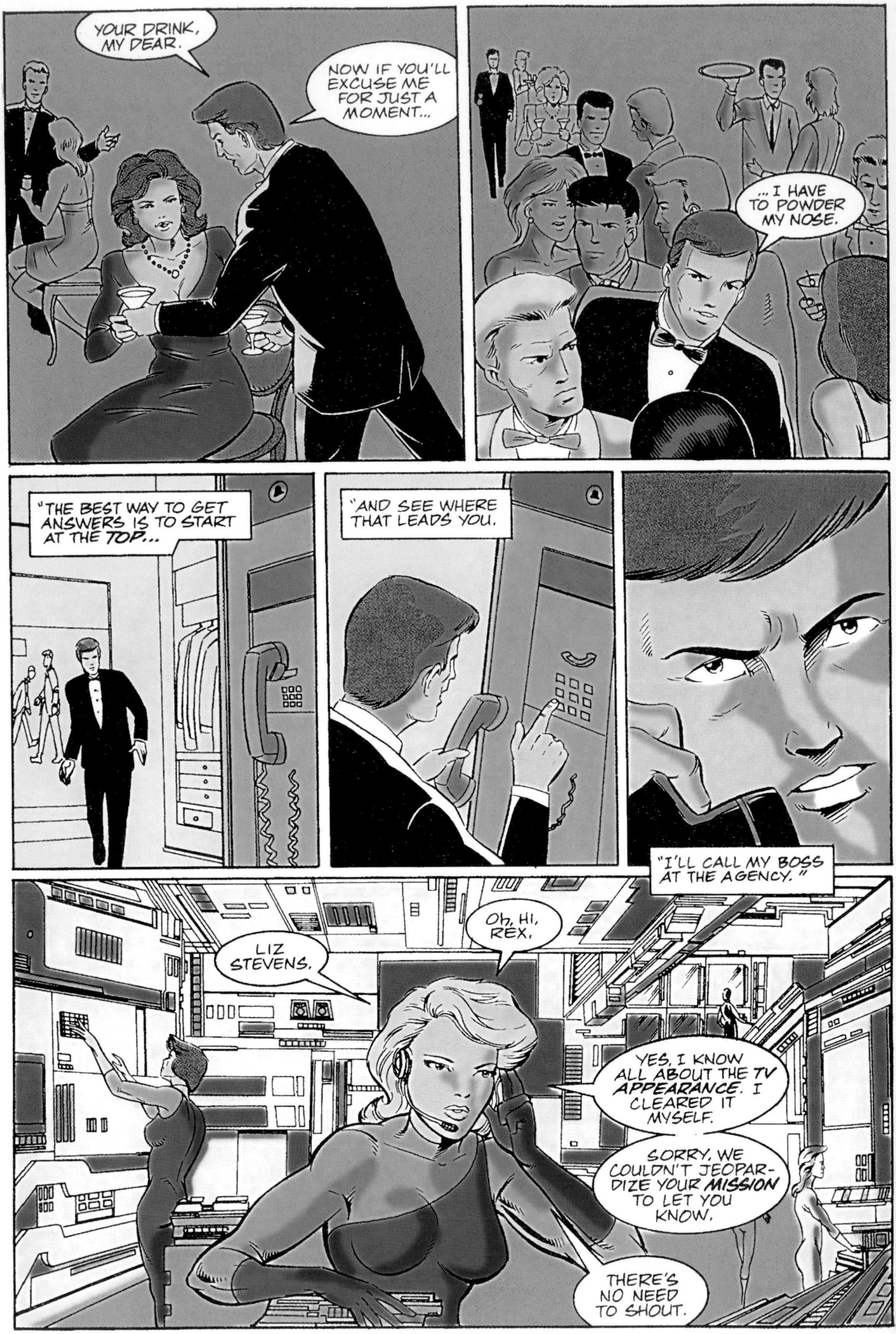
YOUR DRINK, MY DEAR.
NOW IF YOU'LL EXCUSE ME FOR JUST A MOMENT...
...I HAVE TO POWDER MY NOSE.
"THE BEST WAY TO GET ANSWERS IS TO START AT THE TOP...
"AND SEE WHERE THAT LEADS YOU.
"I'LL CALL MY BOSS AT THE AGENCY."
LIZ STEVENS.
Oh, HI, REX.
YES, I KNOW ALL ABOUT THE TV APPEARANCE. I CLEARED IT MYSELF.
SORRY, WE COULDN'T JEOPARDIZE YOUR MISSION TO LET YOU KNOW.
THERE'S NO NEED TO SHOUT.

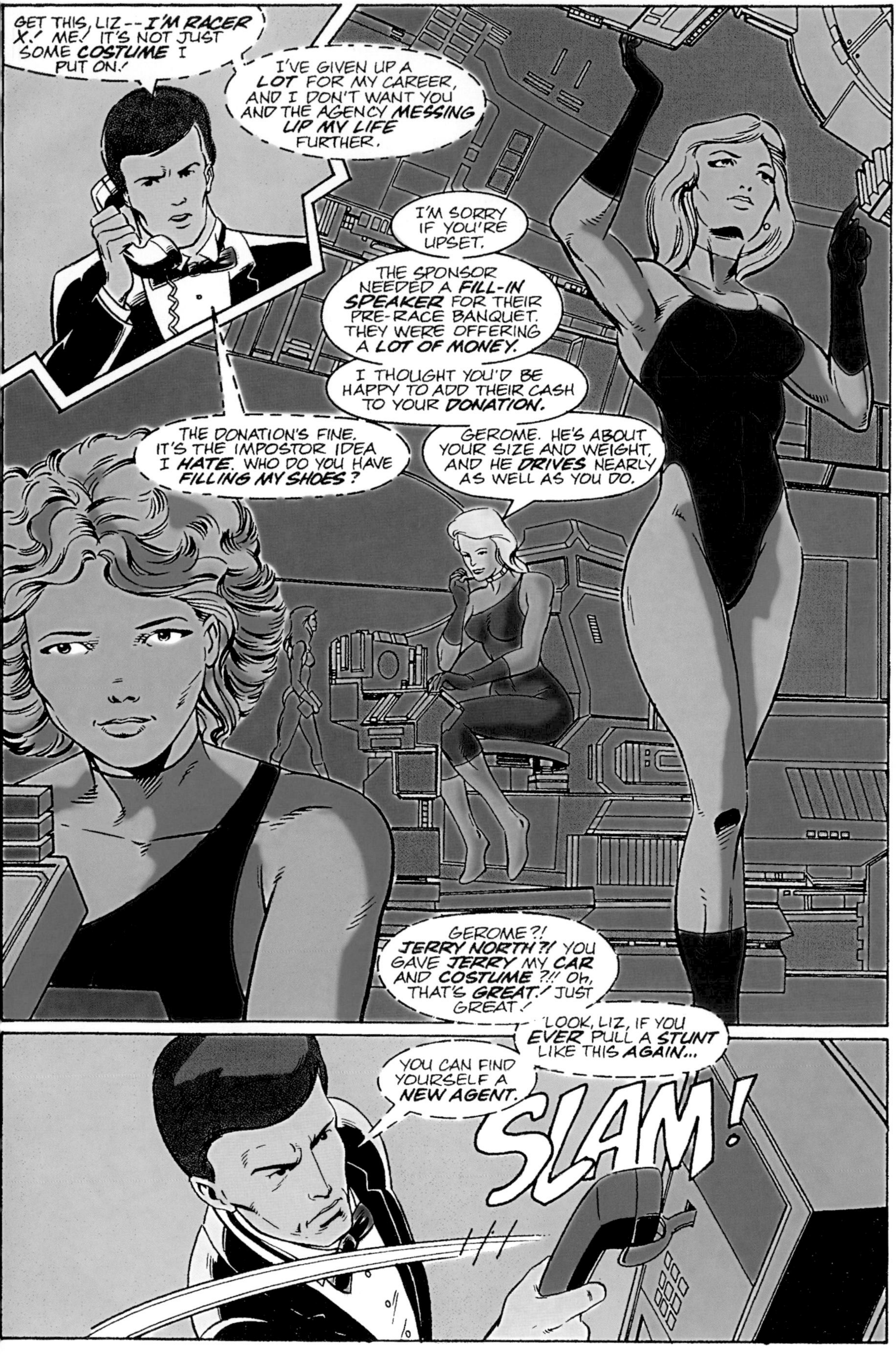
GET THIS, LIZ-- I'M RACER X.! ME! IT'S NOT JUST SOME COSTUME I PUT ON.!
I'VE GIVEN UP A LOT FOR MY CAREER, AND I DON'T WANT YOU AND THE AGENCY MESSING UP MY LIFE FURTHER.
I'M SORRY IF YOU'RE UPSET.
THE SPONSOR NEEDED A FILL-IN SPEAKER FOR THEIR PRE-RACE BANQUET. THEY WERE OFFERING A LOT OF MONEY.
I THOUGHT YOU'D BE HAPPY TO ADD THEIR CASH TO YOUR DONATION.
THE DONATION'S FINE. IT'S THE IMPOSTOR IDEA I HATE. WHO DO YOU HAVE FILLING MY SHOES?
GEROME. HE'S ABOUT YOUR SIZE AND WEIGHT, AND HE DRIVES NEARLY AS WELL AS YOU DO.
GEROME?! JERRY NORTH?! YOU GAVE JERRY MY CAR AND COSTUME?!! Oh, THAT'S GREAT.! JUST GREAT.!
LOOK, LIZ, IF YOU EVER PULL A STUNT LIKE THIS AGAIN...
YOU CAN FIND YOURSELF A NEW AGENT.
SLAM!

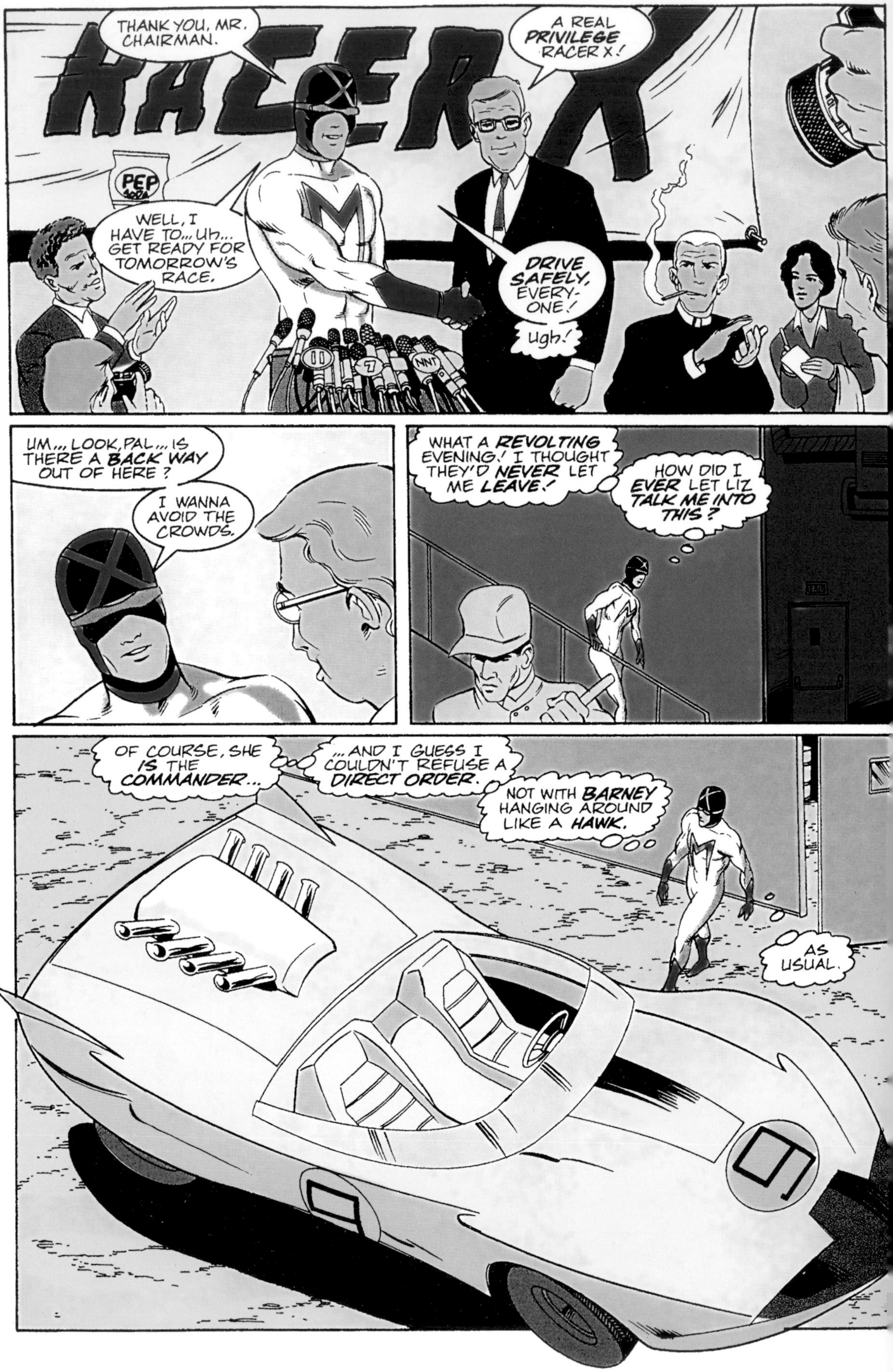
RACER X
THANK YOU, MR. CHAIRMAN.
A REAL PRIVILEGE RACER X!
PEP SODA
WELL, I HAVE TO... Uh... GET READY FOR TOMORROW'S RACE.
DRIVE SAFELY, EVERY-ONE!
Ugh!
UM... LOOK, PAL... IS THERE A BACK WAY OUT OF HERE?
I WANNA AVOID THE CROWDS.
WHAT A REVOLTING EVENING! I THOUGHT THEY'D NEVER LET ME LEAVE!
HOW DID I EVER LET LIZ TALK ME INTO THIS?
OF COURSE, SHE IS THE COMMANDER...
...AND I GUESS I COULDN'T REFUSE A DIRECT ORDER.
NOT WITH BARNEY HANGING AROUND LIKE A HAWK.
AS USUAL.

I'LL JUST DROP OFF THE CAR, CHANGE OUT OF THIS *GOOFY* COSTUME...

...DROP THIS PACKAGE AT MY *FOLKS'* HOUSE...

mom Dad

...AND HEAD BACK TO BASE FOR SOME WELL DESERVED...

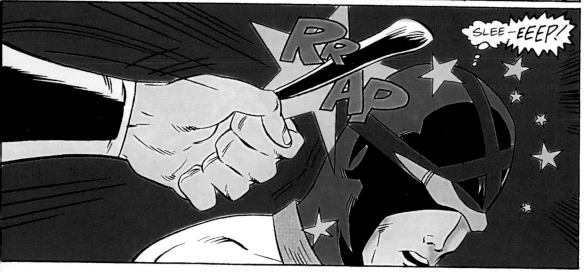

RRAP

SLEE-EEEP!

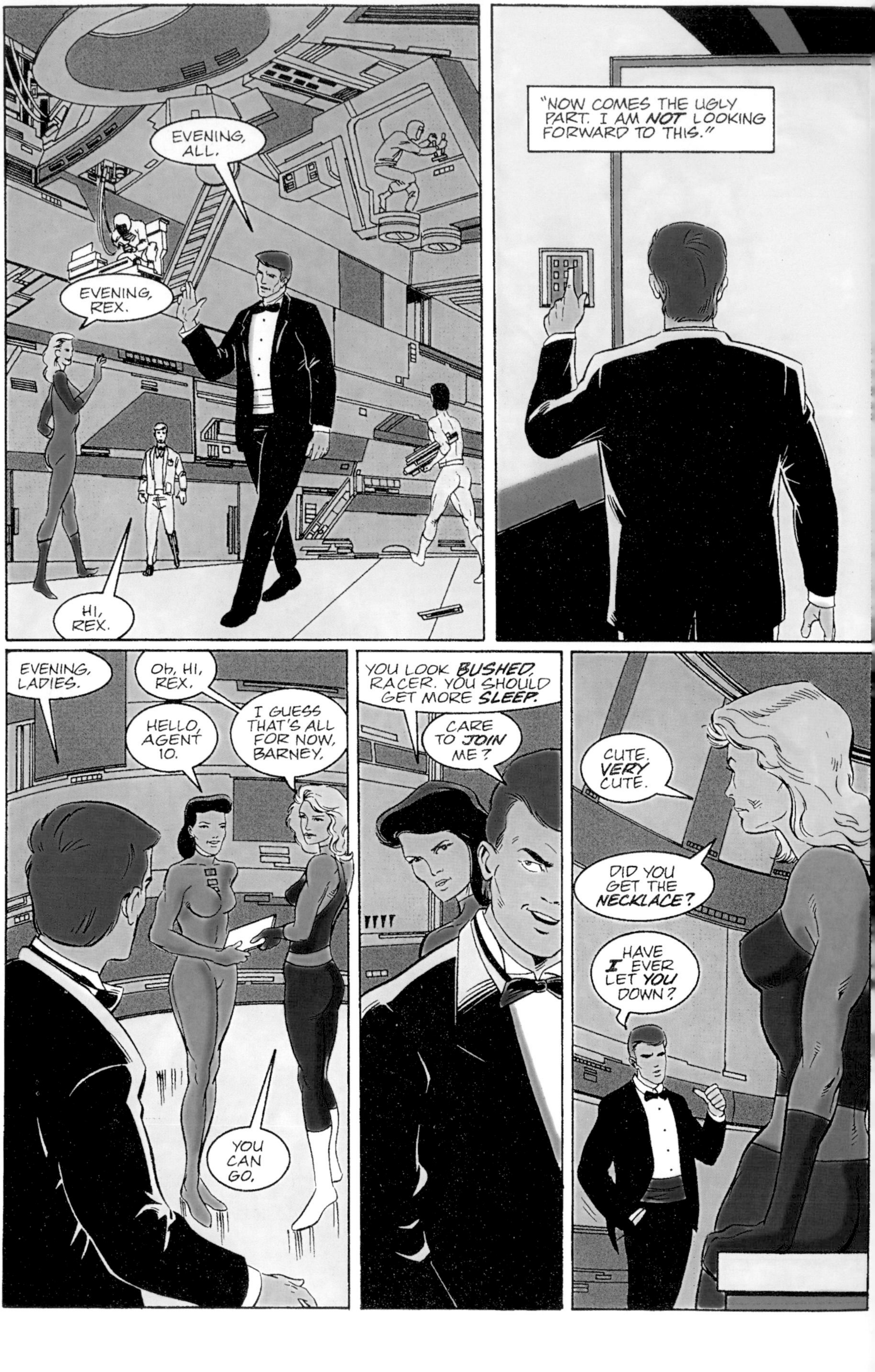
EVENING, ALL.
EVENING, REX.
HI, REX.
"NOW COMES THE UGLY PART. I AM NOT LOOKING FORWARD TO THIS."
EVENING, LADIES.
Oh, HI, REX.
HELLO, AGENT 10.
I GUESS THAT'S ALL FOR NOW, BARNEY.
YOU CAN GO.
YOU LOOK BUSHED, RACER. YOU SHOULD GET MORE SLEEP.
CARE TO JOIN ME?
CUTE. VERY CUTE.
DID YOU GET THE NECKLACE?
HAVE I EVER LET YOU DOWN?

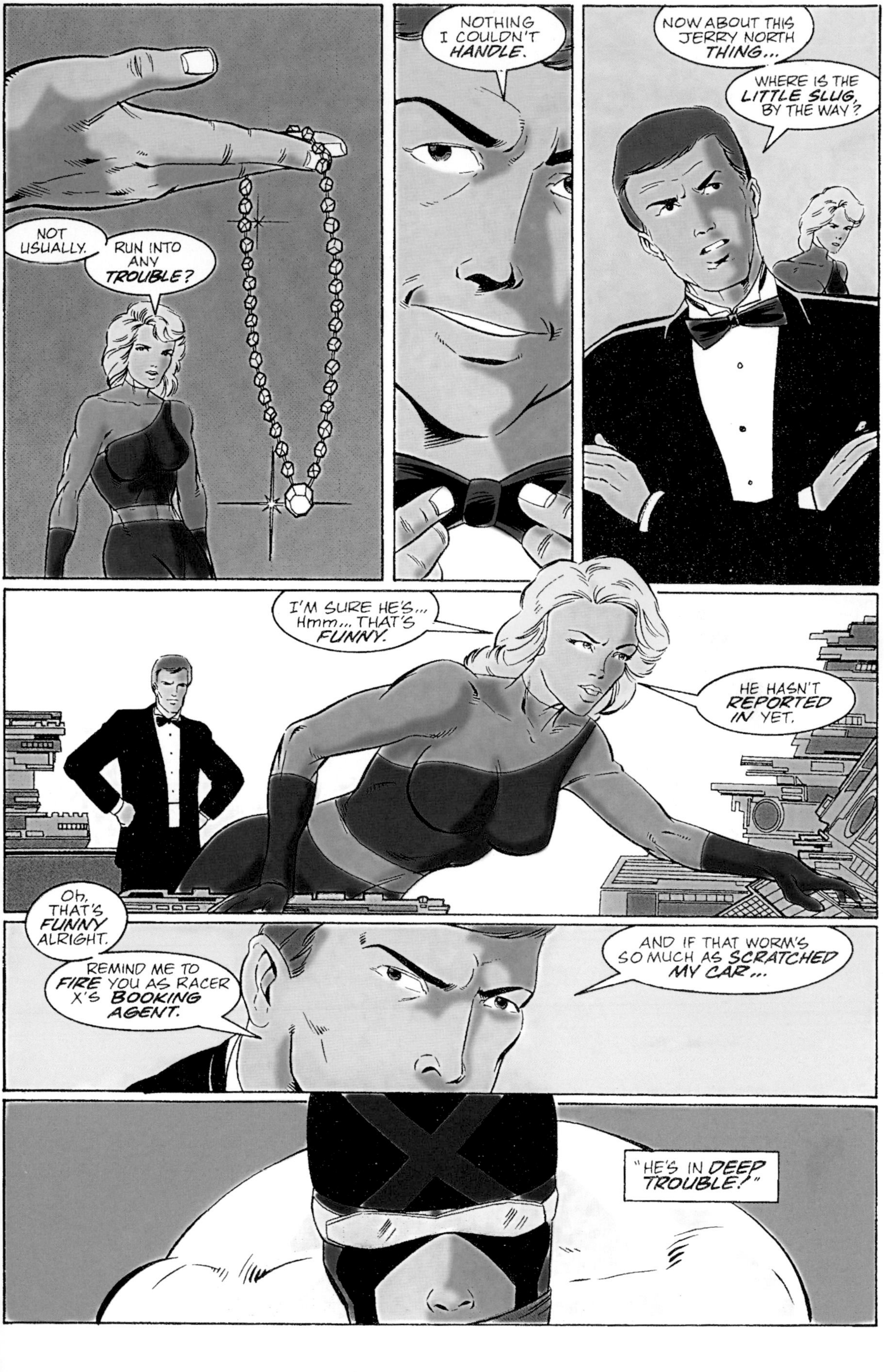
RUN INTO ANY TROUBLE?
NOT USUALLY.
NOTHING I COULDN'T HANDLE.
NOW ABOUT THIS JERRY NORTH THING...
WHERE IS THE LITTLE SLUG, BY THE WAY?
I'M SURE HE'S... Hmm... THAT'S FUNNY.
HE HASN'T REPORTED IN YET.
Oh, THAT'S FUNNY ALRIGHT.
REMIND ME TO FIRE YOU AS RACER X'S BOOKING AGENT.
AND IF THAT WORM'S SO MUCH AS SCRATCHED MY CAR...
"HE'S IN DEEP TROUBLE!"

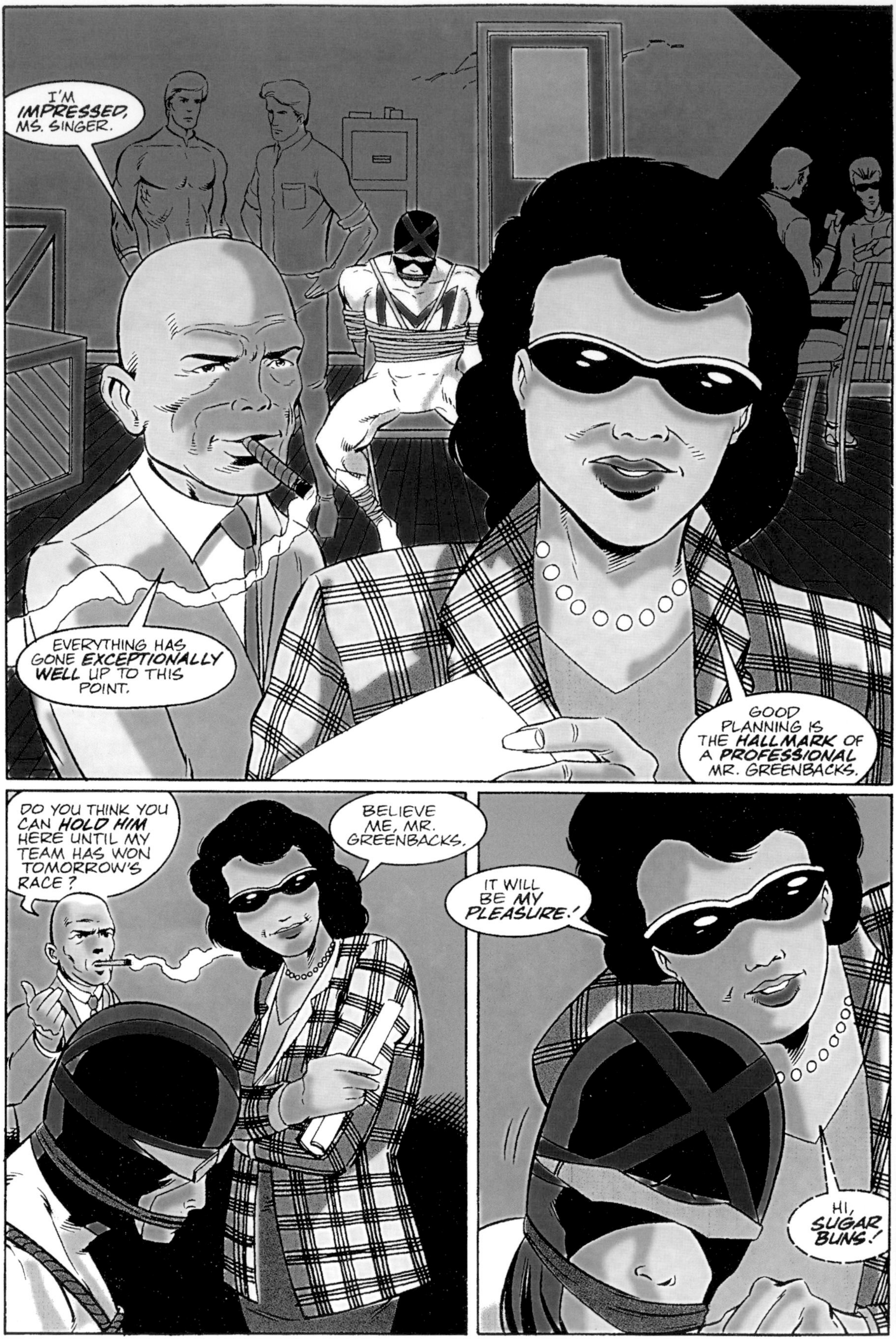
I'M IMPRESSED, MS. SINGER.
EVERYTHING HAS GONE EXCEPTIONALLY WELL UP TO THIS POINT.
GOOD PLANNING IS THE HALLMARK OF A PROFESSIONAL MR. GREENBACKS.
DO YOU THINK YOU CAN HOLD HIM HERE UNTIL MY TEAM HAS WON TOMORROW'S RACE?
BELIEVE ME, MR. GREENBACKS.
IT WILL BE MY PLEASURE!
HI, SUGAR BUNS!

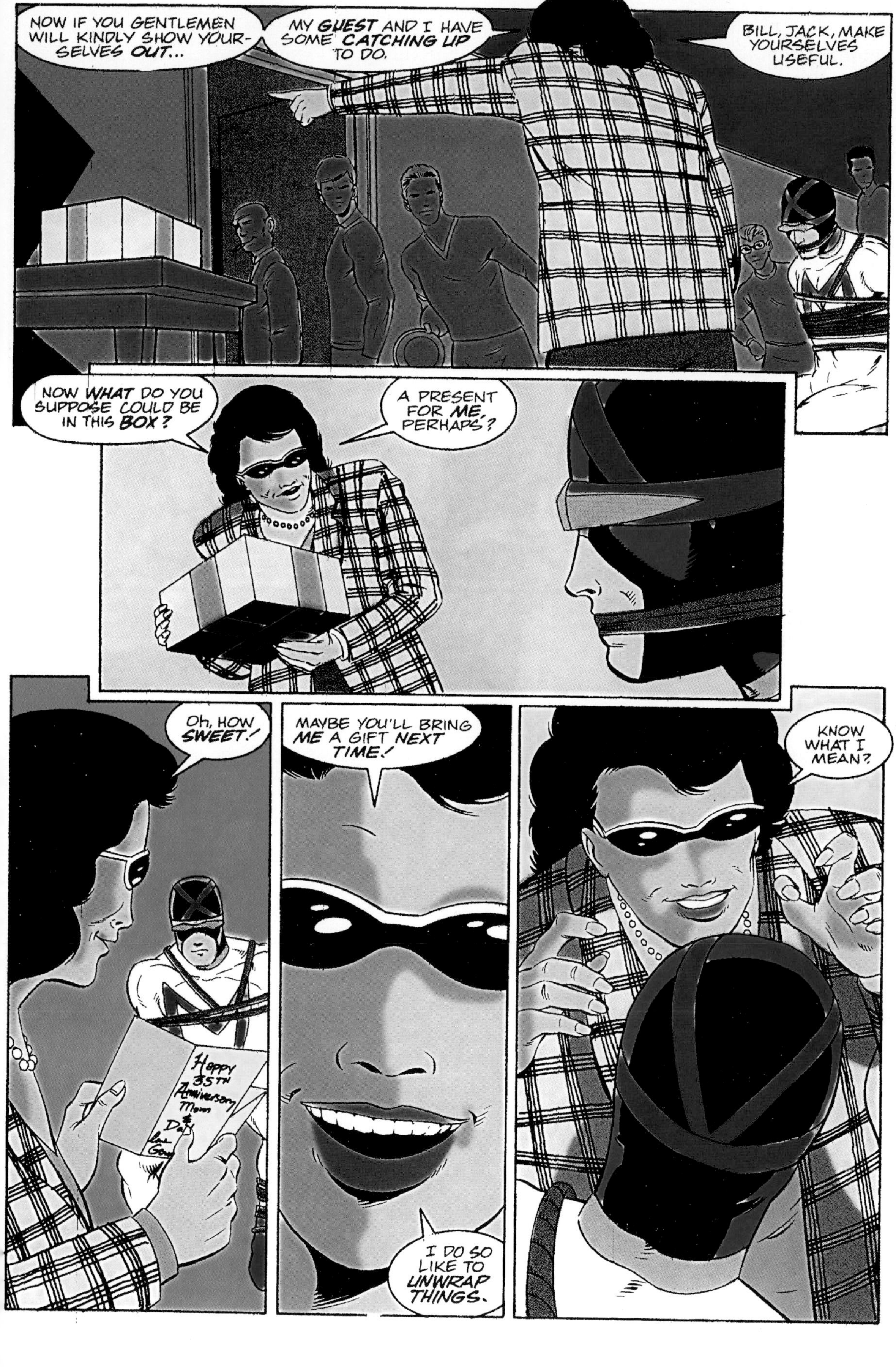
NOW IF YOU GENTLEMEN WILL KINDLY SHOW YOUR-SELVES OUT...
MY GUEST AND I HAVE SOME CATCHING UP TO DO.
BILL, JACK, MAKE YOURSELVES USEFUL.
NOW WHAT DO YOU SUPPOSE COULD BE IN THIS BOX?
A PRESENT FOR ME, PERHAPS?
Oh, HOW SWEET!
Happy 35TH Anniversary Mom & Dad
MAYBE YOU'LL BRING ME A GIFT NEXT TIME!
I DO SO LIKE TO UNWRAP THINGS.
KNOW WHAT I MEAN?

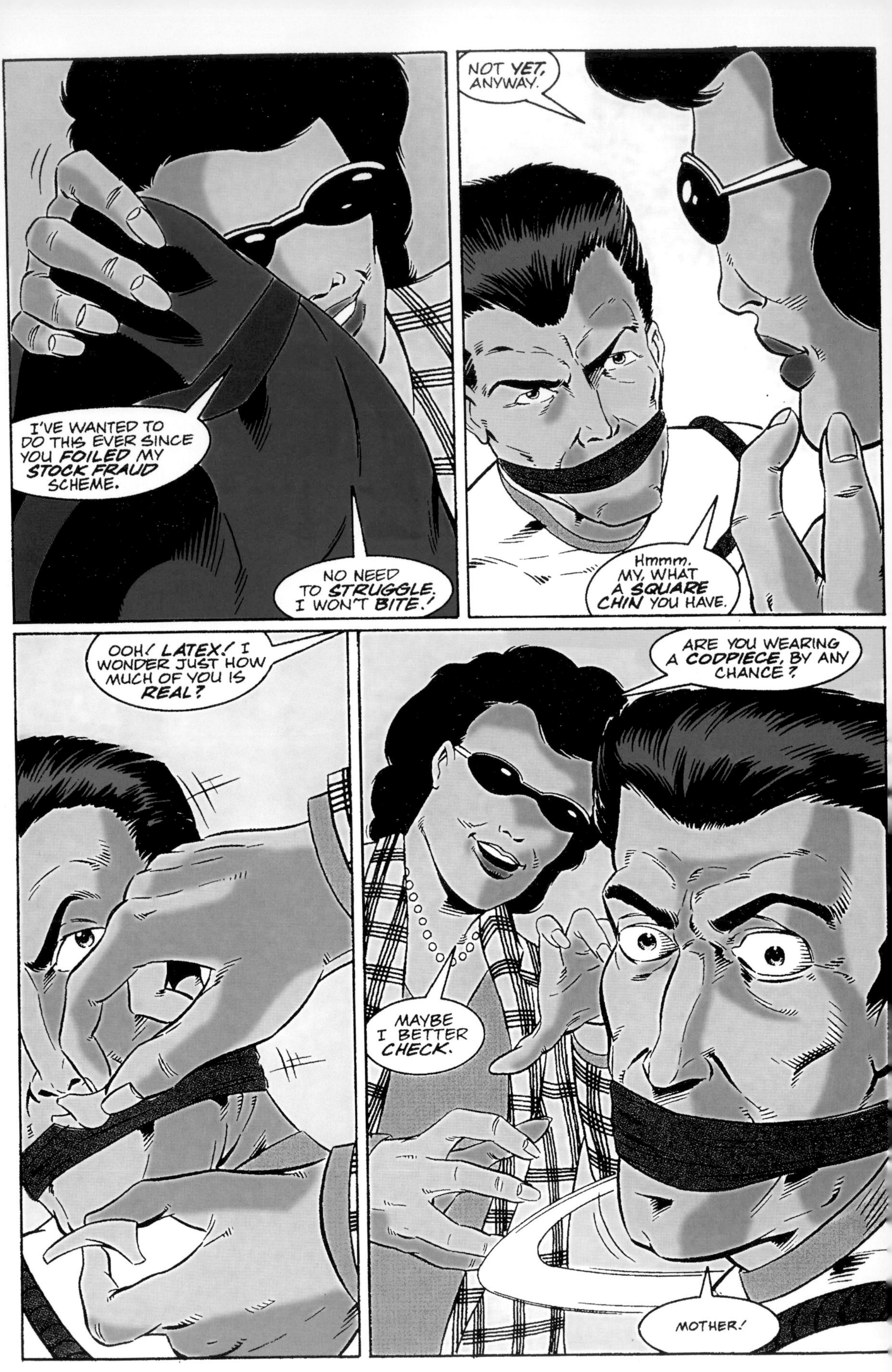
I'VE WANTED TO DO THIS EVER SINCE YOU FOILED MY STOCK FRAUD SCHEME.
NO NEED TO STRUGGLE. I WON'T BITE!
NOT YET, ANYWAY.
Hmmm. MY, WHAT A SQUARE CHIN YOU HAVE.
OOH! LATEX! I WONDER JUST HOW MUCH OF YOU IS REAL?
ARE YOU WEARING A CODPIECE, BY ANY CHANCE?
MAYBE I BETTER CHECK.
MOTHER!

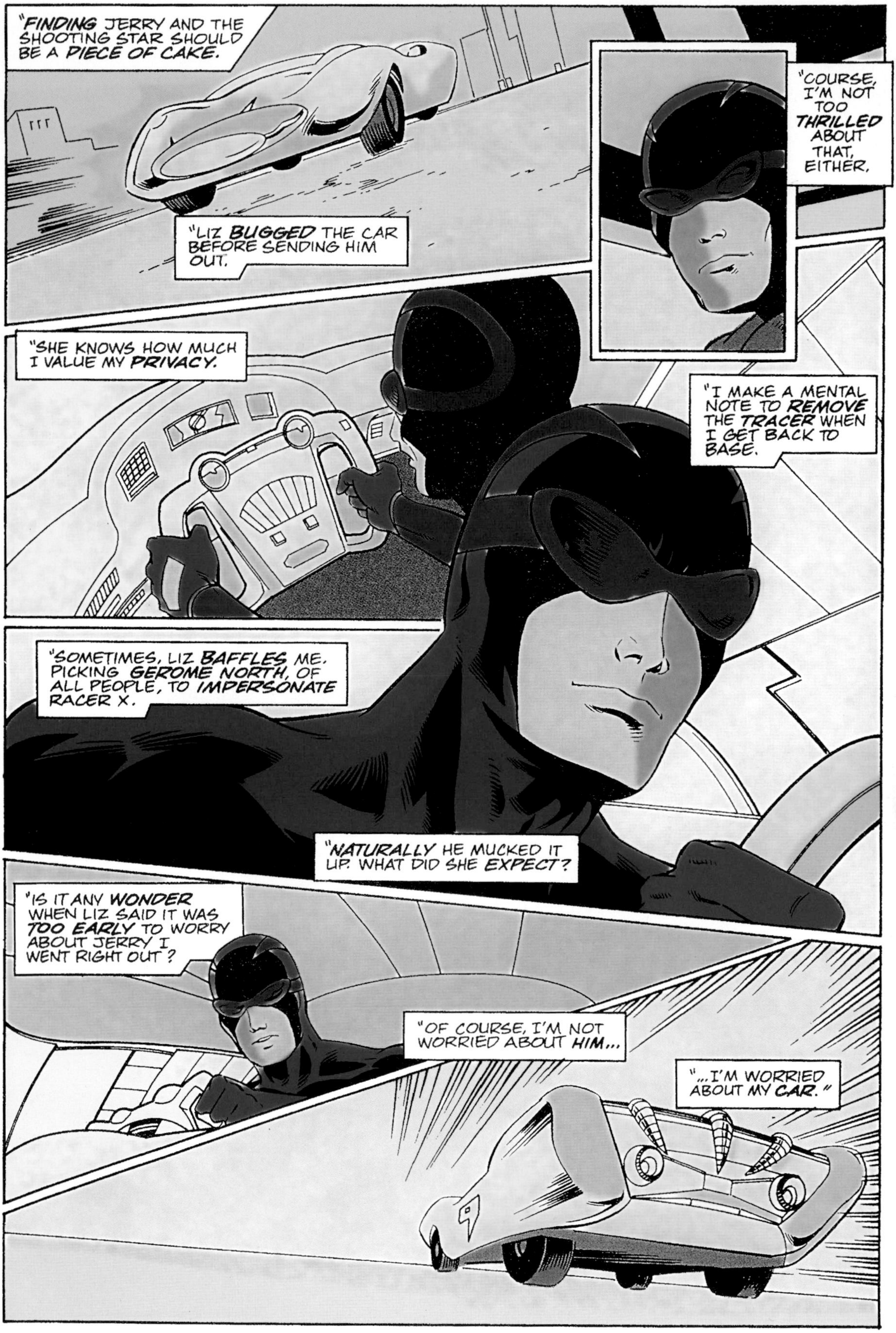
"FINDING JERRY AND THE SHOOTING STAR SHOULD BE A PIECE OF CAKE.
"LIZ BUGGED THE CAR BEFORE SENDING HIM OUT.
"COURSE, I'M NOT TOO THRILLED ABOUT THAT, EITHER.
"SHE KNOWS HOW MUCH I VALUE MY PRIVACY.
"I MAKE A MENTAL NOTE TO REMOVE THE TRACER WHEN I GET BACK TO BASE.
"SOMETIMES, LIZ BAFFLES ME. PICKING GEROME NORTH, OF ALL PEOPLE, TO IMPERSONATE RACER X.
"NATURALLY HE MUCKED IT UP. WHAT DID SHE EXPECT?
"IS IT ANY WONDER WHEN LIZ SAID IT WAS TOO EARLY TO WORRY ABOUT JERRY I WENT RIGHT OUT?
"OF COURSE, I'M NOT WORRIED ABOUT HIM...
"...I'M WORRIED ABOUT MY CAR."

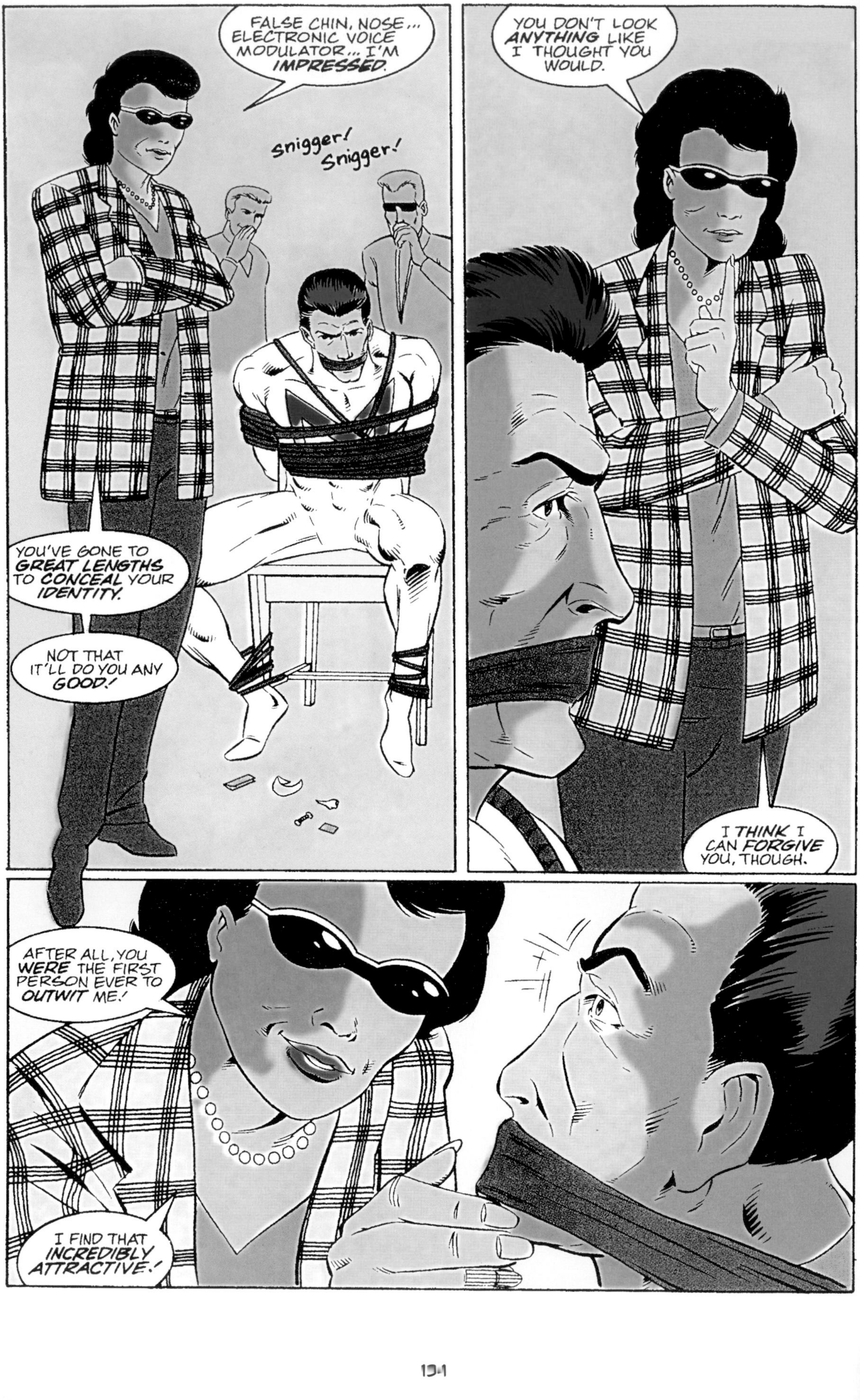
FALSE CHIN, NOSE... ELECTRONIC VOICE MODULATOR... I'M IMPRESSED.
snigger! snigger!
YOU'VE GONE TO GREAT LENGTHS TO CONCEAL YOUR IDENTITY.
NOT THAT IT'LL DO YOU ANY GOOD!
YOU DON'T LOOK ANYTHING LIKE I THOUGHT YOU WOULD.
I THINK I CAN FORGIVE YOU, THOUGH.
AFTER ALL, YOU WERE THE FIRST PERSON EVER TO OUTWIT ME!
I FIND THAT INCREDIBLY ATTRACTIVE!

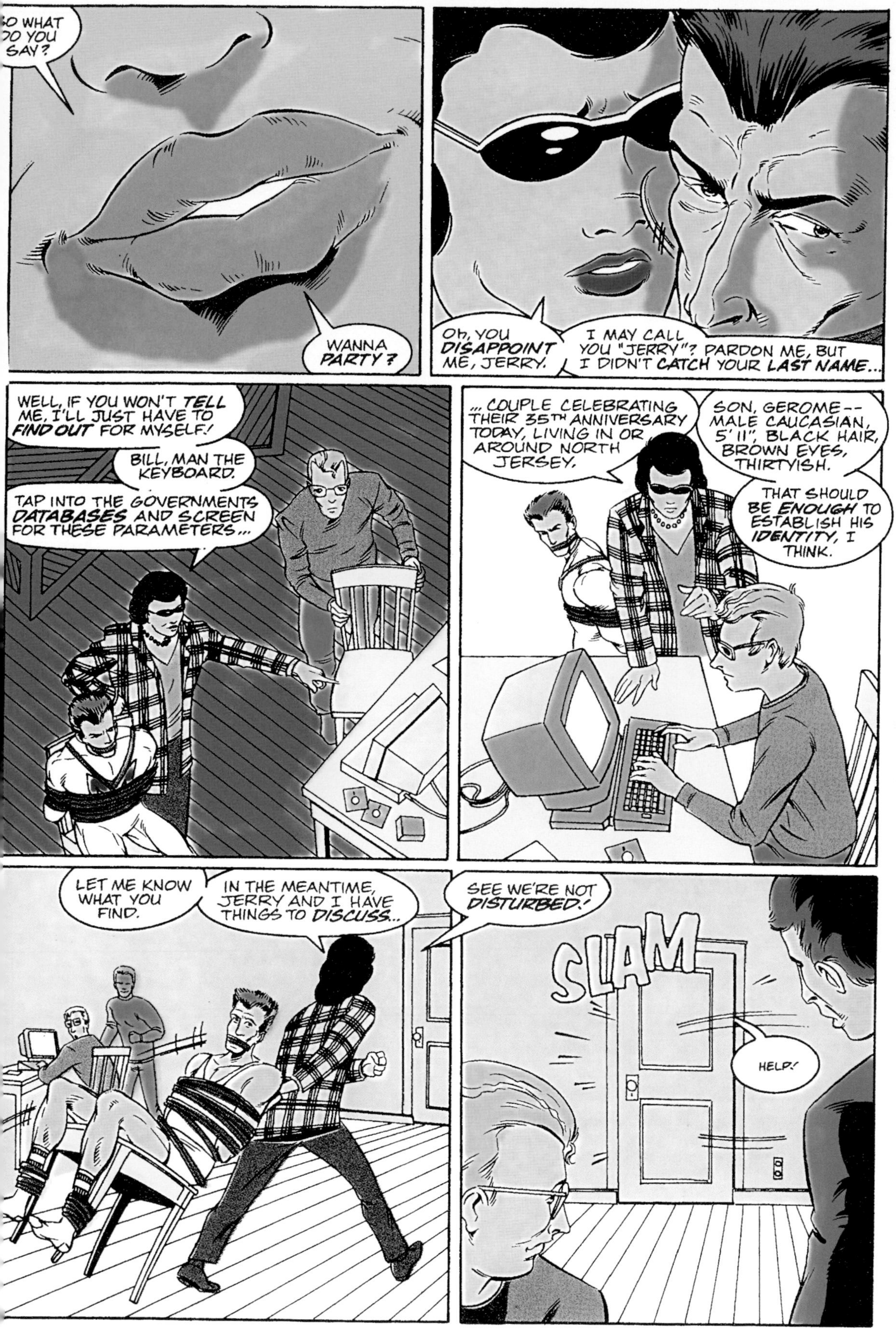
SO WHAT DO YOU SAY?
WANNA PARTY?
OH, YOU DISAPPOINT ME, JERRY.
I MAY CALL YOU "JERRY"? PARDON ME, BUT I DIDN'T CATCH YOUR LAST NAME...
WELL, IF YOU WON'T TELL ME, I'LL JUST HAVE TO FIND OUT FOR MYSELF!
BILL, MAN THE KEYBOARD.
TAP INTO THE GOVERNMENTS DATABASES AND SCREEN FOR THESE PARAMETERS...
...COUPLE CELEBRATING THEIR 35TH ANNIVERSARY TODAY, LIVING IN OR AROUND NORTH JERSEY.
SON, GEROME-- MALE CAUCASIAN, 5' 11", BLACK HAIR, BROWN EYES, THIRTYISH.
THAT SHOULD BE ENOUGH TO ESTABLISH HIS IDENTITY, I THINK.
LET ME KNOW WHAT YOU FIND.
IN THE MEANTIME, JERRY AND I HAVE THINGS TO DISCUSS...
SEE WE'RE NOT DISTURBED!
SLAM
HELP!

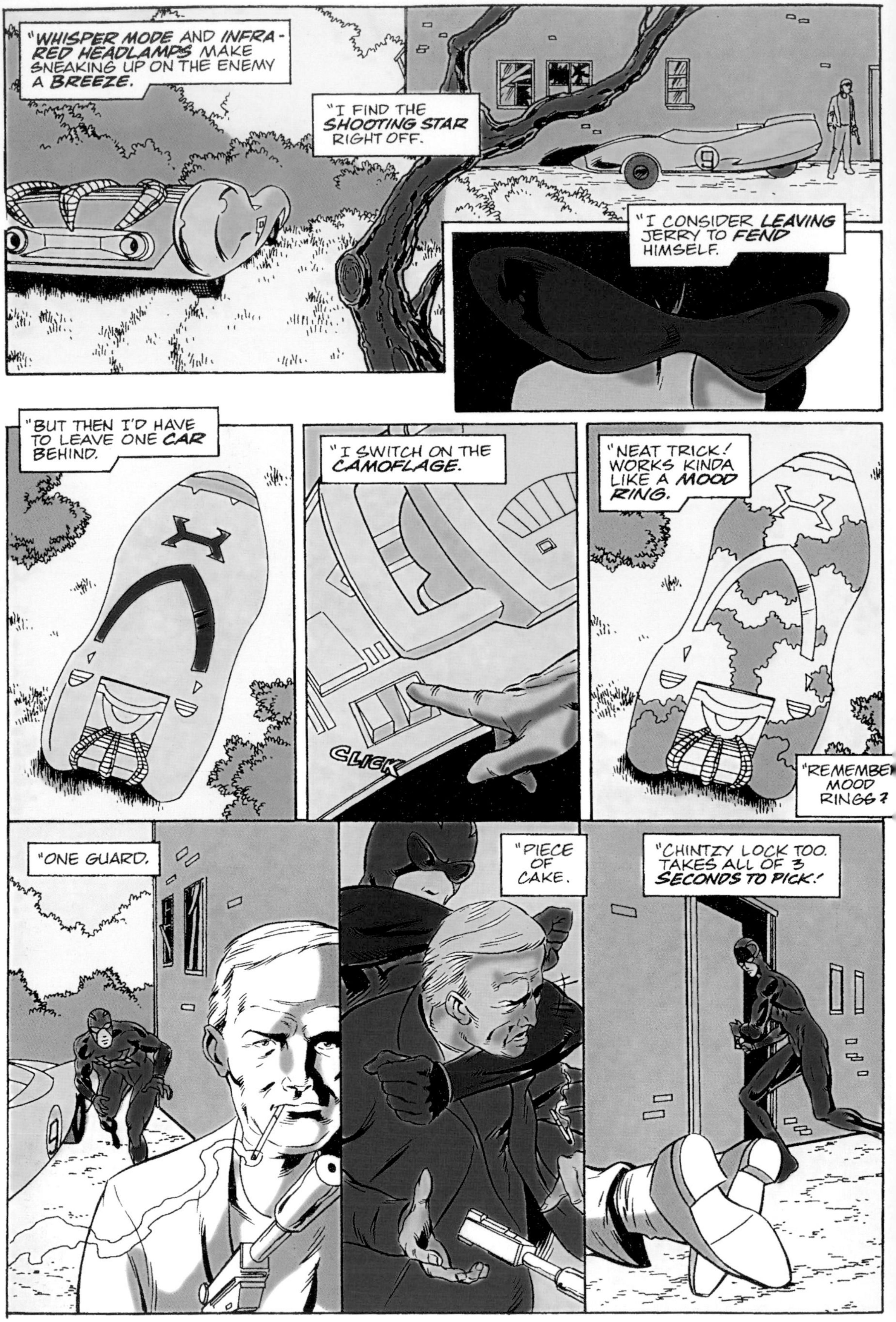

"WHISPER MODE AND INFRA-RED HEADLAMPS MAKE SNEAKING UP ON THE ENEMY A BREEZE.
"I FIND THE SHOOTING STAR RIGHT OFF.
"I CONSIDER LEAVING JERRY TO FEND HIMSELF.
"BUT THEN I'D HAVE TO LEAVE ONE CAR BEHIND.
"I SWITCH ON THE CAMOFLAGE.
CLICK
"NEAT TRICK! WORKS KINDA LIKE A MOOD RING.
"REMEMBE MOOD RINGS?
"ONE GUARD.
"PIECE OF CAKE.
"CHINTZY LOCK TOO. TAKES ALL OF 3 SECONDS TO PICK!

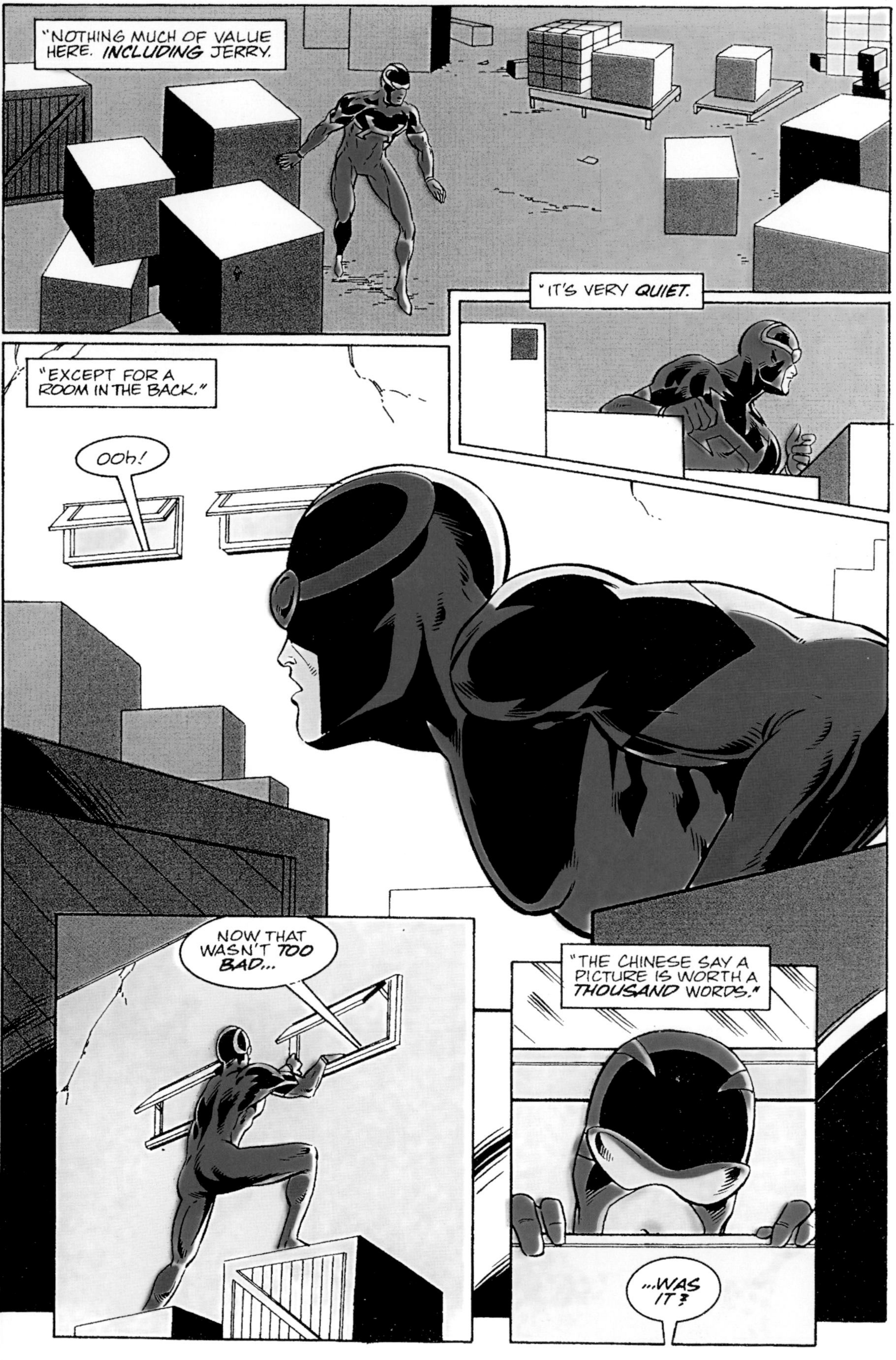
"NOTHING MUCH OF VALUE HERE. INCLUDING JERRY.
"IT'S VERY QUIET.
"EXCEPT FOR A ROOM IN THE BACK."
OOh!
NOW THAT WASN'T TOO BAD...
"THE CHINESE SAY A PICTURE IS WORTH A THOUSAND WORDS."
...WAS IT?

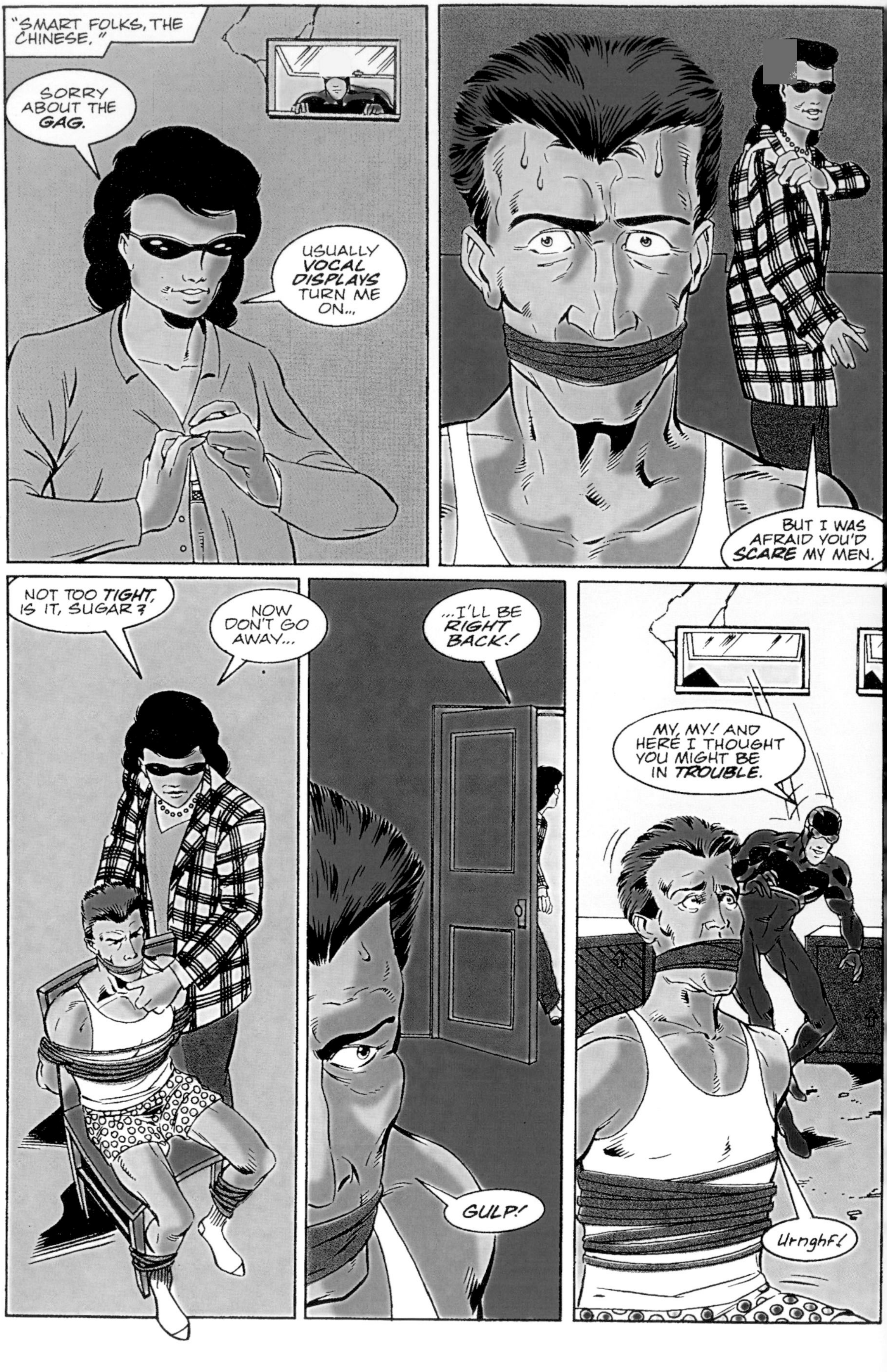
"SMART FOLKS, THE CHINESE,"
SORRY ABOUT THE GAG.
USUALLY VOCAL DISPLAYS TURN ME ON...
BUT I WAS AFRAID YOU'D SCARE MY MEN.
NOT TOO TIGHT, IS IT, SUGAR?
NOW DON'T GO AWAY...
...I'LL BE RIGHT BACK!
GULP!
MY, MY! AND HERE I THOUGHT YOU MIGHT BE IN TROUBLE.
Urnghf!

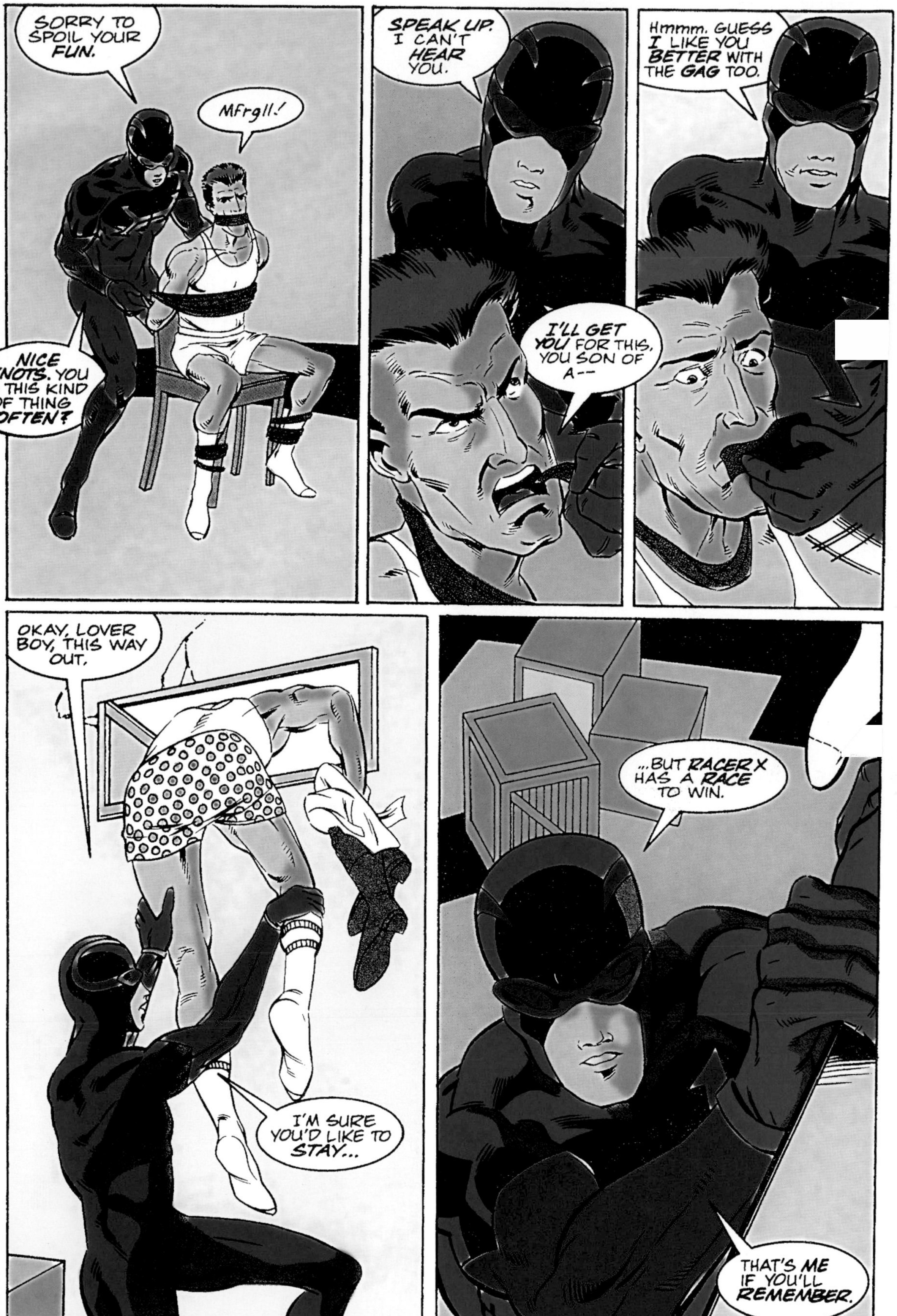
SORRY TO SPOIL YOUR FUN.
Mfrgll!
NICE
NOTS. YOU
THIS KIND
F THING
OFTEN?
SPEAK UP. I CAN'T HEAR YOU.
I'LL GET YOU FOR THIS, YOU SON OF A--
Hmmm. GUESS I LIKE YOU BETTER WITH THE GAG TOO.
OKAY, LOVER BOY, THIS WAY OUT.
I'M SURE YOU'D LIKE TO STAY...
...BUT RACER X HAS A RACE TO WIN.
THAT'S ME IF YOU'LL REMEMBER.

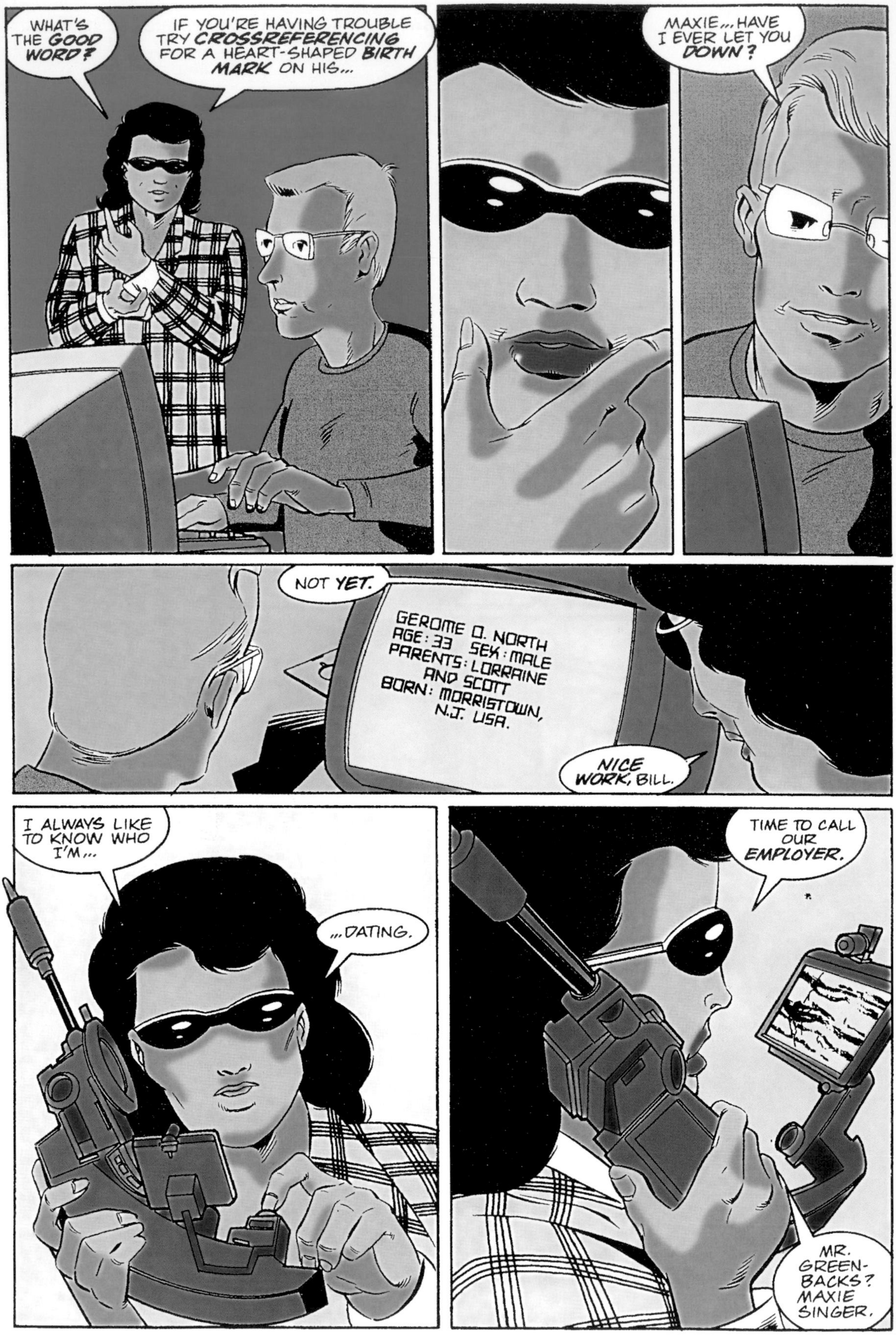
WHAT'S THE GOOD WORD?
IF YOU'RE HAVING TROUBLE TRY CROSSREFERENCING FOR A HEART-SHAPED BIRTH MARK ON HIS...
MAXIE... HAVE I EVER LET YOU DOWN?
NOT YET.
GEROME O. NORTH
AGE: 33 SEX: MALE
PARENTS: LORRAINE AND SCOTT
BORN: MORRISTOWN, N.J. USA.
NICE WORK, BILL.
I ALWAYS LIKE TO KNOW WHO I'M...
...DATING.
TIME TO CALL OUR EMPLOYER.
MR. GREENBACKS? MAXIE SINGER.

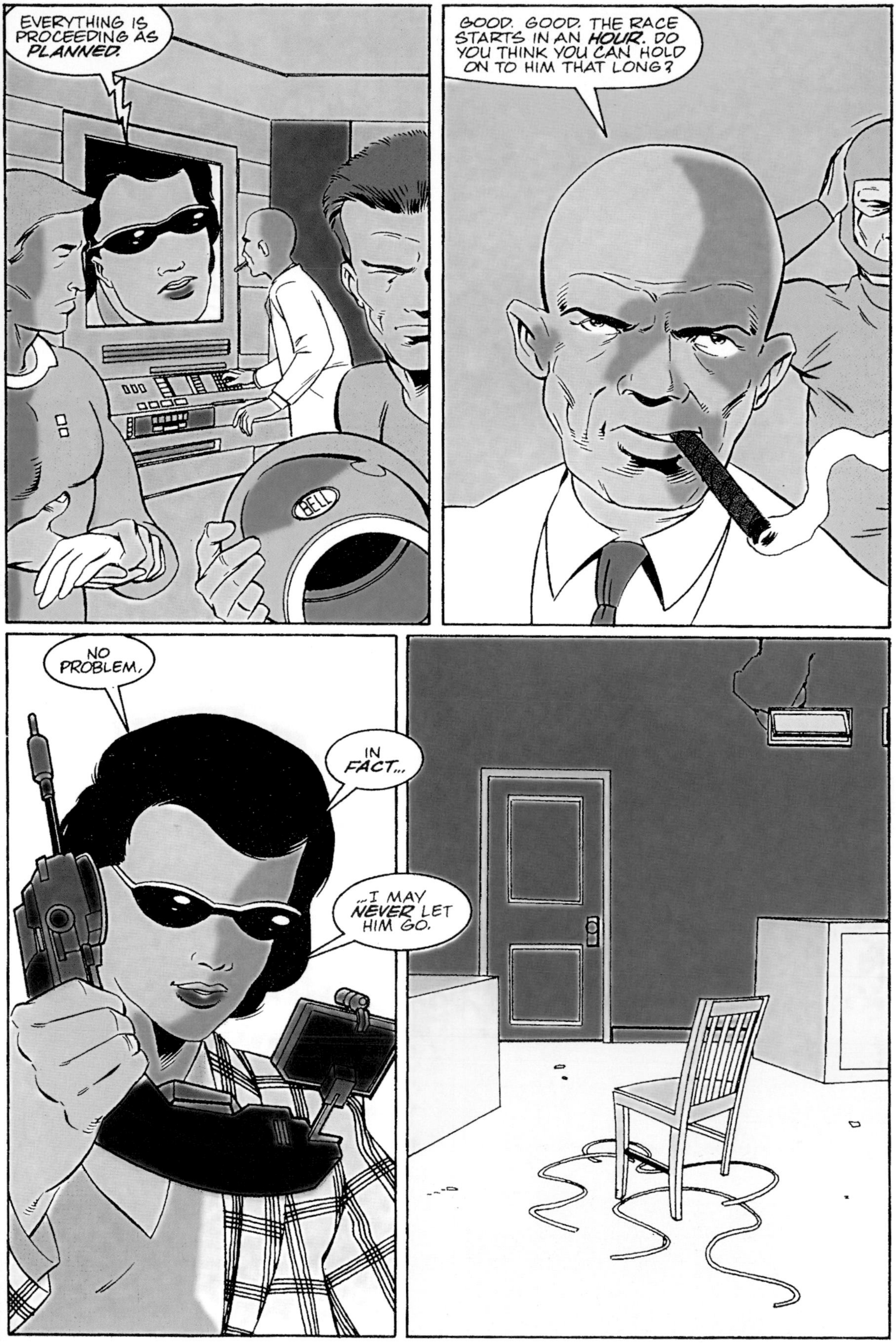
EVERYTHING IS PROCEEDING AS PLANNED.
BELL
GOOD. GOOD. THE RACE STARTS IN AN HOUR. DO YOU THINK YOU CAN HOLD ON TO HIM THAT LONG?
NO PROBLEM.
IN FACT...
...I MAY NEVER LET HIM GO.

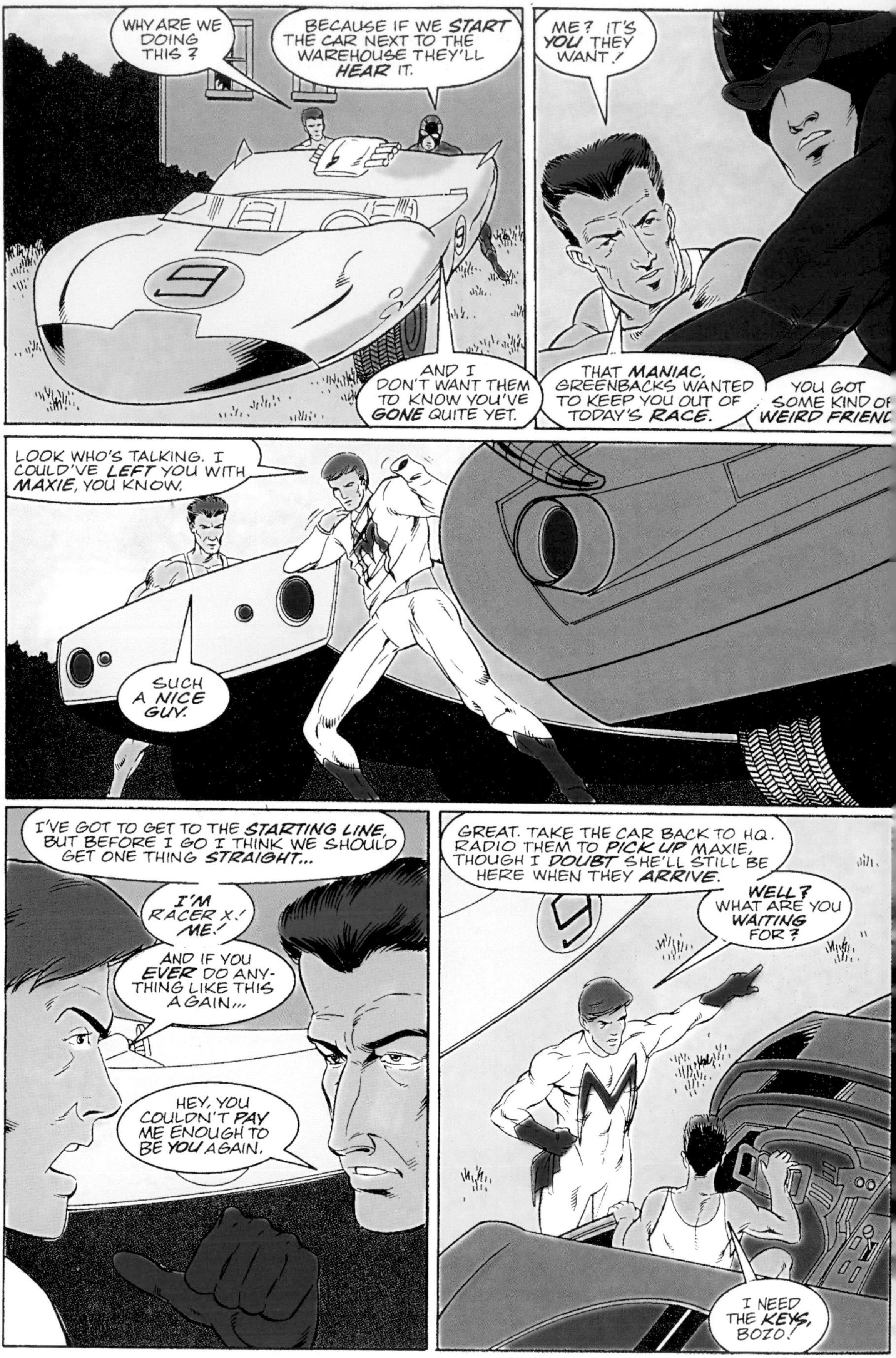
WHY ARE WE DOING THIS?
BECAUSE IF WE START THE CAR NEXT TO THE WAREHOUSE THEY'LL HEAR IT.
AND I DON'T WANT THEM TO KNOW YOU'VE GONE QUITE YET.
ME? IT'S YOU THEY WANT!
THAT MANIAC, GREENBACKS WANTED TO KEEP YOU OUT OF TODAY'S RACE.
YOU GOT SOME KIND OF WEIRD FRIEND
LOOK WHO'S TALKING. I COULD'VE LEFT YOU WITH MAXIE, YOU KNOW.
SUCH A NICE GUY.
I'VE GOT TO GET TO THE STARTING LINE, BUT BEFORE I GO I THINK WE SHOULD GET ONE THING STRAIGHT...
I'M RACER X! ME!
AND IF YOU EVER DO ANY-THING LIKE THIS AGAIN...
HEY, YOU COULDN'T PAY ME ENOUGH TO BE YOU AGAIN.
GREAT. TAKE THE CAR BACK TO HQ. RADIO THEM TO PICK UP MAXIE, THOUGH I DOUBT SHE'LL STILL BE HERE WHEN THEY ARRIVE.
WELL? WHAT ARE YOU WAITING FOR?
I NEED THE KEYS, BOZO!

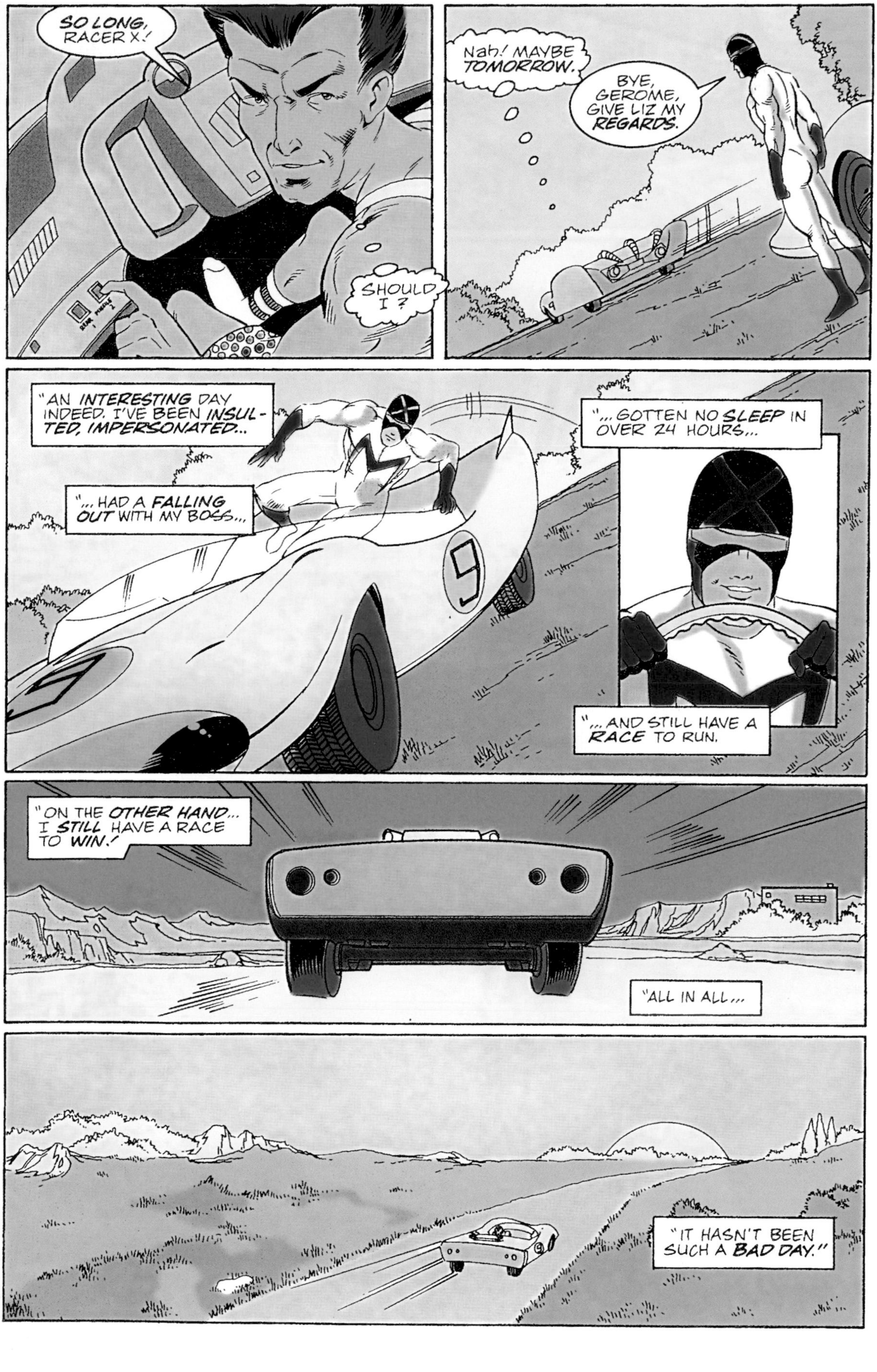
SO LONG, RACER X!
SHOULD I?
Nah! MAYBE TOMORROW.
BYE, GEROME, GIVE LIZ MY REGARDS.
"AN INTERESTING DAY INDEED. I'VE BEEN INSULTED, IMPERSONATED...
"...HAD A FALLING OUT WITH MY BOSS...
"...GOTTEN NO SLEEP IN OVER 24 HOURS...
"...AND STILL HAVE A RACE TO RUN.
"ON THE OTHER HAND... I STILL HAVE A RACE TO WIN!
"ALL IN ALL...
"IT HASN'T BEEN SUCH A BAD DAY."

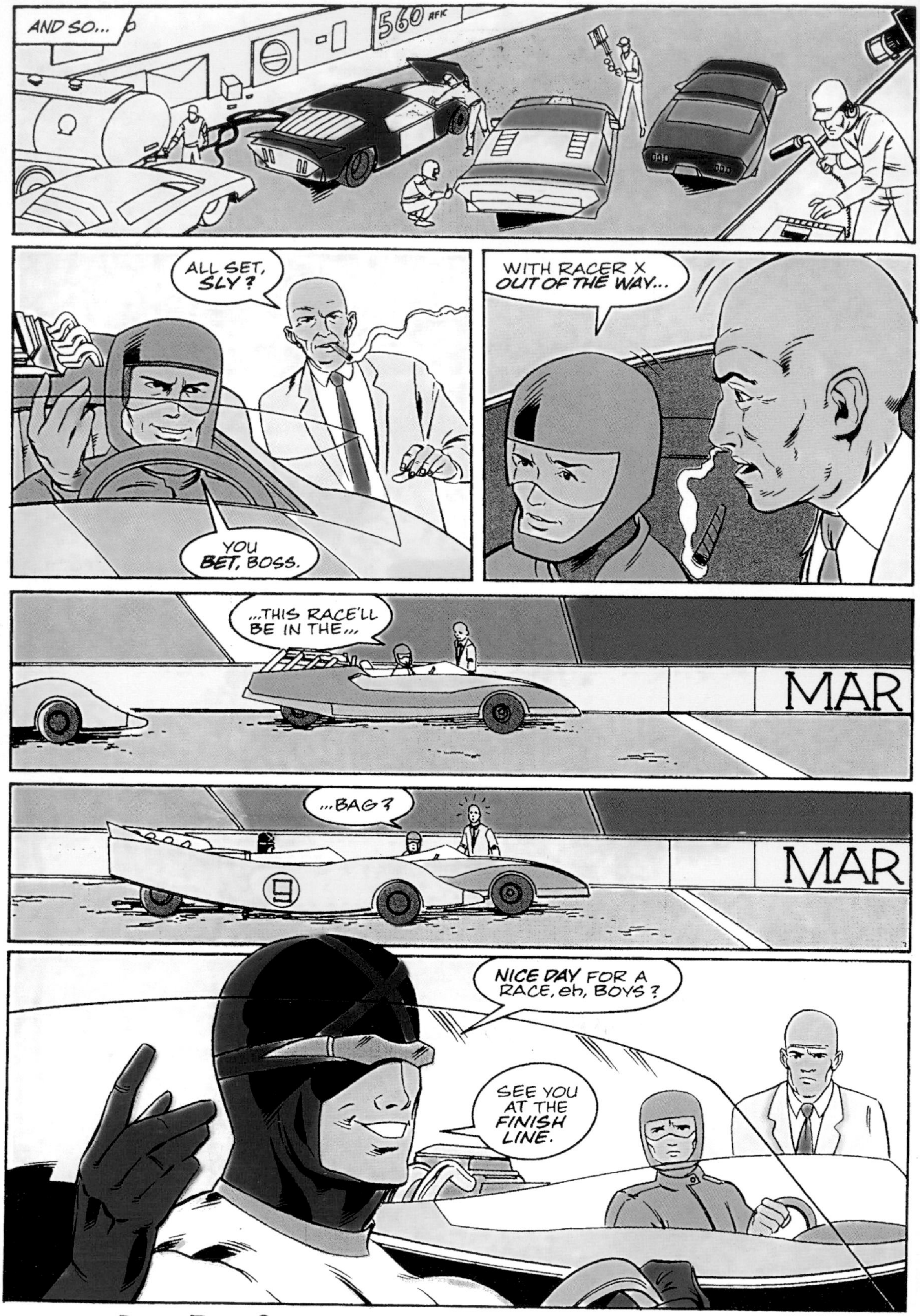
AND SO...
560
ALL SET, SLY?
YOU BET, BOSS.
WITH RACER X OUT OF THE WAY...
...THIS RACE'LL BE IN THE...
MAR
...BAG?
MAR
NICE DAY FOR A RACE, eh, BOYS?
SEE YOU AT THE FINISH LINE.

next: A CHRISTMAS STORY (AND A SPECIAL GUE ARTIST